VULNERABILITY ANALYSIS FOR TRANSPORTATION NETWORKS

CONTENTS

PREFACE

Transportation network reliability has featured in transportation research for some decades, perhaps first as an interesting academic aside, but then—in the aftermath of the great Kobe earthquake of 1994 when substantial parts of that region's infrastructure were destroyed—as a topic of vital interest to governments and transportation agencies. Research in the 1990s focused on travel-time reliability and network connectivity reliability. The former topic has become an important consideration in transport economics and project evaluation, though not without controversy (but that is a story for another time). The latter was concerned with the ability to find a path between any two points through a disaster-struck network. Was the network still intact? Were there alternative paths that could be used?

A series of international workshops were held in the 1990s where researcher presented and discussed their work on network reliability, culminating in the establishment of the triennial *International Symposia on Transportation Network Reliability* (INSTR), with the first INSTR held at Kyoto University in July 2001. In that event four researchers, a Swede, a New Zealander, and two Australians, started to talk about something slightly different: network vulnerability. What happened in networks that were damaged but still operating in some degraded state? When could they cope? How serviceable were they? How could this be measured? What if the damaged network was still fully connected but the available path (or detour) was so much longer than the disrupted path that its use was not logical, let alone practical? What were the critical elements in a network, where failure would have the largest effects, and how to protect them? How could the risk of failure be assessed?

These questions in fact have spurred a decade and a half of intense international research activity, which is still ongoing, and with new players emerging—as well as a growing list of influences from the modern world that can affect vulnerability and infrastructure performance, with major implications for transportation network planning, design, and operations. Beyond the natural disasters that have been part and parcel of concerns on vulnerability, issues such as climate change, international terrorism, and post-disaster relief have come to prominence. A recent report by the OECD[1] has stressed the importance of vulnerability in its review of the potential effects of extreme weather and climate change on the performance of transportation systems. As society places more reliance on its infrastructure systems and their ability to provide safe, efficient, and equitable services on call; as we stress those systems more and more through growing demand that pushes system capacity; and as our expectations of system performance grow and we demand more from the transportation system while squeezing its spare capacity, the concepts of vulnerability become more relevant and important. This book explores these issues and considers the issues inherent in vulnerability analysis, the methods proposed and adopted to assess vulnerability, to identify critical infrastructure, locations and facilities, and the metrics proposed and techniques employed in those methods. It seeks to define an integrated approach to vulnerability analysis that uses the common features (such as data requirements) behind the alternative approaches while maintaining the rounded, multidimensional insights that are possible by using the full set of those approaches.

The book charts the development of transportation network vulnerability analysis and the widening spread of the research on that topic. It also describes a personal journey for the author, from those early beginnings in Kyoto to the present day. The author began the writing believing himself to be an expert in the field and while that belief is still there to a large degree (and is reinforced by the ongoing citations of a couple of his papers in the new published research), he has learnt much more about the topic in compiling this work than he ever knew at the start. That is a valuable thing. Knowledge is ever expanding, and the holders and developers of knowledge are diverse and spread across the globe. There is no single repository of knowledge or, indeed, wisdom. That has always been the case—for example, think of Newton, Leibnitz, and the calculus. At the same time knowledge is ephemeral. Transportation engineers of the 1920s were using trip distribution models, origin–destination matrices, and desire line maps, yet that knowledge disappeared (presumably due to economic depression and a world war) until it was reinvented from scratch, by necessity, in the 1950s. To keep knowledge of a topic alive and growing needs constant attention and development. The author hopes that this book will provide

[1] ITF (2016). Adapting transport to climate change and extreme weather: Implications for infrastructure owners and network managers. International Transport Forum, ITF Research Reports, Paris: OECD Publishing. Retrived from http://dx.doi.org/10.1787/9789282108079-en.

a significant step toward the disclosure of the state of the art in vulnerability analysis and the *raison d'être* to preserve, extend, and utilize the accomplishments in the field. Much has been done, but there is much more still possible—and required.

The starting point for the discussion is the need to maintain reasonable levels of serviceability, i.e., function, in a transportation system, and how this can be assessed. An inherent part of this assessment is the notion of risk; what are the implications and potential impacts of a system failure (full or partial). No system can ever be completely immune from degradation, therefore a risk analysis is required to indicate the potential damage of a failure event and the likely costs of safeguards to minimize that damage. Risk has two dimensions: the probability of an event and the (expected) magnitude of its impact. Risk is then represented as the product of the probability and the magnitudes, resulting in an expected outcome for an event. The potential combination of events is also apparent, and the risk analysis can handle this situation too—as discussed by Nicholson and Dalzeill[2] in their consideration of the road network of the North Island of New Zealand, and the potential simultaneous occurrence of volcanic eruptions and snowstorms in parts of that network. In normal life we perhaps tend to overvalue extreme events—or, perhaps, undervalue the more minor ones. The airplane crash is seen as severe, the road crash death toll perhaps less so, although the cumulative outcomes may actually indicate the reverse. Managers of transportation and other infrastructure systems need to consider the risks in economic, social, and political terms. Whatever the socio-political milieu, the availability of sound data and proper risk analysis are essential for informed decision making and network vulnerability analysis is now a core part of it. This is the theme developed early in the book, and it leads to the twin definitions of vulnerability relating to serviceability (ability of a transportation system to function at an acceptable level under different circumstances) and accessibility (ability of a transportation system to facilitate acceptable levels of participation in socioeconomic activities in a region).

Transportation systems belong to a wider class of infrastructure systems, which also include water supply, drainage, wastewater and sewerage, telecommunications, and gas and electricity supply systems. In modern times, governments around the world are paying special attention to "critical

[2] Nicholson, A. J., & Dalziell, E. (2003). Risk evaluation and management: A road network reliability study. In M. G. HBell, and Y. Iida (Eds.), *The Network Reliability of Transport* (pp. 45–59). Oxford: Elsevier.

infrastructure," meaning both the systems and their components subject to degradation. Vulnerability analysis is often concerned with the identification of critical components, providing planners and managers with information on those components of the greatest risk of failure—meaning of course those components whose failure would engender the greatest consequences as the product of probability and impact. In Chapter 2 the book considers critical infrastructure, first in broad terms including discussion of the potential interactions and interdependencies between different infrastructure systems, and then in terms of transportation systems specifically. The focus is on land transportation system networks, which split into two broad types: road networks and railway networks, each of which have their own features. The differences between them largely relate to the operating rules for traffic using the network, the technologies employed in vehicle propulsion and movement, and the nature of the traffic flows on them. Rail networks perhaps have more complexity than road networks, but road networks are inhabited by numerous individual decision makers (drivers, riders, pedestrians, and others) and the decisions made by one or more individuals can strongly influence the way that a system operates. The study of vulnerability and resilience in infrastructure systems is now widespread, with resilience being concerned with the time and effort required for a disrupted system to return to its normal operating conditions after the event.

To study network vulnerability an understanding of the structure of networks and how the elements of nodes and links connect together is required first. It then requires understanding of the ways in which transportation flows occur in networks. The former is the study of network topology. This provides basic knowledge about the network and how flows through it will use different components. Transportation analysts have by and large ignored network topology in the past, leaving it to the mathematicians and the telecommunications engineers. Yet topological analysis can reveal much core information on how any network will function. Study of transport flows—and hence network usage—requires knowledge and application of the theories and models used by transportation analysts to represent the traffic flows and the resultant network operating conditions. The basics of traffic flow theory lie in the particular description of continuity of flow for road traffic; that there are two main variables to describe flow in a single traffic stream (traffic volume and traffic density); that density (the number of vehicles per unit length of road) is the primary variable; and that the ratio of density to volume yields the average speed of the traffic stream along a road at a given instant of time. Traffic volume (the rate at which vehicles pass an observation point over time) is insufficient to properly describe the traffic state on the road, for a low volume may imply either light traffic flow or a major bottleneck. Density will reveal the true state. The "macroscopic flow diagram" illustrates these characteristics and can also show the observed phenomenon of the "capacity drop"—if a traffic stream is disrupted at a density exceeding a critical value then the flow regime degrades and maximum achievable volumes are significantly less than those experienced before the disruption. This condition will continue until there is a substantial drop in density, which can only come from reduced demand to use the road.

The question of travel demand is a key consideration in transportation network analysis, including vulnerability analysis. Travel demand is summarized by the origin–destination pattern and corresponding origin–destination matrices (the numbers of travelers wishing to move from a given origin point to designated destination points across the network). For vulnerability studies, the starting point for travel demand analysis is route choice, i.e., the paths that travelers take in making their journeys. Route choice is modeled using "traffic assignment" models, which route the trips along the links in the network between each origin and destination in response to the conditions (travel time or travel costs) experienced on the network. This situation where the number of trips to be made and the destinations of those trips are fixed is known as inelastic travel demand. Full or partial network failures (e.g., a blocked or congested link) may alter the available and preferred routes for some journeys. The extent of these alterations is at the heart of vulnerability analysis. However, route choice is not the only travel decision that people make: when to travel (departure time choice), where to travel to (destination choice), how to travel (transport mode choice), and indeed whether to travel at all (in a given time period) are also decisions to be made. Prolonged network failure or chronic congestion may make travelers reconsider their earlier choices. Such changes are termed as elastic travel demand. Elastic travel demand has still to be properly considered in the existing methods for vulnerability analysis.

The development of traffic congestion, which certainly contributes to loss of serviceability in a network, is a key part of the vulnerability equation. In particular, this is because congestion manifests itself in different forms. There is the regular, cyclic "recurrent" congestion which is part of everyday life: the morning rush hour, the business hours, the evening peak, the off peak hours, and the wee hours of the morning. Cyclic patterns also span the days of the week, the weeks, and seasons of the year. We know about these patterns and generally work within them. Some congestion is a natural part of network operations, particularly in urban areas. On the other hand, there is incident-based "non-recurrent" congestion, which can strike "at random" and disable small (or sometimes large) parts of a network for durations from minutes to days. Incidents range from vehicle breakdowns blocking a lane and road crashes to police operations and structural collapses. Some are quickly dispelled, others take longer and demand considerable resources to remedy. Other influences including natural phenomena (e.g., floods, blizzards, landslides, and earthquakes) and manmade events (e.g., roadwork and road and track maintenance, road closures for special events, and construction zones) can also affect network operations and congestion levels. Then there are the occasional malevolent events including sabotage and terrorist attacks which can cause immediate distress, or worse, and leave longer lasting impacts. Vulnerability analysis has to be cognizant of all these potentials.

At the same time vulnerability analysis is important in rural and regional areas as well as our cities. Rural road and rail networks tend to be sparse, with few alternative routes available. A network disruption can cause isolation and economic harm in a locality—think of the dairy farm unable to ship its milk to the dairy because of a single road closure or bridge collapse. Traffic congestion is rarely a major concern in rural regions, but accessibility and connectivity are. Natural hazards from extreme weather and environment are perhaps more prone to affect rural transportation networks. Rural communities are often less privileged in terms of their access to services and facilities than their urban cousins. The road network is often their only transport connection to the outside world. Loss of connectivity may have profound implications for health, education, and economic wellbeing in rural areas.

The issues are explored in depth in Chapters 3—5 of this book.

The crux of vulnerability analysis is then to provide tools that assist transportation planners and decision makers in identifying potential points of weakness in their networks—critical locations and infrastructure—and then assist in developing plans to protect those locations or provide ready alternatives in case of disruptions. The research on which this book is based identified four broad methods for vulnerability analysis:

1. Risk-based inventory assessment, which considers the infrastructure assets across the system and rates those assets at greater risk of failure or disruption due to traffic and environmental influences
2. Topologically based assessment, which considers network structure and connectivity, and identifies the nodes and links most critical for flows

through the network, as well as the locations where failure may have the gravest effects on network operations

3. Serviceability-based assessment, which is concerned with the impacts on network operations of failures and disruptions at different locations and may be used to identify critical locations in terms of those impacts, with a focus on transport and traffic
4. Accessibility-based assessment, which is similar to serviceability assessment but is more concerned with socioeconomic impacts outside the network traffic operations.

The book describes each of these methods and provides examples of their applications. It also considers the applications of the methods to road-based transportation and to (rail-based) public transport. Most of the reported studies have dealt with road networks, but public transport vulnerability analysis has emerged as a substantial area of transportation research since 2010. Chapter 6 of the book deals exclusively with studies of public transport networks.

The various methods share some features as well as having their own, unique characteristics. Recognizing the common features, mainly in the topological description of networks, provides the basis for a future integrated approach to vulnerability analysis that is outlined in the latter chapters of the book. The different methods for analysis can be seen in terms of layering of additional detailed data—asset information and travel demand patterns—on top of the basis connectivity information. Development and application of this integrated approach to vulnerability analysis should provide the firm and comprehensive footing for its full inclusion in transportation planning and systems analysis. We have the knowledge to enable this, and the software platforms, such as geographical information systems (GIS), to facilitate it. The author wishes that this book will provide the necessary blueprints.

There are many people, family, friends, and colleagues, who have helped me, inspired me, and have contributed to the development of vulnerability analysis in concept, theory, and application. There are others who have encouraged and helped me in the preparation of this book. My grateful thanks are extended to them all. I must single out the following: Glen D'Este, for his trail-blazing insights and uncanny knack for describing complex phenomena in ways that all of us can readily understand; Michael Bell, for his authority, novel thinking, and expert advice; Sekhar Somenahalli, my GIS guru and "go to" person; my PhD student "Susi" Susilawati, for her GIS expertise, analytical skills, and "can do" enthusiasm; my Masters student Sally Freeman for her modeling skills and willingness to experiment in the analysis; Alan Nicholson, for his insights into vulnerability, risk, and exposure; Katja Berdica, for her foresight and innovation; Erik Jenelius and Lars-Goran Mattsson, for their innovation, acumen, and leadership in vulnerability analysis; Jan Husdal, for his original work and innovation in accessibility-based methods; and William Lam, for his ongoing encouragement and support. Special thanks are due to Jackie Bowler and the interlibrary loans team in the UniSA Library, who helped me uncover some rare gems that might otherwise have gone unnoticed. Brian Romer and Kattie Washington at Elsevier also deserve my thanks, to Brian for the invitation to write this book, to Kattie for her advice and guidance in keeping me "on track", and to both of them for their constant support and encouragement during the authoring process. Finally, to my wife Marg, my inspiration and guiding light always, for her encouragement and support—and indeed for her substantial proofreading skills, used to good effect in this work.

CHAPTER ONE

Introduction

In the late evening of Sunday, January 5, 1975, the bulk-ore carrier MV "Lake Illawarra" was sailing up the Derwent River in Tasmania, past the city of Hobart on its way to the Electrolytic Zinc Works located close to Risdon. This journey had been made many times before, and at this stage the ship had to sail under the Tasman Bridge. On that evening, however, something was wrong. The "Lake Illawarra" was more than 120 m off course, so that instead of negotiating the navigation channel through the central span of the bridge it struck a glancing blow against one pier and then crashed broadside on into its neighbor. Both piers were demolished, a third pier severely damaged, and three spans of the bridge fell into the estuary. The falling debris struck the vessel which then sank in 35 m of water. Four cars crossing the bridge plunged into the water. Seven crew members died, along with five motorists. This was tragedy enough, but the implications of what might have happened had the collision taken place during a peak demand period were traumatic.

Next morning the full extent of the disaster started to become apparent. Hobart was cut into two. The nearest river crossing was nearly 30 km upstream on poor quality roads, a detour of perhaps 2 h. While 28% of Hobart's population lived on the eastern side of the Derwent, the central business district (CBD) and 94% of the jobs in the city were on the western side, along with the city's major hospitals and other vital facilities and services. The city was paralyzed in the aftermath. Immediate emergency plans were initiated, with an air force helicopter available for emergency medical cases and army landing barges on standby to move ambulances and other emergency vehicles when required. The small existing passenger ferry system was augmented, using vessels brought expressly from Sydney Harbour. A temporary bailey bridge was constructed 5 km upstream of the Tasman Bridge, and opened to traffic in December 1975. The Tasman Bridge was repaired, although it lost its pleasing symmetry. Thus eventually "normal service" could be resumed. Today the Bowen Bridge stands at the site of the bailey bridge, so Hobart has two, separated river crossings—on either

Vulnerability Analysis for Transportation Networks
ISBN: 978-0-12-811010-2
http://dx.doi.org/10.1016/B978-0-12-811010-2.00001-0

side of the zinc smelter. Lock and Gelling (1976) provided a salutary account of the Tasman Bridge disaster and its immediate aftermath from the perspective of the transportation planner.

Here are the inklings of the study of transportation network vulnerability, the impacts of the failure or loss of critical components of transportation infrastructure. More so is the need for planning and scenario investigation of potential impacts of network failures and the identification of critical locations and infrastructure in a network. This interest, and its importance, has long been recognized, for instance Lee (1946) detailed the substantial works done by the British Government to protect its national railway system during World War II, through the installation of additional section of rail track and loops. Unfortunately that paper only indicated the sites selected and the works implemented at them. It did not reveal how the site selection was undertaken.[1]

In the present age, the need for vulnerability analysis has widened considerably. Sadly, the organized violence of warfare still exists, and human error of the type involved in the Tasman Bridge disaster is always hovering, but other issues have also become more prominent. Natural disasters such as earthquakes can devastate transportation infrastructure, and while this is an historical problem the increased reliance of societies, economies, and communities on that infrastructure heightens the potential consequences. Extreme weather and its impacts, such as flooding, wild fires, and landslides also present threats to the infrastructure, and climate change stands to exacerbate these. The incidence of terrorism in the early 21st century provides an additional, malevolent threat, especially to public transport systems—urban transit is an open system with large numbers of people occupying constrained spaces and may thus provide attractive targets for those who wish to create mayhem.

This book attempts to describe the development and application of analytical methods aimed at describing potential vulnerabilities in transportation systems, in diagnosing the potential causes of those vulnerabilities and identifying vulnerabilityprone locations, and suggesting remedies to overcome those problems. It does so by drawing on the substantial body of international research and investigation on the topic.

[1] An interesting comment reflecting the situation of the day was Lee's final conclusion in his paper, that "all these wartime works have been constructed at Government expense, and remain Government property. Their ultimate fate is a matter for negotiation between the Government and the individual railway companies ..." (Lee, 1946, p. 183).

1.1 ORIGINS OF NETWORK VULNERABILITY ANALYSIS

Network vulnerability emerged as a significant area in transportation planning research over the last 15 years or so. While the main driver was the need to consider the performance and impacts of degraded networks, vulnerability analysis became important for researchers and planners for two reasons: (1) the development of concept and theory regarding vulnerability, and (2) the application of the new theory to large-scale, complex transportation networks, usually road networks or urban public transport networks. The degree of complexity of real world networks requires computation efficiency as well as theoretical development for the implementation of vulnerability analysis. The theoretical developments are therefore grounded in realism, by necessity.

In broad terms, network vulnerability deals with the socioeconomic impacts and transport systems performance of degraded transport networks. Thus network vulnerability is not just an interesting topic for research by transport network modelers, it is also of great importance to modern society. Degraded network performance from system failures, disaster situations, or even traffic congestion can have significant social and economic impacts. Network failures, whether full or partial or whether due to natural or man-made events, are of great significance. These failures can range from disasters such as earthquakes and bridge collapses, whose effects may persist for long periods of time, to incident-based congestion episodes of relatively short duration but still with large social and economic impacts. Transportation agencies need well-defined concepts and validated models and tools to test networks for their robustness and resilience to failure at different locations, as an integral part of network design and incident management planning, and indeed planning for emergencies.

The concept of network vulnerability is still relatively new, and it is important to define what is meant by vulnerability. For instance, there are several possible responses to the reduced performance of a degraded network, or in dealing with the perceived risks of degradation at different locations. In some cases, an appropriate response may be to upgrade key transport infrastructure, for instance, by raising structures above expected maximum flood levels or by adding more capacity. But sometimes this simply makes the network more reliant on those key links and more vulnerable to their failure. An alternative approach is to add links to the network. These links may normally be redundant but provide alternative routes when key network links are broken (e.g., see Lee, 1946). At the urban-network level there may already be many such latent alternative routes, but at the regional or national strategic network level this is less likely to be the case. Extra links would make the transport network more robust, but this may add unnecessary cost to the provision of transport infrastructure. The questions are:

1. Where are these locations of potential network vulnerability?
2. What is the best response?

The starting point for study of network vulnerability is the study of transportation network reliability, which has been the subject of intense international research interest since the Kobe earthquake of 1995.

1.2 NETWORK RELIABILITY AND VULNERABILITY

Transport network reliability is the subject of considerable international research interest in recent years (Bell & Cassir, 2000; Bell & Iida, 2003; FHWA, 2016; Lam, 1999; OECD, 2010; Taylor, 2013). Much of this research has focused on congested urban road networks and the probability that a network will deliver a required standard of performance. The urban studies are important, but they are not the only areas of concern, especially when considering the wider implications of transport systems performance. At the regional and national strategic level, accessibility, regional coverage, and interurban connectivity are the primary considerations. In these sparse networks, "vulnerability" of the network can be more important than "reliability," because of the potentially severe adverse consequences of network degradation. As noted by the Australian Bureau of Transport and Regional Economics (BTRE, 2002) in its analysis of the effects of flooding on road access,

> *the vast distances involved means that access to alternative services (such as hospitals and business) often do not exist … disruption costs to households, businesses and communities can therefore be more important in rural and remote communities.*

In both urban and rural areas, the concept of vulnerability or incident audit—the proactive determination of locations in a transport network that may be most sensitive to failure and where network failure may have the gravest consequences—requires detailed research. The transport planner may seek opportunities to reduce vulnerability—and the community will demand such action.

Network reliability became an important research topic in transport planning during the 1990s, although some elements had been the subject of research interest for some time before that (e.g., Herman & Lam, 1974; Lee, 1946; Richardson & Taylor, 1978; Taylor, 1982, 2013). The Kobe earthquake of 1995 and its aftermath stimulated an interest in reliability of connectivity. This is the probability that a pair of nodes in a network remains connected—i.e., there continues to exist a connected path between them—when one or more links in the network have been cut. Bell and Iida (1997) provided an analytical procedure for assessing connectivity reliability, and a summary of the procedure is given by Iida (1999). Subsequent research was directed at degraded networks, usually urban road networks subject to traffic congestion, in which the network remained physically intact but the performance of one or more links could be so severely affected by congestion that their use by traffic is curtailed. This led to the definition of two additional forms of reliability: travel-time reliability and capacity reliability, as described below.

Travel-time reliability considers the probability that a trip between an origin–destination pair can be completed successfully within a specified time interval (Bell & Iida, 1997). This can be affected by fluctuating link flows and imperfect knowledge of drivers when making route choice decisions (Lam & Xu, 2000). One measure of linking travel-time variability is the standard deviation of the distribution of individual travel times (e.g., Bates, Polak, Jones, & Cook, 2001; Fosgerau & Karlstrom, 2010; Taylor, 2017). Measures of travel-time variability are useful in assessing network performance in terms of service quality provided to travelers on a day-to-day basis (FHWA, 2016; OECD, 2010). Thus travel-time variability can be seen as a measure of demand satisfaction under congested conditions.

A supply-side measure of network performance in congested networks is capacity reliability (Taylor, 2013; Yang, Lo, & Tang, 2000). Capacity reliability is defined as the probability that a network can successfully accommodate a given level of travel demand. The network may be in its normal state or in a degraded stated (say due to incidents or road works). Chen, Yang, Lo, and Tang (1999) defined this probability as equal to the probability that the reserve capacity of the network is greater than or equal to the required demand for a given capacity loss due to degradation. Yang et al. (2000) indicated that capacity reliability and travel-time reliability together could provide a valuable transport network design tool. Taylor (1999, 2000) demonstrated how the concepts of travel-time reliability and capacity reliability could be used in planning and evaluating traffic management schemes in an urban area.

From the above review, we may conclude that the standard approaches to transport network reliability have focused on network connectivity, travel-time reliability, and capacity reliability. While this provides valuable insights into certain aspects of network performance, reliability arguments based on probabilities and absolute connectivity may obscure potential network problems, especially in large-scale, sparse, regional or national networks. In these networks, the consequences of disruption or degradation of the network become important. For example, D'Este and Taylor (2001) used the extreme example of the Australian national strategic land transport system to illustrate the potential consequences of the severance of certain transport connections in this multimodal network. In this example the system reliability was considered, in terms of a cut to the Eyre Highway and transcontinental rail line on the Nullarbor Plain between Perth and Adelaide, for instance, by flood (a perfectly plausible scenario), see Figure 1.1. The overall network remains connected and the probability that the route in question is cut by flood or other natural cause is very small (but not zero, for it has happened), so the travel-time and capacity reliabilities are high. Therefore the established measures of network reliability discussed above would not indicate any major problem with the network. However, the consequences of network failure are substantial in real terms—in this case the next best feasible path through the network involves a detour of some 5000 km! In reality the alternative route via Broome would not be used—it is more likely that shipments would be delayed or canceled thereby producing a different but no less significant economic impact. Nicholson and Dalziell (2003) pointed to similar circumstances in their study of the regional highway network in the center of the North Island of New Zealand, a region subject to both snowstorms and volcanic eruptions.

These examples illustrate the concept of network vulnerability and the difference between network reliability and vulnerability. The concept of vulnerability is more strongly related to the consequences of link failure, irrespective of the probability of failure. In some cases, link failure may be statistically unlikely, but the resulting adverse social and economic impacts on the community may be sufficiently large to indicate a major problem warranting remedial action—akin to taking out an insurance policy for an extremely unlikely yet potentially catastrophic event. For example, consider the impact on a rural community of loss of access to markets for its produce and to vital human services (such as hospital). Low probability of occurrence and network performance elsewhere does not offset the consequences of a network failure. Thus network reliability and vulnerability are related concepts; while reliability focuses on connectivity and probability, vulnerability is more closely aligned with network weakness and consequences of failure.

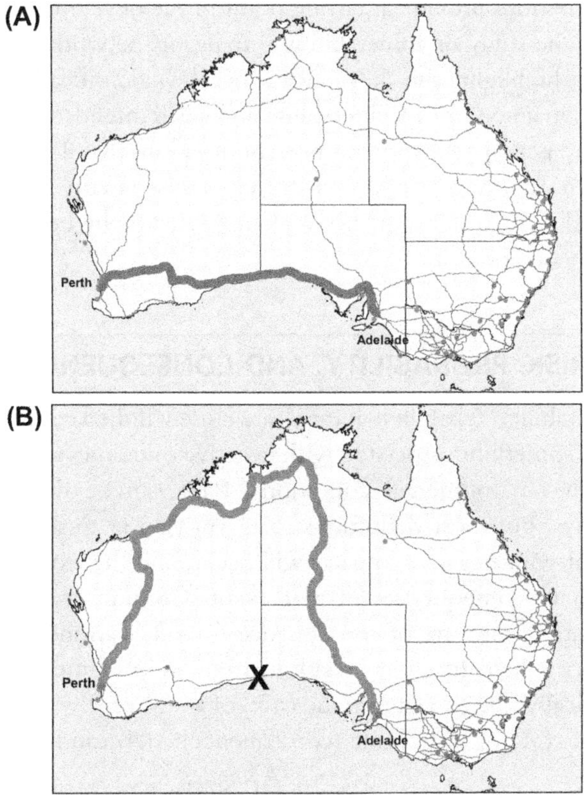

Figure 1.1 Effect of a loss of connectivity in the Australian National Highway System (NHS) network—shortest path from Perth to Adelaide in (A) full network and (B) network with Eyre Highway cut, a detour of 5000 km.

Berdica (2002) proposed that vulnerability analysis of transport networks should be regarded as an overall framework through which different transport studies could be conducted to determine how well a transport system would perform when exposed to different kinds and intensities of disturbances. From her study of the road network in central Stockholm, she suggested three main questions that might be posed in these studies:

1. How do interruptions of different critical links affect system performance, and to what extent?
2. How is network performance affected by general capacity reductions, and possible changes to traffic management and road space allocation in a subregion of the network?
3. How is the system affected by variations in travel demand?

These questions provide a starting point in the development of a methodology for the study of vulnerability in transport networks and infrastructure. They highlight the key issues of the identification of critical components in a network. Vulnerability analysis is intended to address these questions and perhaps the more important questions that flow from them—when we know where the vulnerable elements or critical locations (the "weakest links") of a transport network are, what is the best response, and what can we do about it?

1.3 RISK, PROBABILITY, AND CONSEQUENCE

Vulnerability, reliability, and risk are closely linked concepts. In broad terms, risk is something associated with negative outcomes for life, health, or economic or environmental conditions. Risk can be defined in many different ways, but most definitions focus on two factors: the probability that an event with negative impacts will occur, and the extent and severity of the resultant consequences of that event. Commonly, the product of probability and a measure of consequence is used as an index of risk. This can be shown schematically as a "risk matrix," as in Figure 1.2.

Theoretically, the expected value (risk) of an event A with probability of occurrence $\Pr\{A\}$ of magnitude (consequence) $X(A)$ can be written as

$$E(A) = \Pr\{A\}X(A) \tag{1.1}$$

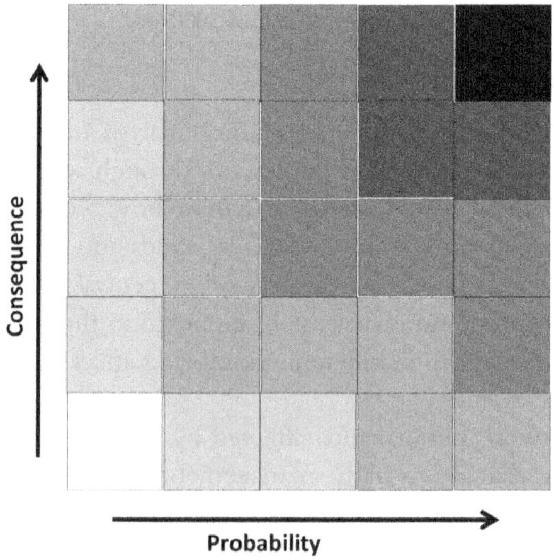

Figure 1.2 Conceptual risk matrix.

This value can be used in comparisons of different events possible in a given environment.

Risk and reliability analysis is mostly concerned with the top-right sector of the matrix where increasing probability and increasing consequences are combined. Nicholson and Dalziell (2003) applied this framework to the risk assessment of transport networks in New Zealand. They measured risk as simply the sum of the products of the event probabilities and the economic costs of the event (e.g., the expected annual economic cost of a given event). Their risk evaluation process involved the following steps:

1. Establish the context (i.e., the technical, financial, legal, social, and other criteria for assessing the acceptability of the risk).
2. Identify the hazards (i.e., the potential causes of closure).
3. Analyze the risks (i.e., identify the probabilities, consequences, and expectations).
4. Assess the risks (i.e., decide which risks are acceptable and which are unacceptable).

If any risk is found unacceptable, it needs to be managed. This generally involves either (1) treating the unacceptable risks, using the most cost-effective treatment options, or (2) monitoring and reviewing the risks (i.e., evaluating and revising treatments).

The study of vulnerability extends this risk assessment framework in several important ways. First, it extends the region of interest to areas of high consequences, and low or unquantifiable (but nonzero) probability of occurrence—on the basis that measurement of occurrence probability and consequences (human and economic) is imprecise for many types of incidents, and society may well consider some consequences to be unacceptable and worthy of safeguarding against, despite the uncertainty about their probability of occurrence (e.g., Evans, 1994). Second, vulnerability analysis provides a framework for targeting risk assessment. One of the key conclusions of the Nicholson-Dalziell risk assessment of the New Zealand highway network was that it is impractical and financially infeasible to conduct detailed geophysical and other risk assessment across an entire transport network. The costs of deriving accurate location-specific risk probabilities across a range of risk factors are too high to make it viable—what is needed is a way of targeting risk assessment resources to get best value from them. Vulnerability analysis provides another way of approaching this problem. It can be used to find structural weaknesses in the network topology that render the network vulnerable to consequences of failure or degradation. Resources can then be targeted at assessing these "weak links". Third, vulnerability auditing admits a more proactive and targeted approach to the issue of transport network risk assessment and mitigation.

1.4 CAUSES OF VULNERABILITY

The sources of network vulnerability are varied, and are explored in more detail in Chapter 2, where Berdica's (2002) spectrum of potential threats to transportation infrastructure is discussed in Section 2.4. Four broad areas for consideration are:

1. system operation, capacity, and congestion;
2. infrastructure systems management and maintenance;
3. demographic change, regional development, and economics; and
4. climate and environment.

Considerations of these areas collectively raise the question of the criticality of infrastructure systems and their components as integral parts of wider society and economy.

1.4.1 System Operation and Congestion

A transportation system operating at or near its capacity can be tipped over into a congested state by small perturbations in travel demand, traffic flows, or available capacity. In day-to-day life traffic flow perturbations are commonplace; a sudden braking maneuver or lane change by one vehicle can cause a delay propagating back along the affected traffic lanes, potentially bringing the traffic to a stop or even leading to a rear-end collision. Once traffic movement has been interrupted, there may be a considerable time period before the traffic stream can be restored to its earlier state, even with the intervention by responsible agencies (police and transportation agency). The effects of such disturbances can be explained by known traffic flow theory, such as the "macroscopic flow diagram." This theory is introduced in Chapter 3 and applied to vulnerability analysis in Chapter 4. Fluctuations in demand can occur due to many circumstances, for example special events which impose an unusual additional travel load on a section of a network, or the late arrival of a scheduled (public transport) service which then coincides with the arrival of other services leading to an excessive pulse of demand at a railway station. Chapter 6 includes an examination of this phenomenon. A sudden decrease in capacity can occur due to a vehicle breakdown, which blocks a lane or track, requiring the traffic to find detours or to merge ad hoc with other traffic on the road. Chapters 3 and 4 include discussion of this circumstance, and especially (Chapter 4) the significant effects of nonrecurrent congestion (i.e., congestion due to random events such as road crashes, the occurrence, severity, and location of which cannot be predicted).

1.4.2 Infrastructure Management and Maintenance

Infrastructure systems and networks need ongoing monitoring, maintenance, and rehabilitation to keep them in satisfactory operating condition, and often need remedial treatments over time to cater for changing demands and technology. A case in point would be bridge strengthening on highway networks so that older bridges can safely handle increased traffic loads, especially increased mass of heavy goods vehicles. Freight transport economics, consumer demand, and vehicle technological developments impose trends for increased size and mass of goods vehicles, but this is only acceptable if the elements of road infrastructure are structurally capable of handling the new vehicles and their loads. Many countries have undertaken major bridge rehabilitation and replacement programs on their highway systems in the last few decades. These programs of necessity require reductions in road capacity in the vicinity of the affected structures, often for extended periods of months or more while the works are completed. This leads to a general transient reduction in network capacity, which can then be tested by the fluctuations in demands cited above. Chapter 4 deals with vulnerability analysis directed to ensuring the serviceability of transportation networks.

1.4.3 Regional Development and Economics

Population growth, demographic change, economic development (with new industries and employment creation), and, certainly in developing countries, the concomitant growth in motorization and vehicle ownership can place strains on existing transportation infrastructure, and require the provision for new and improved infrastructure. This is a complex process of planning, resource provision, design, construction, and implementation, which is time-consuming. The availability of the new infrastructure may also lag development by considerable time periods. The extent to which governments can control the location and intensity of new developments can assist in defining the need for and scheduling of new infrastructure to keep up with the development, but in the meantime the transportation system may be vulnerable to the shocks of demand and capacity discussed above. In addition, certain locations and facilities in the region may assume new levels of heightened criticality for the operation of an infrastructure system. Chapter 5 provides a discussion of methods for vulnerability analysis directed at consideration of the wider economic and social impacts of network degradation or failure.

1.4.4 Climate and Environment

Climate change is a compounding factor for consideration in the present age. Account has long been taken of the effects of local environment and climate on the design and operation of transportation systems at the local level. If the climate is changing, then the relevant design parameters need to be adapted to include the new and near-future circumstances for the location. Effects such as sea-level rise and increased risk of flooding would be two cases in point. The occurrence of extreme weather events may also be influenced by climate change. This would include both the increased frequency and intensity of events already experienced in a region, such as blizzards, heat waves, or hurricanes, but also the inception of new types of events in regions that had not experienced these previously (the spread of hurricane activity to previously immune areas would be one case). Future infrastructure systems may therefore need to be designed and maintained to cope with the new environments, remembering that the engineering design life of infrastructure components such as road pavement, rail tracks, culverts, and bridges ranges from 15 to 80 years; time periods well within the span of the climate-change scenarios. Chapter 4 deals with issues of extreme weather and climate change in terms of their potential effects on network vulnerability. The recent OECD report (ITF, 2016) on the impacts of severe weather and climate change on the performance of transportation assets and infrastructure provides a useful reference source for consideration of the potential impacts.

1.5 CRITICAL INFRASTRUCTURE

Considerations of critical infrastructure are now a major concern in many countries (Murray and Grubesic, 2007). The concern stems from a variety of causes, including the state of development, condition, and level of use of existing infrastructure systems, especially transport networks; difficulties associated with public-sector provision for new infrastructure; public—private partnership arrangements for infrastructure provision, and perceptions of risks and threats to infrastructure from both natural disasters (e.g., floods, fire, or earthquake) and human malevolence such as acts of sabotage, war, or terrorism. A pertinent question is then how to identify critical locations in an infrastructure network? For example, the road transport network is large, wide, and diverse in nature. Are there particular locations or facilities in that network where loss or degradation of certain road sections (links) will have significant impacts? How should such impacts be assessed? Thus there are needs for the development and application of a methodology to assess risk and vulnerability of transport networks. Methods and decision-support tools are needed that allow planners and policy makers to make rational assessments of threats to facilities and infrastructure; the consequences of network degradation and failure at various locations and under different circumstances; and what to do about these. Social and economic benefits flow from the ability to plan for and manage the impacts of transport network degradation to minimize wider consequences on economic, employment, trade, and social activities in cities and regions.

Chapter 2 of this book considers critical infrastructure and the interactions between infrastructure systems.

1.6 DEFINITIONS OF VULNERABILITY

Transport network vulnerability as a research topic in its own right owes its origins to Berdica (2002) and D'Este and Taylor (2003). For Berdica, vulnerability was:

> *a susceptibility to incidents that can result in considerable reductions in road network serviceability.*

Serviceability is itself related to the nodes and links in a road network, and was defined as:

> *the possibility to use that link/route/road network during a given time period.*

This general notion of vulnerability continues in widespread use, see for instance Berdica and Mattsson (2007), Jenelius and Mattsson (2012), and Jenelius, Petersen, and Mattsson (2006).

D'Este and Taylor (2001, 2003) defined vulnerability by using the notion of accessibility, i.e., the ease by which individuals from specific locations in a region may participate in activities (e.g., employment, education, shopping, trade, and commerce) that take place in other physical locations in and around the region, and by using a transport system to gain access to those locations. Then transport network vulnerability is defined in the following terms:

- *A network node is vulnerable if loss (or substantial degradation) of a small number of links significantly diminishes the accessibility of the node, as measured by a standard index of accessibility.*
- *A network link is critical if loss (or substantial degradation) of the link significantly diminishes the accessibility of the network or of particular nodes, as measured by a standard index of accessibility.*

This definition requires the use of an accessibility metric that is sensitive to network topology and network operating conditions.

Thus there are two alternative but related definitions in general use for transport network vulnerability. Each has its own field of application. Berdica's serviceability definition is useful for considering "short-term" (hours-days-weeks) disruptions, degradations, and failures in a network. It is also concerned with network operations and the effects of those on network degradation. Serviceability can also be seen as a supply-side view of vulnerability. The D'Este-Taylor definition is perhaps more useful for long-term (weeks-months-years) disruptions, degradations, and network failures. It is primarily concerned with the wider socioeconomic impacts of network degradation, and may also be seen as a demand-side view of vulnerability.

1.7 STRUCTURE AND CONTENT OF THE BOOK

This book presents an overview of the concepts, theories, and methods adopted for vulnerability analysis of transportation networks, dealing with the identification of critical locations and infrastructure components in those networks, the estimation of the potential impacts of network degradation or failure, and the planning and design for remedial actions in the case of failures.

Chapter 2 considers critical infrastructure systems with a focus on transportation. It includes the potential reliance of the transportation system on other infrastructure systems, such as the energy supply system, so that the interaction between systems is also an issue. Vulnerability and resilience are also discussed, and the chapter concludes with the outline of a general framework for vulnerability analysis.

The main body of the book lies in Chapters 3–6. Chapter 3 introduces the main approaches to vulnerability analysis: risk-based inventory analysis, topology-based analysis, serviceability-based analysis, and accessibility-based analysis. It provides the conceptual and theoretical bases for these different approaches, and provides an account of risk-based inventory studies as well as an introduction to topological methods. Chapter 4 focuses on the serviceability methods, which relate mainly to road networks and aim to ensure the ongoing functionality of the network. Chapter 5 discusses the accessibility-based methods, which are intended for studies involving the wider social and economic impacts of network deficiency. Chapter 6 is devoted to vulnerability analysis of public transport systems, largely urban rail (subway, underground, or metro) systems, for which topological methods have been developed. In addition, new developments can be found for serviceability analysis of transit systems in both static and dynamic modes.

Chapter 7 is a synthesis chapter. It provides a vehicle for the future comprehensive study of vulnerability, which can include an amalgam of the four approaches in an integrated framework that uses the common features of network structure used by the different methods as well as catering for the particular data input needs of each. This indicates the way forward for the development and application of an integrated suite of vulnerability analysis tools with identification of the best areas of application for each tool. Chapter 8 discusses the needs for additional research, to fill in gaps in present knowledge as well as extending that knowledge, and presents a research agenda for these purposes.

Vulnerability analysis is set to become an integral part of the planning, design, and management of transportation systems. The author anticipates that this book can be a primary facilitator of that development.

REFERENCES

Bates, J., Polak, J., Jones, P. M., & Cook, A. (2001). The valuation of reliability for personal travel. *Transportation Research E: Logistics and Transportation Review, 37*(2–3), 191–229.

Bell, M. G. H., & Cassir, C. (Eds.). (2000). *Reliability of transport networks*. Baldock, Herts: Research Studies Press.

Bell, M. G. H., & Iida, Y. (1997). *Transportation network analysis*. Chichester: John Wiley and Sons.

Bell, M. G. H., & Iida, Y. (Eds.). (2003). *The network reliability of transport*. Oxford: Elsevier.

Berdica, K. (2002). An introduction to road vulnerability: What has been done, is done and should be done. *Transport Policy, 9*(2), 117–127.

Berdica, K., & Mattsson, L.-G. (2007). Vulnerability: A model-based case study of the road network in Stockholm. In A. T. Murray, & H. Grubesic (Eds.), *Critical infrastructure: Reliability and vulnerability* (pp. 81–106). New York): Springer.

BTRE. (2002). *Benefits of flood mitigation in Australia*. Report 106. Canberra ACT: Bureau of Transport and Regional Economics.

Chen, A., Yang, H., Lo, H. K., & Tang, W. H. (1999). A capacity related reliability for transportation networks. *Journal of Advanced Transportation, 33*(2), 183–200.

D'Este, G. M., & Taylor, M. A. P. (2001). Modelling network vulnerability at the level of the national strategic transport network. *Journal of the Eastern Asia Society for Transportation Studies, 4*(2), 1–14.

D'Este, G. M., & Taylor, M. A. P. (2003). Network vulnerability: An approach to reliability analysis at the level of national strategic transport networks. In M. G. H. Bell, & Y. Iida (Eds.), *The network reliability of transport* (pp. 23–44). Oxford: Elsevier.

Evans, A. W. (1994). Evaluating public transport and road safety measures. *Accident Analysis and Prevention, 26*, 411–428.

FHWA. (2016). *FHWA climate resilience pilot program*. Washington, DC: Federal Highways Administration, US Department of Transportation. Retrieved from http://www.fhwa.dot.gov/environment/climate_change/adaptation/.

Fosgerau, M., & Karlstrom, A. (2010). The value of reliability. *Transportation Research Part B: Methodological, 44*, 38–49.

Herman, R., & Lam, T. (1974). Trip time characteristics of journeys to and from work. In D. J. Buckley (Ed.), *Transportation and traffic theory* (pp. 57–85). Sydney: A H and AW Reed.

Iida, Y. (1999). Basic concepts and future directions of road network reliability analysis. *Journal of Advanced Transportation, 33*(2), 125–134.

ITF. (2016). *Adapting transport to climate change and extreme weather: Implications for infrastructure owners and network managers*. International Transport Forum, ITF Research Reports. Paris: OECD Publishing. Retrieved from http://dx.doi.org/10.1787/9789282108079-en.

Jenelius, E., & Mattsson, L.-G. (2012). Road network vulnerability analysis of area-covering disruptions: A grid-based approach with case study. *Transportation Research Part A: Policy and Practice, 46*(5), 746–760.

Jenelius, E., Petersen, T., & Mattsson, L.-G. (2006). Importance and exposure in road network vulnerability analysis. *Transportation Research Part A: Policy and Practice, 40*(7), 537–560.

Lam, W. H. K. (Ed.). (1999). Special issue on transport network reliability. *Journal of Advanced Transportation, 33*(2).

Lam, W. H. K., & Xu, G. (2000). Calibration of traffic flow simulator for network reliability assessment. In M. G. H. Bell, & C. Cassir (Eds.), *Reliability of transport networks* (pp. 139–157). Baldock, Herts: Research Studies Press.

Lee, C. E. (May/June 1946). New works for wartime traffic – 2. *The Railway Magazine, 92*(563), 177–183.

Lock, J. B., & Gelling, M. J. (1976). The Tasman bridge disaster – before and after. *Australian Road Research, 6*(2), 9–16.

Murray, A. T., & Grubesic, H. (Eds.). (2007). *Critical infrastructure: Reliability and vulnerability*. New York): Springer.

Nicholson, A. J., & Dalziell, E. (2003). Risk evaluation and management: A road network reliability study. In M. G. H. Bell, & Y. Iida (Eds.), *The network reliability of transport* (pp. 45–59). Oxford: Elsevier.

OECD. (2010). *The reliability of travel time*. Research Report. Paris: International Transport Forum, Organisation for Economic Cooperation and Development.

Richardson, A. J., & Taylor, M. A. P. (1978). Travel time variability on commuter journeys. *High-Speed Ground Transportation Journal, 12*(1), 77–99.

Taylor, M. A. P. (1982). Travel time variability – the case of two public modes. *Transportation Science, 16*(2), 517–521.

Taylor, M. A. P. (1999). Dense network traffic models, travel time reliability and traffic management II: Application to reliability. *Journal of Advanced Transportation, 33*(2), 235–251.

Taylor, M. A. P. (2000). Using network reliability concepts for traffic calming – permeability, approachability and tortuosity – in network design. In M. G. H. Bell, & C. Cassir (Eds.), *Reliability of transport networks* (pp. 217–242). Baldock: Research Studies Press.

Taylor, M. A. P. (2013). Travel through time: The story of research on travel time reliability. *Transportmetrica B: Transport Dynamics, 1*(3), 174–194.

Taylor, M. A. P. (2017). Fosgerau's travel time reliability ratio and the Burr distribution. *Transportation Research Part B: Methodological, 97*, 50–63.

Yang, H., Lo, H. K., & Tang, W. H. (2000). Travel time versus capacity reliability of a road network. In M. G. H. Bell, & C. Cassir (Eds.), *Reliability of transport networks* (pp. 119–138). Baldock: Research Studies Press.

CHAPTER TWO

Critical Infrastructure, Services, and Locations

Functioning infrastructure systems are essential for modern societies. These systems provide us with energy, water, telecommunications, and transportation, and they remove solid and liquid wastes. Our economic, financial, and social activities all depend on infrastructure systems, networks, and the services they offer. Transportation and communications infrastructure systems are also vital in dealing with emergencies and disaster relief, including considerations of population evacuation, the ability of emergency services to reach an affected area and individual locations within it, and to ensure the necessary coordination of rescue and humanitarian resources required. The provision, management, upkeep, and maintenance of infrastructure is a major task for governments and the private sectors alike, and society expects these systems to be fit for purpose, adequately provided and provisioned, and available as required, if not "on demand." Failure or service degradation in an infrastructure system can have significant impacts on economic and social activities. Flows of information, personal mobility, and the physical movement of goods all require infrastructure systems, and indeed there are interdependencies between systems that are of concern. Failures can be local, regional, or global—affecting an entire system—but even localized failures are significant for the individuals and enterprises affected; this realization is one of the key tenets of vulnerability analysis.

Some infrastructure systems are deemed to be "critical," which in broad terms means that they are so important to a community or society that they need to be designed, managed, and protected to minimize the opportunity of failure or of becoming unavailable. Energy, water, transportation, and telecommunications systems would certainly fall into this category. The chance of failure or significant degradation can never be completely eliminated, and so the resilience of a system—its ability to be reinstated, to recover, or to "bounce back" in a short period of time—is of interest. Infrastructure system failure, resilience, and criticality are all issues that can be addressed using vulnerability analysis. In particular, the identification of specific elements, locations, and facilities most at risk in a particular

Vulnerability Analysis for Transportation Networks
ISBN: 978-0-12-811010-2
http://dx.doi.org/10.1016/B978-0-12-811010-2.00002-2

infrastructure system is a key task providing vital inputs into system planning, design, and management.

Consideration of risk is an important feature, with risk being taken to represent the overall product of the probability of a failure in a system, at a specific location, and the consequences of such a failure.

This introduction is couched in broad terms, and there is a need to establish and provide more specific definitions of concepts such as criticality, resilience, and interdependency. Further, an examination of the nature of transportation infrastructure systems, their components and physical representation, and the ways they are used is required, to indicate why the study of network vulnerability is important. This chapter provides this necessary background as an underpinning for the study and analysis of network vulnerability.

2.1 INFRASTRUCTURE NETWORKS AND SYSTEMS

Infrastructure exists in the form of systems and networks, with the following prominent applications (Rinaldi, Peerenboom, & Kelly, 2001):

- transportation;
- water supply, wastewater removal, and treatment;
- telecommunications;
- electrical power;
- oil and gas;
- banking and finance;
- government services;
- emergency services;
- medical and health care;
- food and agriculture; and
- goods movement and supply chains.

A general characteristic of these infrastructure systems is that they tend to be spread geographically and thus are represented by networks, with nodes of activity and/or connection and links between the nodes. Each system will have both physical and virtual facets. The physical facets include the structures, assets and facilities, and connections between them. The virtual facets include the operating rules and systems under which the infrastructure operates, and the policy, governance, and regulatory environment in which the infrastructure is placed. For a transportation system the physical facets include roads or rail lines, intersections and interchanges, stops, stations, and pickup points, and the depots, parking, storage facilities, and refueling stations. The virtual facets include the traffic operating rules and control systems applied to the infrastructure. The latter indicates a further point that an infrastructure system may depend on other infrastructure systems for its operations. For example, modern traffic control systems use telecommunications systems for the flows of information that are required for the system operation. Thus a failure in one system may lead to degraded performance of another. Physical proximity is also an issue affecting the performance of different infrastructure systems. For instance, a road bridge in a transportation network may be used to carry pipes and cables for other infrastructure systems (e.g., water and telecommunications) across a waterway. Damage to the bridge may then affect the operation of these other systems as well. In many cities water, sewerage and gas pipelines, and underground power cables are located in a road reserve or indeed under the road pavement. Maintenance and repair work on these facilities—which constitute a large part of the activity generally known as "roadwork"—may thus lead to capacity reduction and disruptions in the operation of a road traffic system.

An overall picture of the system conditions and interrelating factors is shown in Figure 2.1, which presents six separate dimensions for consideration of infrastructure systems and the relationships between different systems. These dimensions cover the characteristics of a given infrastructure, its possible states of operation, types of interrelations with other systems, the

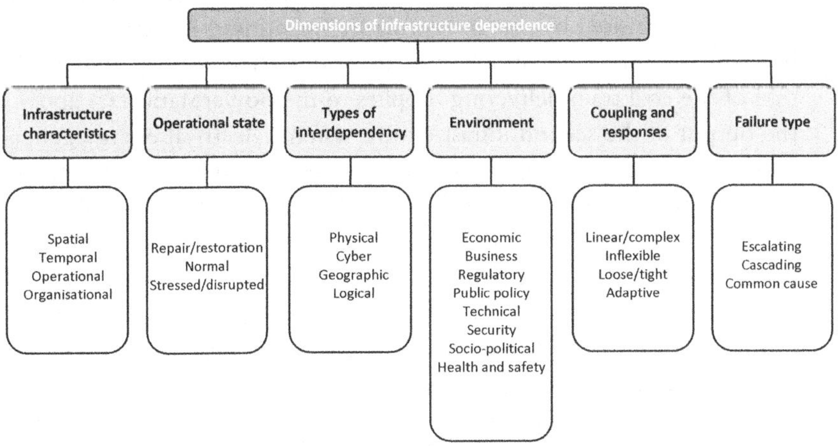

Figure 2.1 Dimensions of infrastructure interdependencies. *Adapted from Rinaldi, S. M., Peerenboom, J. P., & Kelly, T. K. (December 2001). Identifying, understanding and analyzing critical infrastructure interdependencies.* IEE Control Systems Magazine, *11–25.*

economical, technological, security, and governance environment in which it exists, the degree of linkage or coupling with other systems, and the types of failure that can be experienced. Thus the level of independence, dependence, or interdependence between infrastructure systems has to be considered. According to Rinaldi et al. (2001), one infrastructure system is dependent on another, if there is a unidirectional relationship between the pair, i.e., one system depends on the other but the second one does not depend directly upon the first. Thus an electric passenger rail system, such as a subway system, is dependent on the electrical power system. Infrastructure dependency then exists when the state of one infrastructure system influences or is correlated with the state of another. Two infrastructure systems are interdependent when there is a bidirectional relationship between them, that is, the operating state of each system affects or is influenced by the state of the other. An electric rail system used to haul coal to a power station would be an example of two interdependent infrastructure systems. The rail system requires the electrical energy from the power system to operate, and the power generating infrastructure requires the fuel brought to it by the rail system. In general, if we wish to take a holistic view of the operation of a set of infrastructure systems, it is perhaps best to consider interdependency as the overriding perspective.

Interdependencies exist in a number of forms, as illustrated in Figure 2.1. Four types of interdependencies are shown in the figure:

- *Physical interdependency*, which occurs when there is a physical linkage between the inputs and outputs of two systems, i.e., some commodity produced or treated by one infrastructure (its output) is used by another infrastructure in its operations (thus an input to that system). If, as in the case of the coal train delivering supplies to the power station (as above), the output of the second infrastructure system (electrical energy generation) is itself an input to the first, then a degradation in the performance of one system can lead to a degraded performance of the other. Positive feedback may occur, with changes in the operating state of one system having effects on the other, to its further detriment.
- *Cyber interdependency* is found when the operating state of an infrastructure system depends on the transmission of information through an information infrastructure, such as a telecommunications system. As modern infrastructure systems have become more and more dependent on information gathered across the system (such as traffic volumes at different intersections in a road system), or taken from other systems

(such a GPS satellites for location and vehicle tracking), and base their optimal operating states on the ready availability of reliable and accurate information, the transportation infrastructure has become more and more cyber-dependent.

- *Geographic interdependency* is found when a local environmental event, such as a traffic accident, roadwork, road closure for a special event, an extreme weather event, flooding, wildfire, or an earthquake, leads to changes in the operating states of a set of infrastructure systems. Such interdependency generally reflects the close proximity of the systems, such as co-location or sharing of common facilities (e.g., power, water, and telecommunications systems using a road bridge to span a river). While the performance of one system and the change in its operating state may not directly affect the other systems, their performances may be correlated because of their proximity to, or involvement in, the environmental event. Multiple infrastructure systems can be affected simultaneously under geographic interdependence.
- *Logical interdependency* between two infrastructure systems occurs when the state of each depends on the state of the other, through a connection or mechanism that is not a physical, cyber, or geographic connection. Logical dependency is thus a "catch all" for other forms of dependency, such as those resulting from public-policy decisions, public-sector service provision, or private-sector investment decisions. For instance, the contraction of health and education services from small rural communities to larger urban centers may have an effect on the operation of the road transport system as residents of outlying areas have to travel further to access these services.

Infrastructure characteristics, as also indicated in Figure 2.1, influence system operations and interdependency. The principal characteristics of an infrastructure system include spatial or geographic scales, temporal scales, operational factors, and organizational characteristics. These scales are particularly important for transportation infrastructure, which is characterized by its distribution over geographical regions and the requirement that it can operate at all times under a wide range of environmental conditions.

In terms of geographic (or spatial) scale, transportation infrastructure operates at the local (precinct) level, the metropolitan level, the regional level, the state/provincial level, the national level, the international level, and the intercontinental level. The composition of the infrastructure may be described in hierarchical terms, following the taxonomies described by Perrow (1984) and Rinaldi et al. (2001), as follows:

- Item (or part), the smallest component of a system that can be identified in an analysis. A traffic light standard would be one item in a road transport system.
- Unit, a functionally related collection of parts, such as a road intersection, which would include the parts such as traffic lights, traffic islands, designated traffic lanes, and pedestrian crossing facilities.
- Subsystem, an array of units, such as the set of intersections along an arterial road.
- System, a grouping of subsystems, such as the set of arterial roads, highways, and local streets that comprise the traffic network in a city or region.
- Infrastructure, a complete collection of similar systems, such as the road network in a state or province.
- Interdependent infrastructures, which (as described above) form the interconnected web of infrastructures and environment. Road and rail transportation systems often operate in the same locations, and can interact with each other in different ways, e.g., delays to road traffic at level crossings, or the connections between urban passenger rail services and feeder buses at suburban train stations.

In addition, the road traffic system can also be seen as comprising three interrelated systems: the road infrastructure itself, the users of the road system (vehicles, drivers, cyclists, pedestrians, and public transport), and the environment (topography, light conditions, climate, and weather). This designation is widely employed in the studies of road safety (Ogden, 1996). This consideration leads to a further concern: the factors (internal and external) affecting the performance of an infrastructure system. With our focus on transportation systems and networks, we can identify three broad groupings of such factors:

1. *Supply factors*, relating to the coverage (in time and space) and capacity of the different components (items, units, and subsystems) of a transport system. Urban road networks tend to be dense, with many alternatives available between separated locations in the network, whereas rural road networks may be sparse, with few alternative routes available. Even when there are alternative routes, some of these may be inadequate or inconvenient. Public transport networks, especially suburban networks and intercity networks, tend to be directional in nature, e.g., providing good access to a city center but poor, if any, access between adjacent

suburbs, while high-speed rail networks may provide good connections between some towns and cities and bypass others. Road link and intersection capacities can also be limited, or subject to degradation due to vehicle breakdowns, crashes, roadwork, and weather events (e.g., floods).

2. *Demand factors*, which relate to the mobility requirements of a community and the travel intentions and behavior of individuals, in terms of their needs to travel, and where, when, and how they wish to travel.
3. *External factors*, such as weather conditions and (transport) energy supply, population growth that affects the utilization and provision of system capacity, environmental factors, and climate change, which may lead to changes in environment and population distribution.

2.2 ROAD AND PUBLIC TRANSPORT NETWORKS

The content of this book is directed at transportation infrastructure and common transportation networks, mainly at land transportation—road and rail—in the first instance, although the methods for vulnerability analysis can be applied more widely. The inherent purpose of any transportation system is to provide for the movement of people and goods between different locations in a region, and thus the system is largely represented by a network of nodes and links which provide the paths for travel (a set of connected links) in the region, and in which the nodes represent junction points (where changes in direction can take place) or terminal points (origins and destinations) in the region. There are well-known techniques for network analysis and for modeling flows on transportation networks, as described in de Dios Ortuzar and Willumsen (2011). This current work assumes that the reader will have some knowledge of travel demand modeling and network analysis techniques. However, some of the methods and results are basic inputs in vulnerability analysis. Thus it is necessary to provide some background on these. One vital consideration is the description of transportation networks and their potential components, first in terms of physical characteristics (by network type) and then in terms of approaches to network analysis. This is a necessary step in considering critical infrastructure systems and critical components of those systems.

While water and air transport networks are of concern, the emphasis in this discussion is largely on road and rail systems and networks. Network configuration and topology is important, but so are the vehicles that use these networks and the control systems that are applied to them.

2.2.1 Road Networks

Road networks constitute a major public asset in most jurisdictions. For instance, the road network of Australia and New Zealand comprises over 900,000 km of roads valued at more than $200 billion, the single largest community asset in Australasia (Austroads, 2015). The road asset includes kilometers of road pavement (often expressed as lane-km to account for multilane roads), as well as other components (units) such as bridges, tunnels, culverts, car parking stations, and fueling stations. Road networks provide for both through movements across a region and for access to properties and facilities within it. The network is often split into (interconnected) subnetworks in terms of the jurisdictional and legal responsibility for ownership and maintenance of road facilities, with national highway systems, the responsibility of national or federal governments, main road systems, the responsibility of state or provincial transportation agencies, and local roads and streets, the responsibility of local government. Increasingly, many parts of the world now have significant toll road facilities, largely urban highways and intercity routes in private hands. One outcome of these ownership arrangements is that different design standards and maintenance regimes can be applied on different parts of the road network in the same region, which can have consequences if a major road is blocked or unavailable and heavy volumes of traffic have to detour by other roads. This can be an important factor for vulnerability analysis, and plans and operational management decisions based on that analysis.

Different components in a road system will have different design lives, so that a road sign may last for 10–15 years, a road pavement be designed for satisfactory performance over 20–25 years, and a road bridge designed to provide good performance for 80 years. Life cycle analysis for individual transport assets, and the set of assets comprising a given road, is important, especially when concerns about environmental changes over time, such as ongoing urban development or climate change, are pertinent.

Road networks also cater for two dimensional flows and indeed for two-way flows on individual links, a point of difference between them and some other infrastructure networks such as water supply and electrical power generation. They are also populated by myriad decision makers—individual travelers—whose travel decisions can have significant impacts on the operation of the transport system. Electrons, water, and gas molecules do not have that capability. The human influences on travel behavior thus have to be accounted for in any consideration of transportation network performance. A large range of vehicle types, from bicycles to heavy goods vehicles, may have to be accommodated on a road network and on the individual road links in it.

One subtle point of differentiation between road networks and public transport networks is that the former are ubiquitous, intended to provide for access widely across a region, and available for use at any time by a variety of vehicles and users. This is often not the case for transit services.

2.2.2 Public Transport Networks

Public transport (transit) networks possess similar characteristics to road networks but have some additional features and perhaps operate under more restrictive control systems. The additional features include the necessary presence of stops and stations where passengers can access or alight from the transit services, a necessary part of the system operation. Catering for passenger movements thus imposes particular tasks in system operation and perhaps for differentiation of services, especially but not uniquely, for rail systems, where a mixture of local (frequently stopping) and express services may exist. Transit systems operate with fewer (but often larger) vehicles, often quite homogenous in performance characteristics, and with more restrictive operational rules, especially in guided path system such as railways, where overtaking opportunities are few and limited to places where sections of parallel tracks, sidings, or spur lines can be provided. The flows of public transport vehicles may best be described as granular in nature, as they consist of a few large vehicles with relatively long headways separating them. This is particularly the case for railway systems.

According to Vuchic (2007) a public transport system can be defined in terms of three dimensions:

1. its right-of-way (ROW) class;
2. the system technology employed, which is made up of four basic elements: support, guidance, propulsion, and control; and
3. the type of service provided.

The ROW for a transit line is the spatial area on which the transit vehicles operate. There are three basic classes of ROW:

- The lowest class (Vuchic's classification "Category C") comprises surface streets with mixed traffic, typified by urban bus operations, and sometimes streetcars. The transit vehicles may have special priority treatments such as exclusive bus lanes, but these are only nominally separated from other traffic, e.g., by painted lane markings, and so other road users can—and sometimes must—encroach on that space. Transit services operating in this environment are subject to the general traffic congestion found on the road.

- The second ROW class is longitudinal separation, where some form of kerbing, physical barrier or grade separation exists to keep other traffic clear of the transit services, which can then proceed largely unimpeded—although there may be strong interactions between transit and other traffic at crossing points and road intersections. Light-rail transit often operates in this environment.
- The highest class of ROW is fully controlled access, where the transit service operates on an exclusive track completely separated from other transport modes, with grade separation between the track and intersecting transport. A metro (or subway) system is a good example. Fully controlled access transit may operate above ground, below ground, or at ground level. Regional rail systems with widely spaced at-grade crossings (protected by signals and boom or gate barriers) can also be regarded as belonging to this ROW class, at least for the transit mode, since the crossings have little practical effect on transit line performance (as long as the crossing facilities are functioning properly).

Transit system technology relates to the mechanical features of the transit vehicles and trackways in terms of support, guidance, propulsion, and control:

- Support is the vertical contact between the vehicle and the riding surface, for instance as rubber tire on road pavement or steel wheel on steel rail, with other support types such as air cushions or magnetic levitation also possible.
- Guidance relates to the means of steering or lateral guidance of the vehicle, with rail vehicles guided by rail flanges and the shape of the wheel surfaces. Note that a rail system and its wheel-rail assembly integrate support and guidance.
- Propulsion is defined by the type of propulsion unit (engine or motor) and energy source (e.g., diesel fuel or electricity) and the method of traction.
- Control is the means employed to regulate and separate the movements of the vehicles in a system, with longitudinal separation as the key especially in rail-based systems. Control systems can be manual or automatic.

One further characteristic of public transport that is important for vulnerability analysis and that contrasts with road transport is the general "lumpiness" of transit services which results from the granular flow characteristics of transit services. While the ROW—the transit network—is in place at all times,[1] the ability to access and use the system depends on the availability of a transit vehicle to the potential traveler. Thus service frequency by destination is an important consideration. If no vehicle is present, the system cannot be used. This is an important consideration for vulnerability analysis in public transport networks.

2.3 NETWORK TOPOLOGY AND NETWORK ANALYSIS

Network topology is the general topic relating to the structure and connections in a network (of nodes and links), with the form, shape, and connectivity of a particular network affecting the ease of movement through it, the potential for alternative paths between nodes, and the vulnerability of the network in the face of loss or degradation of some part of it. Vulnerability analysis is concerned in large part with identifying those components or regions within a network where failure or degradation will have the most important effects.

Albert, Jeong, and Barabasi (2000) provided a binary classification of network types for complex networks of the kinds to which transportation networks generally belong: (1) exponential networks in which there is considerable homogeneity between the nodes in the way that most nodes are connected by very similar numbers of links, and (2) scale-free networks which exhibit considerable heterogeneity between nodes whereby most nodes have only one or two links as connections but a few nodes have large numbers of links. As a broad example, road networks tend to be exponential, whereas the internet (or worldwide web) is scale-free. A general result (Albert et al., 2000) is that a scale-free network can be very robust in the face of random attacks (failures) of nodes in the network, whereas exponential networks suffer progressively increasing performance when subject to random node failures (escalating failure). On the other hand, targeted attacks—aimed specifically at nodes with high connectivity—can have much more severe effects in the scale-free networks (and potentially lead to cascading failure).

[1] For the case of rail-based transport and perhaps bus rapid transit (BRT) systems the transit ROW is visually obvious at all times, even when no transit vehicles are present. This is not the case with buses using the road system, and this observation is sometimes considered as a limitation on the public perception of the availability of bus public transport in an area.

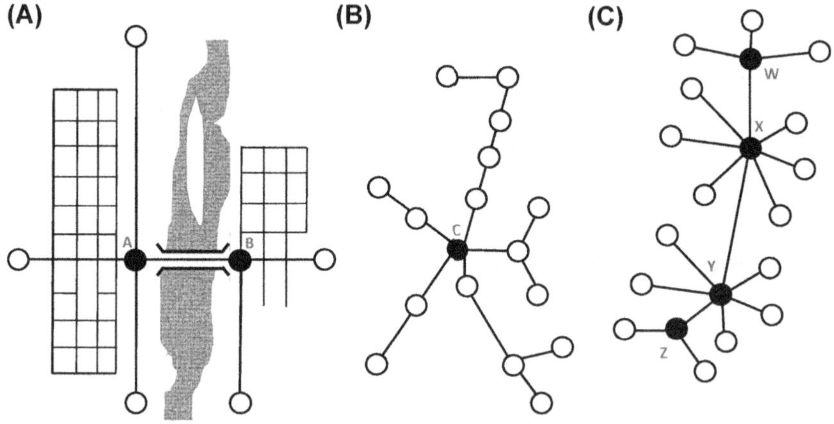

Figure 2.2 Schematic transportation networks as examples—(A) road network for a small city, (B) a radial suburban railway network in a metropolitan area, and (C) a "hub-and-spoke" airline network.

Figure 2.2 provides some schematic examples of different transportation networks that may be described as exponential (Figure 2.2A) and scale-free (Figure 2.2B and C).

Figure 2.2A represents the simple road network for a small hypothetical city. This has a grid pattern and most nodes have either three or four links. The peculiar feature of this network is that it has one connecting link (A—B) between the two main parts of the network. The city straddles a river, and link A—B represents the sole bridge that connects these two parts. The network also contains some links to the "rest of the world," which can be assumed to represent main highways out of town. By inspection the bridge link A—B is a point of weakness in this network. Should it fail, the two parts of the city are cut apart and connectivity in the region around the city may also be badly affected, depending on the availability and proximity of other river crossings.

Figure 2.2B represents a different kind of transportation network, in this case a stereotypical radial suburban rail network in a metropolitan area. There are several rail lines, but the only real connection between lines is at the central railway station (C) taken to be in the city center. This node has five links, while none of the other nodes (stations) in the network has more than three links and most only have one or two. Whereas failure of one of the outer nodes would have little impact on the performance of the other rail lines (unless the train service operating system is based on trains traveling from one side of the network to another rather than all services terminating at station C), failure of node C would quickly bring the whole system to a halt. While this network has some of the characteristics of a scale-free network, it is not really that. Figure 2.2C is, however, closer to a scale-free network. This network represents an aviation system in which airline services are based on a "hub-and-spoke" system, with (in this case) four main airports (W, X, Y, and Z) through which flights are scheduled. Then there is a set of subsidiary airports, all with single link connections to the hubs. Closure of one of the hub airports, especially X or Y, would have significant impacts on system performance. Closure of any of the subsidiary airports would not affect the whole system—though there would be local delay and frustration, the rest of the system would continue to operate (though perhaps with fewer flights than expected). This network, provided as an illustrative schematic, is not complex enough to be classed as scale-free, but it serves to demonstrate the point of difference for scale-free.

Appendix A provides a more detailed treatment of network topology, methods for describing a network for analytical purposes, algorithms for determining paths in a network, and the parameters and metrics that may be used to describe a particular network. However, some basic numerical descriptions and results are useful at this point.

Assume a network $G(N, A)$ comprises a set of N nodes and A (unidirectional) links, and let a_{ij} be the unidirectional link connecting node i to node j. Then, if it exists, a_{ji} is the link from node j to node i, and is a two-way pair of link a_{ij}.[2] A path Ψ_{hd} from origin node h to destination node d exists if there is a connected set of links $(a_{hr}, \ldots, a_{ij}, \ldots, a_{sd})$ from h to d. The cost of travel on this path is L_{hd}, given by

$$L(\Psi_{hd}) = \sum_{a_{ij} \in \Psi_{hd}} c(a_{ij}) \tag{2.1}$$

where $c(a_{ij})$ is the travel cost (time, distance, money, or generalized[3] cost) on link a_{ij}. The minimum cost L_{hd} is given by

$$L_{hd} = \min_{\Psi_{hd}} \{L(\Psi_{hd})\} \tag{2.2}$$

In a connected network there will be at least one minimum path between h and d. Equally, in a degraded network, where one or more nodes

[2] The links shown in Figure 2.2 can be taken to be bidirectional i.e., two-way, so that each of them is represented for purposes of network analysis by a pair of unidirectional links.

[3] The generalized cost of travel is a weighted sum of costs components such as time, distance and money.

or links have failed, there may be no available path between these nodes and so $L_{hd} = \infty$.

Each node i will have $u_i \geq 0$ links feeding into it and $v_i \geq 0$ links leaving it—u_i and v_i do not have to be the same (this would occur in a road network with one-way streets).

The interconnectedness of the network can be described in the first instance by two metrics: (1) the characteristic path length $(\overline{L})$, which is the average length of the minimum paths between all node pairs (h, d) in the network (Latora & Marchiori, 2001), i.e.,

$$\overline{L} = \frac{1}{N(N-1)} \sum_{hd:h \neq d} L_{hd}, \tag{2.3}$$

and (2) the average degree (C^D) of the network, which is the average number of direct connections from a node to all other nodes in the network, i.e.,

$$C^D = \frac{1}{N} k_i = \frac{1}{N} \sum_{j \neq i} \delta_{ij} \tag{2.4}$$

where k_i is the degree of node i, the number of links connecting i to the rest of the network,

$$\delta_{ij} = \begin{cases} 1 & \text{If link } a_{ij} \text{ exists in the network, i.e., nodes } i \text{ and } j \text{ are directly} \\ & \text{connected}^4 \\ 0 & \text{otherwise} \end{cases}$$

and N is the number of nodes in the network. The nodes directly connected to i define the neighborhood of that node.

2.4 DEFINITIONS OF CRITICAL INFRASTRUCTURE

Critical infrastructure is a wide concern and many governments and professional organizations have provided definitions for it. There are also differences in the definitions depending on the perspective of a given agency. National governments are concerned with high level questions, issues, and policies reflecting the overall states and performance of their infrastructure

[4] The N × N matrix $\Delta = [\delta_{ij}]$ is known as the incidence matrix of the network. See also Appendix A.

systems. System planners and managers add concerns about the individual elements, components, facilities, and locations of the infrastructure system, how these interact with each other, and how the system interacts with, or has interdependencies on, other infrastructure systems.

Thus the definition of critical infrastructure in the United States is as follows:

> *The nation's critical infrastructure provides the essential services that underpin American society. Proactive and coordinated efforts are necessary to strengthen and maintain secure, functioning, and resilient critical infrastructure — including assets, networks and systems — that are vital to public confidence and the Nation's safety, prosperity, and well-being.*
>
> *The nation's critical infrastructure is diverse and complex. It includes distributed networks, varied organizational structures and operating models (including multi-national ownership), interdependent functions and systems in both the physical space and cyberspace, and governance constructs that involve multilevel authorities, responsibilities and regulations ...*
>
> *The term "critical infrastructure" has the meaning provided in section 1016(e) of the USA Patriot Act of 2001 (42 U.S.C. 5195(e)), namely systems and assets, whether physical or virtual, so vital to the Unites States that the incapacity or destruction of such systems would have a debilitating impact on security, national economic security, national public health or safety, or any combination of those matters ...*
>
> *The term "resilience" means the ability to prepare for and adapt to changing conditions and withstand and recover rapidly from disruptions. Resilience includes the ability to withstand and recover from deliberate attacks, accidents, or naturally occurring threats or incidents.*
>
> ***The White House (2013)***

Other national governments provide similar types of high-level definitions and directed at their own citizens. For example, the Government of Canada (2010), in its *National Strategy for Critical Infrastructure*, offers the following:

> *Critical infrastructure refers to processes, systems, facilities, technologies, networks, assets and services essential to the health, safety, security or economic well-being of Canadians and the effective functioning of government. Critical infrastructure can be stand-alone or interconnected and interdependent within and across provinces, territories and national borders. Disruptions of critical infrastructure could result in catastrophic loss of life, adverse economic effects, and significant harm to public confidence ...*

> *The National Strategy is based on the recognition that enhancing the resiliency of critical infrastructure can be achieved through the appropriate combination of security measures to address intentional and accidental incidents, business continuity practices to deal with disruptions and ensure the continuation of essential services and emergency management planning to ensure adequate response procedures are in place to deal with unforeseen disruptions and natural disasters.*
>
> ***Government of Canada (2010)***

These definitions are also concerned with both natural, accidental hazards and disaster, and manmade (and sometimes malevolent) incidents, and touch upon both the continuity of normal economic and social activity and the responses to abnormal or emergency situations. This theme continues in other nations' definitions, such as that of Australia:

> *The Australian Government recognises the importance of critical infrastructure, including those parts that provide essential services for everyday life (such as energy, food, water, transport, communications, health and banking and finance). A disruption to critical infrastructure could have a range of serious implications for business (including other critical infrastructure), governments and the community …*
>
> *(Critical Infrastructure) is defined as, "those physical facilities, supply chains, information technologies and communication networks which, if destroyed, degraded or rendered unavailable for an extended period, would significantly impact the social or economic wellbeing of the nation or affect Australia's ability to conduct national defence and ensure national security" …*
>
> *"Significant" in the context of this definition is defined as an event or incident that puts at risk public safety and confidence, threatens our economic security, harms Australia's international competitiveness, or impedes the continuity of government and its services.*
>
> ***Australian Government (2010, 2015)***

At the next level below of government are the organizations, agencies, and professional institutions charged with the provision, management, and operation of infrastructure systems and their components. The definitions used by these bodies reflect their interests and responsibilities, with a narrowing focus on specific infrastructure systems, and how they should be planned, designed, and operated. Thus the American Society of Civil Engineers (ASCE) defines critical infrastructure as:

> *Critical infrastructure includes systems, facilities, and assets so vital that their destruction or incapacitation would have a debilitating impact on national security, the economy, or public safety, health, or welfare. Critical infrastructure may cross political boundaries and may be built, natural, or virtual. Built critical infrastructure includes energy; water and wastewater treatment, distribution, and*

> *collection; transportation; and communications systems. Natural critical infrastructure systems include lakes, rivers, and streams that are used for navigation, water supply, or flood water storage, as well as coastal wetlands that provide a buffer for storm surges. Virtual critical infrastructure includes cyber, electronic, and information systems.*
>
> ***ASCE (2009)***

The ASCE then sets out a set of interrelated guiding principles for the protection of public health, safety, and welfare to be used in the management of critical infrastructure:

1. *Quantify, communicate, and manage risk*, where risk management is the application of a systematic process for identifying, analyzing, planning, monitoring, and responding to risk so that critical infrastructure will meet the service expectations. For the purposes of the guiding principles, risk is defined as a product of the probability that an event may occur and the magnitude of consequences that would result from that event.
2. *Employ an integrated systems approach.* Critical infrastructure requires planning, funding, design, construction, and operation as a system, appropriately integrated with all other interdependent systems. Critical infrastructure systems must also be resilient and sustainable throughout the system's life cycle. The systems must be properly maintained, operated, and modified as necessary to perform effectively under changing conditions.
3. *Exercise sound leadership, management, and stewardship in decision-making processes*, given that the long-term viability of any critical infrastructure system, irrespective of its resilience and sustainability, will ultimately rely on the human and organizational stewardship applied to the system. Effective organizations can control program outcomes through technical oversight, coordination with related projects and activities, appropriate control and change management, and effective communication with project stakeholders. In the absence of sound leadership and management of critical infrastructure, the safety, health, and welfare of the public are at risk.
4. *Adapt critical infrastructure in response to dynamic conditions and practice.* Critical infrastructure systems generally have long life cycles, spanning decades. These projects are normally designed to meet expected performance levels deemed appropriate at the time of design. However, conditions continually evolve and change, and system managers must adopt change-management systems that can effectively address new conditions. Change-management systems need to be flexible and robust,

and must establish discipline in the way critical infrastructure systems are operated, reviewed, maintained, and upgraded throughout their life cycle.

The guiding principles provide the high-level advice on how those responsible for infrastructure systems should fulfill their duties. A clear example of the recognition of those requirements and their application is shown by the US Federal Highways Administration (FHWA) in its framework for assessing the vulnerability of road systems to climate change and extreme weather (FHWA, 2012).

2.4.1 Examples of Critical Infrastructure, Services, and Locations

Figure 2.2 offers some schematic examples of critical infrastructure components in transportation networks, and these are useful precursors to a full discussion of methods for determining critical components. Figure 2.2A shows a critical network link—link AB, the bridge across the river—failure of which would cut the city into two, create significant disruptions for the population, and, depending on the locations of key facilities such as hospitals, could create severe health and safety problems. Figure 2.2B shows a critical node (node C) which is the central railway station for a metropolis. Failure at this node would lead to significant disruption of all urban rail services. Figure 2.2C has at least two critical nodes (X and Y)as airline hubs. Failure or service degradation at either of those would impose restrictions, disruptions, delays, and probably service cancellations for flights in that network.

These examples are only illustrative—although they are very simple versions of actual networks and vulnerability issues in those networks—and may thus be seen as trivial. However, they do highlight certain considerations in the identification of critical components, locations, or services in a transportation network.

These schematic examples lead us toward a view of the basic requirements of vulnerability analysis. The general purpose of this analysis is twofold; first, to anticipate points of weakness where the transport network is vulnerable and network failures will have substantial adverse effects; and second, to suggest remedial measures such as "protecting" vulnerable links or adding links to the network to make it more robust. At first sight it may be tempting to believe that a transport network is most vulnerable simply where link flows are greatest but:

1. alternative routes may be available providing a new equilibrium pattern of flows at little reduction in overall network performance; and

2. considering aggregate flows may obscure significant vulnerabilities in connections between particular origins and destinations.

Therefore the key to diagnosing network vulnerability is the development of analytical tools for identifying network weaknesses because network vulnerabilities may exist that are not obvious from a scan of network activity patterns under normal operating conditions. This is very much the case in large and complex real world networks. The previous considerations of critical infrastructure in this chapter have in large part focused on the consequences of degradation of the network. In other words, if the "best" path through the network is no longer available, how much worse is the second-best option, or the third best, and so on. This suggests an approach based on *n*th best paths though the network or on constrained shortest path algorithms, but in general, algorithms for these problems are inefficient and are seldom included in standard transport network modeling software packages (D'Este, 1997).

An alternative starting point is the probabilistic route choice algorithms, such as those based on the logit model. According to this model, a traveler will choose a particular path from the set of available paths from the required origin to destination on the basis of the utility of that path compared to the alternatives. The measure of utility is travel time or other appropriate generalized costs. The probability of using a particular path will then depend on its relative utility. This argument can be extended to individual links. The probability of using a particular link is a measure of the utility of paths through that link compared to paths through alternative links. Note that for a network without loops, the probabilities for links that comprise a network cut will sum to unity. Therefore if the probability of using a particular link is low, there exist other links with similar or "better" paths. However, if the probability is high then paths through alternative links are inferior. The higher the probability of using a particular link, the greater is the difference between its utility and the utility of paths through alternative links. If that link is cut then the network performance will degrade significantly. In other words, the link probabilities provide a measure of the relative performance of alternative paths and hence of the consequences of network failure.

It follows that the logit-based traffic assignment algorithms can form the basis of a method for identifying vulnerable links in a transport network as follows (D'Este & Taylor, 2003). Assume that the probability of using a path $\Psi(h, d)$ connecting origin h to destination d is directly proportional to the likelihood of use of all links a in the path, then

$$\Pr\{\Psi(h,d)\} = K \prod_{a \in \Psi(h,d)} g(a) = KG(\Psi(h,d)) \tag{2.5}$$

where K is a constant, $g(a)$ is the *link likelihood function*, $G(\Psi)$ is the *path likelihood function*, and $0 \le g(a) \le 1$. A suitable functional form for $g(a)$ is

$$\begin{aligned} g(a) &= \exp(-\theta z(a)) \quad && \text{if } a \text{ is on an acceptable path} \\ g(a) &= 0 && \text{otherwise} \end{aligned}$$

where $\theta \ge 0$ is a constant (path-diversion factor) and $z(a) \ge 0$ is the difference between the travel cost incurred in using link a to travel from node r to node s, and the minimum-cost path between r and s. If $z(a) = 0$ then link a is on a minimum-cost path. Taylor (1979) defined an acceptable path to be one on which each successive node is closer to the destination than its predecessor, in other words each step on an acceptable path takes the traveler closer to the destination.

If $\Omega(r, d)$ is the minimum path potential of node r with respect to destination d, i.e., the minimum travel cost from r to d, then the link a will be on an acceptable path if $\Omega(r, d) > \Omega(s, d)$. The cost difference $z(a)$ is given by $z(a) = \Omega(s,d) + c(a) - \Omega(r,d)$ where $c(a)$ is the travel cost on link a. If a is on a minimum path from h to d then $z(a) = 0$ as $\Omega(r,d) = \Omega(s,d) + c(a)$ by definition (D'Este, 1997).

Equation (2.5) provides a conceptual definition of the probability of use of a path $\Psi(h, d)$ between h and d. The probability that link a will be used for travel between h and d is given by summing the path probabilities of all paths from h to d that use a, i.e.,

$$\Pr\{a,(h,d)\} = \sum_{\Psi(h,d):a \in \Psi(h,d)} \Pr\{\Psi(h,d)\} \tag{2.6}$$

This result is conceptually simple but difficult to use in practice, because it requires definition of all of the acceptable paths between i and j. Bell and Cassir (2002) described a method, the path-flow estimator, for doing so. However, an efficient alternative approach is available. The conditional probability of a trip from h to d using a given that it passes through node r, i.e., $\Pr\{a,(h,d)|r\}$ may be found using an efficient recursive algorithm without the need for explicit determination of all acceptable paths. This conditional probability may be computed recursively using the link weight function $w(a)$ (Taylor, 1979):

$$w(a) = g(a) \qquad \text{if } s = j, \text{ the destination node}$$
$$w(a) = g(a) \sum_{l \in v(s)} w(l) \qquad \text{for all other } s$$

where the summation $\sum_{l \in v(s)} w(l)$ is the sum of the weight functions of all links l in the set $v(s)$, i.e., those links that can be used to leave node s. It then follows that $\Pr\{a, (h, d)|r\} = \frac{w(a)}{\sum_{l \in \beta(r)} w(l)}$, given that $w(a)$ can be computed recursively by considering each node s in forward topological order (i.e., increasing value of path potential $\Omega(s, d)$) from the destination d.

Link probabilities may be used in network scans for the identification of critical network components (links, nodes, routes, or subnetworks). The probability that a trip from h to d uses link a is $\Pr\{a, (h, d)\}$, which can be determined as above. This probability can be used to indicate where to look for the key links where the connection is most vulnerable. In general, the higher the link probability, the greater the adverse impact if that link is broken. This suggests that candidates for the source of network vulnerability will be links with probability higher than some prescribed threshold λ, e.g., $\lambda = 0.6$. Note that if the probability of use is less than one for any link, there is at least one alternative path that avoids that link. The following example illustrates the identification of links where a network is potentially vulnerable. Consider the network shown in Figure 2.3. The number shown alongside each link is a measure of the link cost.

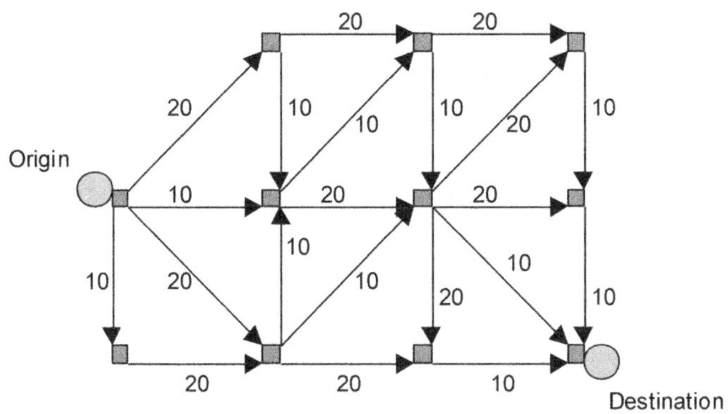

Figure 2.3 Test network—the number shown alongside each link is the link cost.

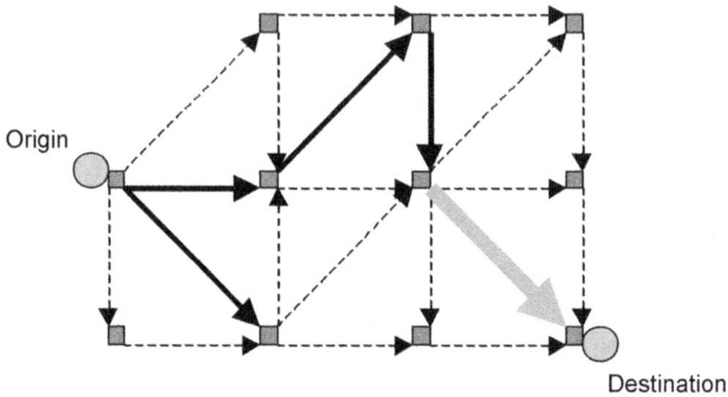

Figure 2.4 Computed link probabilities (logit assignment with $\alpha = 0.1$). Probabilities less than 0.3 are shown with a *thin dashed line,* between 0.3 and 0.6 with a *solid line* and link probabilities greater than 0.6 are shown with a *thick line.*

Figure 2.4 shows the link probabilities after applying the method described above with $\alpha = 0.1$. Probabilities less than 0.3 are shown with a thin dashed line, between 0.3 and 0.6 with a solid line, and link probabilities greater than 0.6 are shown with a thick line. As shown in this figure, there is only one link with a high probability. According to the link probability method, the connection between the indicated origin and destination is likely to be vulnerable to degradation of this link, but relatively insensitive to loss of other links. If this key link is cut then the minimum and expected cost of travel increases by around 25%, whereas if any other link is cut, there is little (if any) impact on network performance. This example illustrates the application of the vulnerability concepts and the analytical technique described above. It also highlights the important phenomenon that all links on the shortest path are not necessarily points of vulnerability. If there is sufficient redundancy in the network then diversion to alternate paths can take place with little degradation of network performance.

Zhu and Levinson (2011) provided a review of a number of disruptions to, and failures of, transportation networks, including the collapse of i-35W bridge over the Mississippi River at Minneapolis in 2007, the collapse of the Tasman Bridge in Hobart, Tasmania in 1975, and the 1996 and 2005 transit strikes in New York.

2.4.2 Identification of Critical Features

The technique illustrated in the previous section provides a method for identifying the network links which are most likely to be vulnerable, so that failure or degradation of these links may lead to the greatest levels of service disruption. A further step is to begin an assessment of the likely levels and extent of disruptions and their potential impacts on network operations, users of the network, and the population and economy of the region served by the network. These issues are dealt with in-depth in the subsequent chapters of this book, but an introduction to the analysis is useful at this stage.

Network disruptions may arise from a number of sources, some of which are natural, some manmade, some accidental and some deliberate, some benign and some malevolent. Figure 2.5 provides a schematic view of a wide range of potential threats to transport infrastructure from the occurrence of natural disasters, adverse weather, technical error, human error, acts of war, and acts of terrorism. Berdica (2002) suggested that these threats can be viewed in terms of both a level of predictability and a level of malevolence, as shown in Figure 2.5. A level of malevolence can readily be ascribed to human behavior, including acts of sabotage, war, and terrorism, but the concept is also applied in more general terms in network reliability studies. Bell (2000) used the game theory involving two players, one a traveler attempting to use the network and the other an "evil entity" who attempts to disrupt the progress of the traveler.

Latora and Marchiori (2005) introduced a general method to identify and assess critical components in an infrastructure network. This requires the definition of an overall performance index $\Phi(S)$ for infrastructure system S. This index needs to be positively related to infrastructure performance, i.e., to have an increasing value as the performance improves (and conversely a decreasing value for degraded performance). As discussed in subsequent

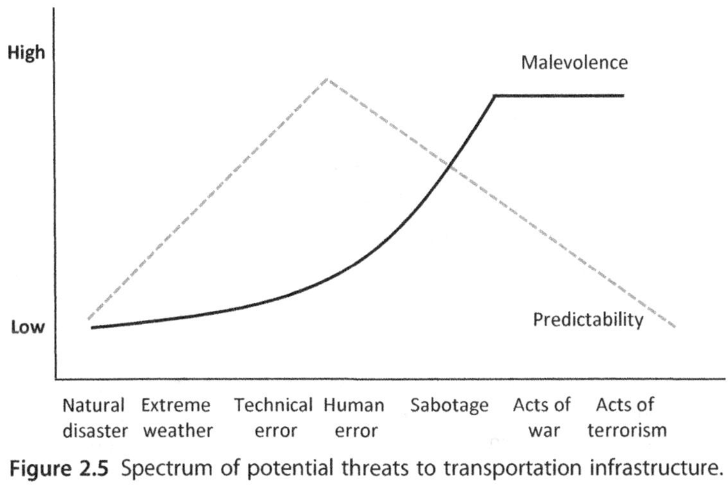

Figure 2.5 Spectrum of potential threats to transportation infrastructure.

chapters, specific formulations of $\Phi(S)$ are defined and used for transportation networks, based on generalized travel costs, economic performance, and accessibility indices, for example see Jenelius, Petersen, and Mattsson (2006) and Taylor and Susilawati (2012).

If $W(S, \sigma)$ is the measured degraded performance of S under damages σ (e.g., full or partial failure of a give link) then

$$Z(S,\sigma) = \frac{\Phi(S) - W(S,\sigma)}{\Phi(S)} = \frac{\Delta\Phi(S,\sigma)}{\Phi(S)} \tag{2.7}$$

is the relative decline in infrastructure performance under damages σ. Examining and comparing $Z(S, \sigma)$ for different σ (i.e., different levels of network failure at different locations) can be used to identify the most critical locations or facilities in the infrastructure (Taylor and Susilawati, 2012).

A current practical implementation of a vulnerability assessment tool for identifying critical elements in engineering asset management is that employed by the FHWA (2012). This framework is summarized in Figure 2.6, and is used by state transportation departments across the United

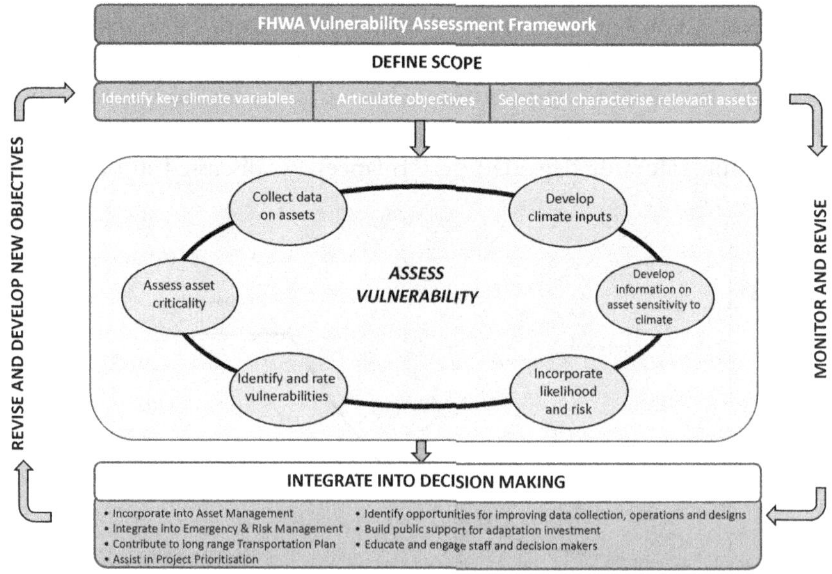

Figure 2.6 The FHWA assessment framework for climate change vulnerability of road assets. *Adapted from FHWA. (2012).* The Federal Highway Administration's climate change and extreme weather vulnerability assessment framework. *Washington, DC: Federal Highway Administration. Retrieved from http://www.fhwa.dot.gov/environment/climate_change/adaptation/.*

States to identify potential risks and hazards to road networks and road assets due to climate change and extreme weather.

The framework provides a definitive, comprehensive system for undertaking climate change vulnerability assessments, yet it leaves considerable scope for the user to decide on the critical features to be studied and in the selection of specific performance indices for the vulnerability assessment. See, for example, the applications of the framework for the Gulf Coast conducted by the US Department of Transportation (FHWA, 2014) and that by the Iowa Department of Transportation (FHWA, 2015). The framework comprises three main stages, each of which contains a number of tasks:

- Define scope:
  - Identify key climate variables
  - Articulate objectives
  - Select and characterize relevant assets
- Assess vulnerability:
  - Collect and integrate data on assets
  - Develop climate inputs
  - Develop information on asset sensitivity to climate
  - Incorporate likelihood and risk
  - Identify and rate vulnerabilities
  - Assess asset criticality
- Integrate into decision making:
  - Incorporate into asset management
  - Integrate into emergency and risk management
  - Contribute to a long-range plan
  - Assist in project prioritization
  - Identify opportunities for improving data collection, operations, and design
  - Build public support for adaptation investment
  - Educate and engage staff and decision makers

In addition, the framework is designed for ongoing improvement of assessment practice, through two feedbacks between decision making and scope definition:

- Develop new or revised objectives
- Monitor and revisit the program scope

2.5 NETWORK RESILIENCE

Network resilience is increasingly considered to be an important aspect of network performance and featured in a number of the definitions of critical infrastructure introduced earlier in this chapter, with The White House (2013) definition of resilience as "the ability to prepare for and adapt to changing conditions and withstand and recover rapidly from disruptions. Resilience includes the ability to withstand and recover from deliberate attacks, accidents, or naturally occurring threats or incidents" providing a good representation. Reggiani (2013) took a similar definition and concluded that, in terms of the assessment of the level of resilience in a transport network, resilience may be described through four key dimensions:

- robustness—avoidance of direct and indirect economic losses,
- redundancy—untapped excess economic capacity (e.g., inventories, suppliers),
- resourcefulness—stabilizing measures (e.g., capacity enhancement and demand modification, external assistance, and optimizing recovery strategies), and
- recovery—optimizing time to return to pre-event functionality.

She also indicated that three measures of the level of resilience of a system should be considered through reductions in the:

1. probability of failures,
2. consequences from failures, and
3. time to recovery.

A convenient representation of the level of system resilience is the "resilience triangle," see Figure 2.7, which indicates the dynamic performance of an infrastructure system subject to an incident which causes a rapid loss of function. With the occurrence of this incident, the system suffers a shock and its performance decreases rapidly. The minimum level of remaining performance is an indicator of the robustness of the system. Remedial plans are initiated and the system starts to recover its functionality, eventually resuming normal operations. The overall loss of function during the incident and recovery (and hence the system vulnerability) is described as the "resilience triangle" (e.g., D'Lima & Medda, 2015). The area enclosed by the triangle indicates the total loss of functionality due to the incident. Mattsson and Jenelius (2015) take this further, by indicating the potential influences of policy and decision making in (1) prior ("ex ante") planning for alternatives and system redundancies which could mitigate (i.e., reduce) the level of decrease of system functionality, and (2) subsequent ("ex post") adaptation

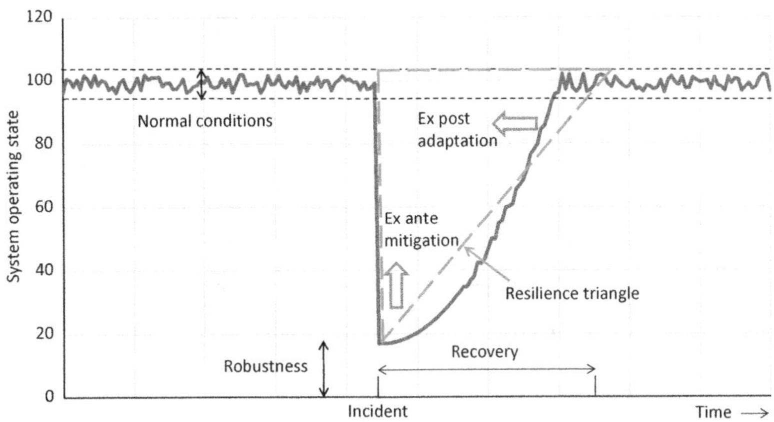

Figure 2.7 Resilience, robustness and recovery: dynamic impacts of an incident, including potential effects of decision making.

(i.e., changes in behavior of system managers and users) which could reduce the total recovery time. These decisions and plans are the basis of resourcefulness for the system. Figure 2.7 shows these features and influences.

The major conclusion of Reggiani (2013) was that as transportation systems normally have a network character, it was therefore plausible that the resilience and vulnerability properties of such spatial networks should be related to the core concept of network connectivity, i.e., the continued existence of usable paths between origin—destination pairs (see also Reggiani, Nijkamp, & Lanzi, 2015). Such ongoing existences suggest the need for the availability of alternative paths and hence, some degree of redundancy in a network.

2.5.1 Redundancy and Alternatives

Figure 2.8 can be used to illustrate the availability of alternative paths through a network and the potential redundancy of network facilities that may then emerge.

Figure 2.8A shows a very simple two-link network containing the minimum path between nodes A and C. This path passes through node B, and comprises the links A—B and B—C. Both of these links are two cost units long, so the length of the minimum path is 4 units. However, a failure at node B would make it impossible to reach C from A. In Figure 2.8B an additional node (D) has been introduced. This network has four links. In this case, there are now two alternative paths from A to C (A—B—C

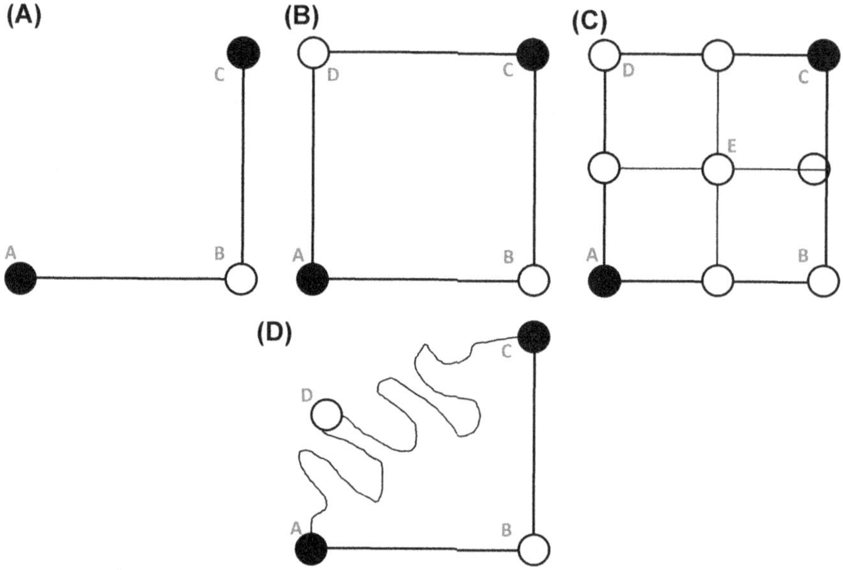

Figure 2.8 Interpretations of network redundancy—(A) minimum path network for A—C, (B) addition of second minimum path, through node D, (C) increased network complexity, and (D) case of alternative path of considerably greater length than the minimum path.

and A—D—C), both of which are minimum paths with four cost units. A failure of either B or D would not affect the connectivity of the network between A and C.

A further extension of the network to nine nodes is given in Figure 2.8C. This network has 12 links, each of one cost unit in length, and there are now six alternative (still minimum) paths four units long between A and C. Two of these paths existed in the network of Figure 2.8B (A—B—C and A—D—C) but now there are four additional paths, all of which pass through the new node E. Thus there are more alternatives available and failure of any one node would have less effect on network connectivity, therefore this network has added resilience.

Figure 2.8D represents one complication that has to be accounted for in network vulnerability analysis. This is a four node network with the same connectivity as that in Figure 2.8B, but the lengths of the links A—D and D—C are considerably greater in this network. This means that although the network is still connected if node B were to fail, the cost and effort involved in traveling along the alternative path through node D may well be wearing, if not prohibitive. As will be discussed in subsequent chapters of this book, the assessment of the extra efforts required to move through a degraded network, or the additional cost involved, or the opportunity lost by having to do so, provides the crux of the network vulnerability analysis methods.

2.6 SUMMARY

This chapter provided an overview of critical infrastructure systems and the place of transportation networks amongst national, regional, and local critical infrastructure systems. It has also outlined some of the issues involved in vulnerability analysis and introduced the basic approach to the determination of critical components and locations within a transportation network. The chapter offered definitions and descriptions of different transportation networks, namely road networks and public transport networks, and highlighted some differences between them. These differences generally relate to additional complexities required in the study of transit systems, where the frequency and availability of transit services must also be considered along with the state and connectivity of the network infrastructure. The chapter concluded with the discussions of a framework for vulnerability analysis and of resilience in network performance.

REFERENCES

Albert, R., Jeong, H., & Barabasi, A.-L. (2000). Error and attack tolerance of complex networks. *Nature, 406*, 378–381.

ASCE. (2009). *Guiding principles for the nation's critical infrastructure.* Reston, VA: American Society of Civil Engineers. Retrieved from www.pubs.asce.org.

Australian Government. (2010). *Critical infrastructure resilience strategy.* Canberra ACT: Attorney-General's Department.

Australian Government. (2015). *National guidelines for protecting critical infrastructure from terrorism.* Canberra ACT: Attorney-General's Department.

Austroads. (2015). *Repositioning for a sustainable future: Austroads strategic plan 2016–2020.* Sydney: Austroads. Retrieved from www.austroads.com.au.

Bell, M. G. H. (2000). A game theory approach to measuring the performance reliability of transportation networks. *Transportation Research B, 34*(6), 533–545.

Bell, M. G. H., & Cassir, C. (2002). Risk-averse user equilibrium traffic assignment: An application of game theory. *Transportation Research B, 36*, 671–681.

Berdica, K. (2002). An introduction to road vulnerability: What has been done, is done and should be done. *Transport Policy, 9*, 117–127.

D'Este, G. M. (1997). Implementing a hybrid route choice procedure in a network modelling context. *Journal of the Eastern Asia Society for Transportation Studies, 2*(3), 737–752.

D'Este, G. M., & Taylor, M. A. P. (2003). Network vulnerability: An approach to reliability analysis at the level of national strategic transport networks. In Y. Iida, & M. G. H. Bell (Eds.), *The network reliability of transport* (pp. 23–44). Oxford: Elsevier.

D'Lima, M., & Medda, F. (2015). A new measure of resilience: An application to the London underground. *Transportation Research Part A: Policy and Practice, 81*, 35–46.

FHWA. (2012). *The Federal Highway Administration's climate change and extreme weather vulnerability assessment framework*. Washington, DC: Federal Highway Administration. Retrieved from http://www.fhwa.dot.gov/environment/climate_change/adaptation/.

FHWA. (2014). *US DOT Gulf Coast study, phase 2*. Report FHWA-HEP-14-053. Washington, DC: Federal Highway Administration. Retrieved from http://www.fhwa.dot.gov/environment/climate_change/adaptation/.

FHWA. (2015). *FHWA climate resilience pilot program: Iowa department of transportation*. Report FHWA-HEP-16-047. Retrieved from www.fhwa.dot.gov/environment/climate/adaptation/2015pilots/.

Government of Canada. (2010). *National strategy for critical infrastructure*. Ottawa: Government of Canada. Catalogue No: PS4−65/2009E-PDF.

Jenelius, E., Petersen, T., & Mattsson, L.-G. (2006). Importance and exposure in road network vulnerability analysis. *Transportation Research Part A: Policy and Practice, 40*(7), 537−560.

Latora, V., & Marchiori, M. (2001). Efficient behavior of small-world networks. *Physical Review Letters, 87*(19), 198701.

Latora, V., & Marchiori, M. (2005). Vulnerability and protection of infrastructure networks. *Physical Review E, 71*, 015103(R).

Mattsson, L.-G., & Jenelius, E. (2015). Vulnerability and resilience of transport systems − A discussion of recent research. *Transportation Research Part A: Policy and Practice, 81*, 16−34.

Ogden, K. W. (1996). *Safer roads: A guide to road safety engineering*. Aldershot: Avebury Technical Books.

de Dios Ortuzar, J., & Willumsen, L. G. (2011). *Modelling transport* (5th ed.). Hoboken, NJ: John Wiley and Sons.

Perrow, C. (1984). *Normal accidents: Living with high-risk technologies*. New York: Basic Books.

Reggiani, A. (2013). Network resilience for transport security: Some methodological considerations. *Transport Policy, 28*, 63−68.

Reggiani, A., Nijkamp, P., & Lanzi, D. (2015). Transport resilience and vulnerability: The role of connectivity. *Transportation Research Part A: Policy and Practice, 81*, 4−15.

Rinaldi, S. M., Peerenboom, J. P., & Kelly, T. K. (December 2001). Identifying, understanding and analyzing critical infrastructure interdependencies. *IEE Control Systems Magazine*, 11−25.

Taylor, M. A. P. (1979). Evaluating the performance of a simulation model. *Transportation Research A, 13*(3), 159−173.

Taylor, M. A. P., & Susilawati. (2012). Remoteness and accessibility in the vulnerability analysis of regional road networks. *Transportation Research Part A: Policy and Practice, 46*(5), 761−771.

The White House. (2013). *Critical infrastructure security and resilience*. Washington, DC: Office of the Press Secretary, The White House. Retrieved from http://www.fas.org/irp/offdocs/ppd/ppd-21.pdf.

Vuchic, V. R. (2007). *Urban transit systems and technology*. Hoboken, NJ: John Wiley and Sons.

Zhu, S., & Levinson, D. (2011). Disruptions to transportation networks: A review. In D. Levinson, H. Liu, & M. G. H. Bell (Eds.), *Network reliability in practice* (pp. 5−20). New York: Springer.

CHAPTER THREE

Methods for Vulnerability Analysis

The focus of this book is on vulnerability analysis as applied to transportation networks. Road and public transport networks are the two areas for particular attention. There are also separate interests in urban, rural, and regional areas, and in provincial, national, and perhaps international land transport networks. These networks and the transport services that use them are major assets for society and for individual communities. As discussed in Chapter 1, vulnerability analysis is concerned with the functional serviceability of a network, its susceptibility to incidents and consequent ability to continue to function adequately, and the identification of locations and components in the network that may be critical to network operations and satisfactory service provision. This chapter reviews the aims and objectives of vulnerability analysis, provides an introduction to the different methods used in it, and discusses the appropriate applications of the methods to different types of networks and problems.

The chapter provides an overview of recent research on the development of a general methodology for transport network vulnerability analysis, based on considerations of the traffic operations and socioeconomic impacts of network degradation. At one level, this involves considerations of alternative paths through a network and the relative probabilities of use of those paths. Whilst probability of use is important in defining potential weak spots in a network, this probability is not of itself a complete measure of vulnerability—the most critical locations in a network will show the most severe (socioeconomic and operational) consequences and impacts resulting from network failure at those locations. The methods therefore consider vulnerability assessment in terms of a planning systems process in which the performance of network components is tested against established performance criteria. The risks and consequences associated with failures at different locations need to be accounted for. Suitable metrics that can be used to interpret the extent and consequence of network failure or degradation need to be defined, tested, and applied.

Vulnerability Analysis for Transportation Networks
ISBN: 978-0-12-811010-2
http://dx.doi.org/10.1016/B978-0-12-811010-2.00003-4

3.1 AIMS AND OBJECTIVES OF VULNERABILITY ANALYSIS

The importance of critical infrastructure systems and the need to identify critical locations and components of infrastructure networks and systems has been made clear. Identification of critical locations gives planners and system managers the potential ability to develop plans to deal with network failure scenarios and to build alternatives (perhaps redundancies) into their systems. Transportation network vulnerability analysis provides a methodological approach to this end, but there is a deeper question to consider: what are the underlying needs for that analysis? The answer lies in a basic tenet of transportation planning: transport is a derived demand. The large majority of travel activities take place because people need to be at another place to conduct their various activities or because some physical items (goods or commodities) need to be delivered to another location. Even travel undertaken for its own apparent sake, e.g., recreational driving, has an underlying purpose, possibly the satisfaction of a psychological need to experience a different environment. Travel is thus a derived demand, undertaken to meet some other purposes. These purposes include economic and social activities, and are thus the drivers of the travel activity. In this wider context, assessment of satisfactory performance of the transportation system should be gauged in terms of the ability to meet those other purposes in timely fashion, satisfactorily, efficiently, and effectively. Thus the broad aim of transportation network vulnerability assessment is to assess the ability of transportation networks to enable social and economic activity in a community, and the society of which that community is part, under a wide range of environmental conditions.

The manifestation of travel activity from the perspective of transportation network analysis is that of travel demand, the numbers of journeys (trips) made between the various origins (sources) and destinations (sinks) in a region over a specified time period (e.g., 24 h of a day). This travel demand is usually represented in the form of an origin–destination matrix (or set of matrices, because the travel demand may be disaggregated by different factors, such as the purpose of the travel). The origin–destination matrix is a table in which each cell represents the number of trips between an origin (the row of the table) and the destination (the column). The row sum gives the total number of trips starting at a given origin while the column sum gives the total number of trips finishing at a given destination. One part of vulnerability analysis is concerned with the numbers of trips able to be completed, i.e., to reach their intended destinations (possibly within a specified time period) in a degraded network (one in which some element, e.g., a link or node of the network has failed, or is operating in a distressed state).

Thus vulnerability analysis must be concerned with the ability of a transportation network to provide service and meet its intended functions of facilitating the daily life of a community. On this score, it should be noted that road networks are intended to serve two broad functions: access and throughput. They provide access to people and businesses by physical connections to the regional road networks, enabling individuals to get to and from properties. They enable throughput for journeys by the connectivity of the road network in providing continuous routes between an origin and a destination. Transport planning has long recognized these twin functions of a road system, and also that, especially in built up areas, it is difficult for a given road to provide both functions simultaneously at acceptable standards. Thus road planning has identified hierarchies of roads, with highways, toll roads, and arterial roads providing for traffic movement across a region, and local roads and streets primarily providing access for people and to properties, connecting them to the main road system. In urban areas characterized by dense network layouts, by and large any road section will have a primary function, either access or throughput, and may have to meet the other function to a much lower degree. Traffic management measures[1] are often employed to ensure that a road section can meet its designated primary function. In regional and rural areas, road networks are sparser and there may be limited alternative connections between any two points, so that a road will, of necessity, serve the twin functions of access and throughput.

There is an issue in a degraded network, especially if a main road section is damaged and unable to meet its traffic carrying function, but detours are available through the surrounding minor road system. These detours may be appropriate in the short term, for example as a response to a traffic incident, such as a road crash or roadwork that temporarily block a main road, but in the long term may not be able to cope due to physical limits on traffic capacity and pavement strength (if the detouring traffic includes large numbers of heavy vehicles), and may reduce amenity for local residents and businesses. Thus system managers need to be able to provide for

[1] For example, curb-side parking restrictions to facilitate throughput on urban arterial roads, and speed control devices and street closure on local streets to improve local amenity by deterring through traffic.

potential long-term alternatives. Continuity in function is also required, especially in regions subject to extreme weather and natural phenomena such as flooding, tornadoes, wildfire, landslides, dust storms, earthquakes, and volcanic activity. There is a need to know the sections of a network that are most at risk in the face of such occurrences.

The broad aim of vulnerability analysis is thus to provide tools that planners and managers can use to examine the potential weaknesses in their networks, and to design plans and strategies to deal with these.

Specific objectives for vulnerability analysis then follow. Using the arguments presented above, three main objectives can be identified.

- Asset management and the protection of networks and their components, which may be best represented in terms of an inventory. This is exemplified by the Federal Highways Administration (FHWA) assessment framework described in Chapter 2 (see Figure 2.5).[2] Network managers need to know the state and condition of their networks and their constituent parts, and how these may vary across the network. They also need assessments of the risks to the various parts of the network posed by climate and environmental conditions, and travel demand patterns. This information can then be used to identify and highlight the elements of a network most vulnerable to risk and those in need of remedial action. This is an ongoing core process in system management, and considers serviceability in terms of the potential failure of network elements in the face of external influences, such as extreme weather events and natural hazards (e.g., floods and earthquakes), and perhaps man-made hazards (such as spills of hazardous materials or road closures as part of police operations).
- Traffic planning and management, in which the ability of the network to continue to meet travel demands under a variety of environmental and operating conditions needs to be assessed. Serviceability here relates to the ability to keep network operations going in the face of incidents. It requires knowledge of traffic movements in the network and the underlying travel demand pattern that generates the traffic. Examination of critical sections of the network in terms of traffic capacity and availability (and condition) of alternative routes is required. Scenario planning, probably using travel demand models and traffic simulation models, can

[2] Chapter 7 describes an integrated framework for vulnerability analysis based on an extension of the FHWA assessment method.

be used to assess the potential impacts of network failure or degradation at different locations. This enables planners and managers to identify key sections of the network that demand particular attention and to develop plans for revised network operations and management in the case of an incident at a given location. The use of a congestion audit approach, in which the sections of a network where failure or degradation is likely to have the most severe impacts, is an important consideration under traffic planning and management. This approach may then be used to determine optimal locations of emergency services and plan for speedy responses to network incidents.
- Regional economic planning and service provision, in which a broader and longer term view of network performance is required. In this perspective, serviceability considers the capability of a network to facilitate the movements of goods and people in efficient and timely fashion, enabling ongoing economic and social activities at acceptable levels of service provision. This includes goods pickup and deliveries to be made according to required schedules, and acceptable access of people to goods and services in a region.

A number of general methods for vulnerability analysis in networks can be applied to meet these objectives.

3.2 OVERVIEW OF CURRENT METHODS

Current methods for vulnerability analysis fall into four main groupings. These are:
- inventory-based risk assessment, concerned with the state of operation of the various elements in the network (generally its physical components and operating systems) and the likely impacts of internal and external factors on the ability of the components to continue functioning
- topologically based methods, which consider the structure and interconnections in a network and seek to identify those network locations (nodes) or elements (links) where failure would have the widest or deepest impact on the network
- serviceability-based methods, which consider the transport-related features of the network, such as link and node capacity, link length, and travel time characteristics, along with topological structure of the network to gauge the likely impacts of network failures on traffic operations and travel demand satisfaction, and

- accessibility-based methods, which consider travel demand in its widest context and which are concerned with the ability of the population of a region (and the individual parts of that region) to continue their normal economic and social activities when the transportation network suffers degradation.

3.3 INVENTORY-BASED RISK ASSESSMENT

The inventory approach examines the makeup of the network and the state of its asset components. It thus provides a detailed picture of the condition of the network. Some measure of the importance of each asset component is then made, using subjective and/or objective means. The levels of risk of damage or impact on the components at different locations can then be assessed. The approach is sometimes termed as risk management approach, and a general framework of a vulnerability risk-assessment model is illustrated in the flowchart of Figure 3.1.

The risk-assessment model relies on existing data sources: (1) the network asset management data commonly held by road and transit authorities, agencies, and operators, and (2) the databases on economic activity, population and demographics, facility locations, weather and climate, and physical environment held by national, state, provincial, regional, and local governments, and pertaining to the region covered by the network. The network asset categories would include:

- road pavement (e.g., lane-km by road type) and rail track (single and double tracks, and lay-buys);
- bridges, tunnels, viaducts, culverts, and flood ways;
- key road segments, including designated evacuation routes;
- transit system assets;
- ports and airports;
- signals and traffic control centers;
- road furniture, signs, control devices, and intelligent transportation system facilities; and
- backup power, communications, fueling, and other emergency operations systems.

The general environmental information required would include:

- population centers, population distributions, and socioeconomic characteristics;
- employment and education centers;
- land-use distributions;

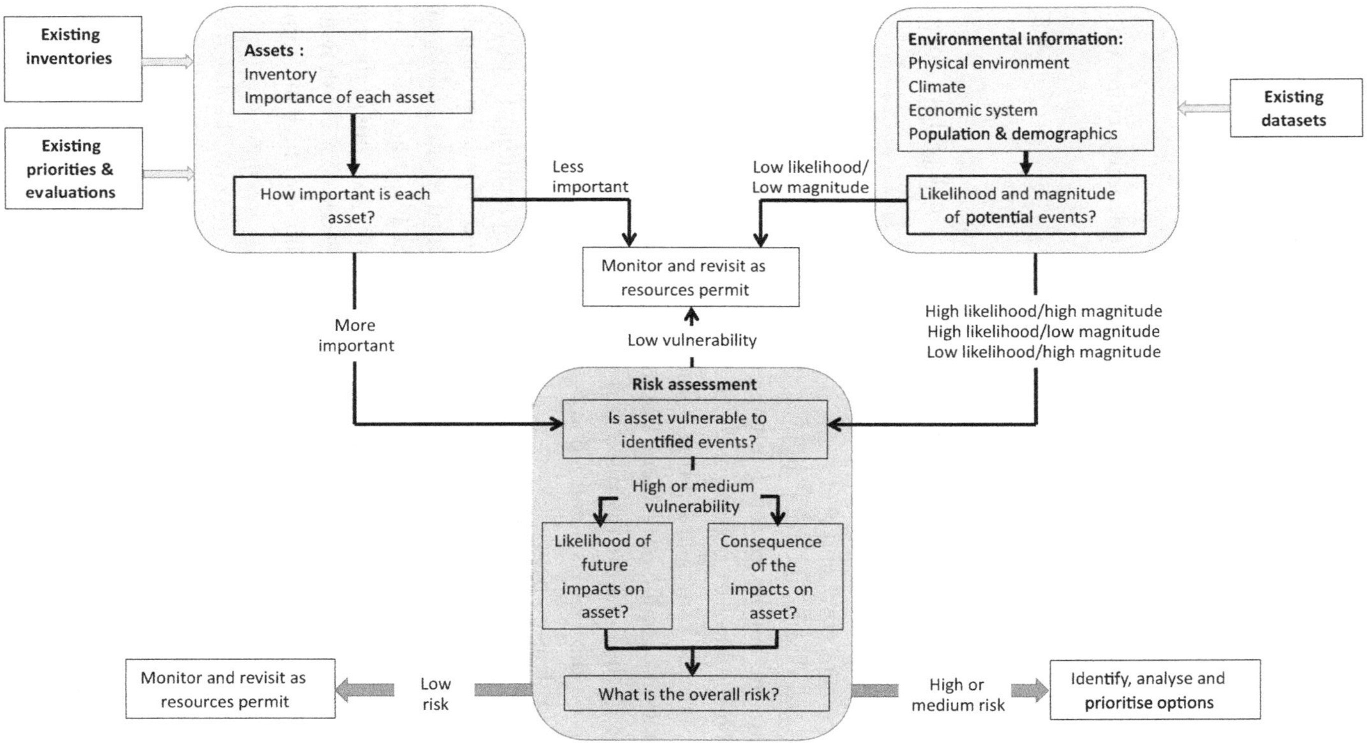

Figure 3.1 General framework of a vulnerability risk-assessment model.

- locations and sizes of medical facilities, energy supply, water supply; and drainage;
- temperature, wind and rainfall data, and flood history;
- physical environment, including rivers and lakes, terrain characteristics, and low-lying areas (flood plains) and vegetation; and
- propensity for extreme weather events and physical disruptions such as earthquakes and wildfires.

The network asset databases would typically include information on the state and location of the assets, including:

- asset age, stage of life, and design lifetime;
- geographic location;
- current and historical performance and condition;
- level of use (e.g., traffic volumes, travel times, and perhaps forecast demands);
- repair and maintenance schedules and costs;
- replacement costs; and
- structural design and materials used.

As indicated in the top left-hand box of Figure 3.1, the network asset information is subject to assessment of importance of the components on the basis of strategic plans and existing priorities. The priorities would include consideration of traffic movement, goods movement, and emergency management. Each asset is then ascribed a broad importance level, with particular attention on those assets identified as of greater importance. Such assets are subject to risk assessment.

The environmental information, especially that pertaining to physical environment, weather, climate, natural disasters, and population distribution, is used to make assessment of expected potential events and hazards likely to impact the network, accounting for both the likelihood of the hazard and the likely magnitude of its impact. This is done in terms of the conceptual risk matrix as described in Chapter 1 (see Figure 1.2). As shown in Figure 3.1, an event or hazard with either high likelihood or high magnitude (inclusive) is then a contender for vulnerability risk assessment.

Assets regarded as less important and events classed as low likelihood and low magnitude are not ignored in the risk-assessment model, but are considered for ongoing monitoring and perhaps further evaluation should new assessment or additional resources be made available for further scrutiny.

Risk-assessment model in Figure 3.1 considers three related questions:

1. To what extent is an identified important asset vulnerable to the projected events? If there is a low vulnerability, this asset should be included for further monitoring. If, however, the asset is assessed as of medium or high vulnerability to the event, then,

2. What is the likelihood of the event and the potential consequences of it on the asset? This enables an estimation of the overall risk (the product of likelihood and consequence) to the asset, so that,
3. If there is high or medium risk level, then options to deal with the risk need to be identified and analyzed so that the options can be prioritized. If the risk is low, then further monitoring is required.

Implementations of a risk management model for network component vulnerabilities include FHWA (2016) and Beer et al. (2015). In both of these cases the events under consideration were related to climate change and long-term impacts on transportation infrastructure. Assessments of vulnerability can be made using the analytical methods described in this book, or by other, possibly subjective, means, such as expert opinion and advice and community consultation. Both the FHWA and Beer implementations used a combination of both approaches, the former with perhaps more emphasis on expert opinion and community consultation. Scott and Dunn (2015) described a link vulnerability rating system for highways in New Zealand, based on an engineering inventory approach which includes both the potential of natural hazards and the road safety performance of individual road sections. This method considers the vulnerability (V_a) of network link a using the product of an exposure index and a consequence index. The exposure index (E_a) accounts for the set of potential hazards identified for the link (and for which the link may be segmented into a number of sections (m_a) to account for different hazards at different locations along the link). Natural hazards are described in terms of the hazard segment length and the "risk profile" for each hazard (HL_{ij} is the hazard length and PR_{ij} is the risk profile factor for hazard i on segment j of the link). They include hazards such as storms and blizzards, landslides, washouts, and flooding. Road safety is included by using the historical crash rate for each segment (CR_j) and a crash severity rating factor PR_j. Consequence of link failure is determined by considering the potential detours in the network undergoing link closure, represented as diversion rating D_a.

Thus the Scott–Dunn link vulnerability metric is given by

$$V_a = E_a D_a \tag{3.1}$$

where the risk of a road closure for a set of hazards is given by

$$E_a = \frac{1}{X} \sum_{j=1}^{m_a} \sum_{i=1}^{n_j} HL_{ij} PR_{ij} + \sum_{j=1}^{m_a} CR_j PR_j \tag{3.2}$$

in which n_j is the number of hazards along the road section j, HL_{ij} is the length of each hazard, PR_{ij} is the "risk profile factor," unique for each type of hazard (and determined using expert judgment, see p. 6 of Scott & Dunn, 2015), CR_j is the annual weighted crash index for section j with severity weight PR_j, and X is a scaling factor.

The diversion rating is given by

$$D_a = \frac{LP_a}{SN_a} \sum_{i=1}^{SN} \frac{CF_i LS_i}{PT_i} \tag{3.3}$$

$SN_a =$ no of subdivided sections (i) on the detour; $LP_a =$ additional length of the detour; $CF_i =$ crash factor for the ith section of the detour, reflecting additional risk of a crash by taking an unexpected route; $LS_i =$ the performance of the ith road section expressed in terms of level of service (see Appendix of Scott & Dunn, 2015 for details on the estimation of LS_i); $PT_i =$ an infrastructure rating gauging serviceability for the ith section of the alternative route (considering expectation of pavement failure)—this factor is based on expert judgment.

A case study application of this method was in the regional road network of the central North Island of New Zealand. It found three bands of vulnerability; high ($V_a > 25$), medium ($7 < V_a \leq 25$), and low ($V_a \leq 7$), largely corresponding to traffic volume with the most vulnerable links located in the mountainous terrain. Scott and Dunn presented this method as an alternative to the use of the more complex models (as described later in this chapter), using a combination of quantitative and qualitative data for evaluation of a road network in which traffic diversions are expected as a result of road closures.

Pokharel and Ieda (2016) described the inventory risk-assessment method adopted by the Japanese Ministry of Land, Infrastructure and Transport, which focuses on the propensity for natural disasters (e.g., earthquakes) in different regions of the road network. This method is described in Section 4.6.

3.4 TOPOLOGICALLY BASED METHODS

Network topology is concerned with the properties and structure of a network, especially the connections between the nodes. Section 2.3 provided a starting discussion on network topology, and Appendix A expands this discussion to summarize the basic characteristics of a network and the metrics used to measure and compare different networks and network configurations. In the basic topological case ("unvalued network"), the existence of a link between nodes i and j is the basic knowledge that is required. The existence of a link is identified in the incidence matrix $\Delta = [\delta_{ij}]$, as introduced in Section 2.3 and described in Appendix A:

$$\delta_{ij} = \begin{cases} 1 & \text{If link } a_{ij} \text{ exists in the network, i.e., nodes } i \text{ and } j \text{ are directly connected} \\ 0 & \text{otherwise} \end{cases}$$

In a metric (or "valued") network, such as a transportation network,[3] each link will have a set of physical properties associated with it. The basic property is the link length (l_{ij}). Other properties such as road type, number of lanes, capacity, and link travel time or cost (see Section 2.3) may also be associated with the link, as applied later in this chapter.

Topological vulnerability is concerned with identification of critical locations (typically nodes) in the network where failure or disconnection of the node will have the maximum impact on network performance and even on the ability of the network to continue functioning. Topological network analysis is therefore largely concerned with the importance of each node—the role it takes in providing for network connectivity—and generally considers two main aspects: network efficiency and node centrality.

One measure of network efficiency was introduced in Chapter 2. The characteristic path length $(\overline{L})$, see Equation (2.3), is the average length of the minimum paths between all node pairs (h, d) in the network (Latora & Marchiori, 2001). The characteristic path length provides one metric of the efficiency of the network, as the lower the value of $\overline{L}$, the higher the speed of movement between any node pair. This metric has a difficulty, however, in that it is not defined if there is a cut (discontinuity) in the network, i.e., if the network is split into separate components due to failure of a link or node, because for some node pairs $L_{ij} \rightarrow \infty$. Thus an alternative measure, the global efficiency $\eta(G)$ is commonly used where G represents the network. The global efficiency is defined as

$$\eta(G) = \frac{1}{N(N-1)} \sum_{i,j \in N; i \neq j} \frac{1}{L_{ij}} \tag{3.4}$$

[3] There may also be physical properties associated with the nodes in a transportation network, such as the type of intersection in a road network or the number of platforms at a station in a rail network.

This metric remains defined in a cut network because $\frac{1}{L_{ij}} \rightarrow 0$ when $L_{ij} \rightarrow \infty$.

In an unvalued network, in which all links may be taken as of unit length, $\eta(G)$ is [0, 1], thus representing a normalized value. The global efficiency $\eta(G)$ equals one in an "ideal" network (in n-dimensional space) where a link connects each and every node pair. There will be $N(N-1)/2$ such links in that ideal network.

In a valued network the global efficiency defined by Equation (3.4) is not normalized, for the links may have different lengths. A normalized global efficiency $E(G)$ can be defined by comparing the shortest path lengths through the network (sometimes referred to as geodesic distances) to the Euclidean straight line distances between the node pairs (Latora & Marchiori, 2001; see also Mattsson & Jenelius, 2015; Porta, Crucitti, & Latora, 2006). If G_{id} is an ideal network with the same nodes as G in which each link a_{ij} has length equal to the Euclidean distance between i and j then

$$\eta\left(G^{id}\right) = \frac{1}{N(N-1)} \sum_{i,j \in N; i \neq j} \frac{1}{L_{ij}^{Euclid}} \tag{3.5}$$

and the normalized global efficiency of the network can be then defined as

$$E(G) = \frac{\eta(G)}{\eta\left(G^{id}\right)} \tag{3.6}$$

As discussed in Appendix A, a similar, alternative normalized measure of global efficiency, the "straightness centrality" defined by Vragovic, Louis, and Diaz-Guilera (2005), can also be considered.

In addition to the global efficiency defined by Equation (3.6), Mattsson and Jenelius (2015) defined a local efficiency $E_{loc}(G_i)$ where G_i is the subgraph of G comprising node i, its neighboring nodes, and the links between them. The local efficiency is

$$E_{loc}(G_i) = \frac{1}{N} \sum_{i \in G} E(G_i) \tag{3.7}$$

Both global and local efficiencies are normalized in the [0, 1] range, and thus these indices can be used to compare different networks or a given network in different states. Global efficiency is a measure of the directness of the connections between all node pairs, while local efficiency indicates the average directness of the connections between the neighbors of a node.

One measure of node centrality was also introduced in Section 2.3, where the average degree (or degree of centrality) C^D was defined in

Equation (2.4). This is the average number of direct connections (k_i) from a node (i) to all other nodes. Two further measures of node centrality for individual nodes are closeness centrality C_i^C and betweenness centrality C_i^B (Freeman, 1979; see also Porta et al., 2006).

Betweenness centrality considers the importance of a node in terms of the proportion of shortest paths which pass through the node. If n_{hd} is the total number of shortest paths between h and d, and $n_{hd}(i)$ is the number of those shortest paths that pass through node i then the betweenness centrality C_i^B is given by

$$C_i^B = \frac{1}{(N-1)(N-2)} \sum_{h,d \in N; h,d \neq i} \frac{n_{hd}(i)}{n_{hd}} \tag{3.8}$$

Betweenness centrality is a measure of the importance of a node in terms of its influence on movement through the network. An equivalent index for link centrality can also be defined, as discussed in Appendix A.

Closeness centrality (Freeman, 1979; see also Porta et al., 2006) is the reciprocal of the average shortest path distance from a node (L_i) to all other nodes, i.e.,

$$C_i^C = \frac{1}{L_i} = \frac{N-1}{\sum_{j \neq i} L_{ij}} \tag{3.9}$$

While this index is useful for a connected network, where it indicates the spatial accessibility of a node, it is not useful for a cut network where some of the L_i may be infinite unless an assumption about the values of L_i can be made. It is also dependent on network size, so that it cannot be readily used to compare different networks.

Topological vulnerability analysis is directed at finding critical locations (nodes) in a network, defined in terms of the potential impacts of failure of those nodes on the overall performance of the network. Performance would be measured by any reduction in network connectivity and the relative increases in minimum path lengths. Its main application is as part of the vulnerability analysis of public transport networks, as described in Chapter 6. Topological analysis can provide a good understanding of the inherent structure of a network and its connections. However, for transportation networks topological vulnerability analysis is generally insufficient for the identification of network weaknesses and for the formulation of strategies and plans to deal with network failures. It takes little account of the physical nature of the network, its components, and their potential susceptibility to natural or man-made hazards. Nor does it account for the intensity, direction, and difficulty of the traffic flows along the network, which are, after all, a primary function of a transportation network. Thus other methods for vulnerability analysis are required. These fall into the two main categories of serviceability analysis and accessibility analysis.

3.5 SERVICEABILITY-BASED METHODS

Serviceability considers the capability of a transportation network to meet its functional requirements (the primary functions of a road network, for instance, and as previously discussed, are traffic movement across a region and accessibility to properties and facilities) under different conditions, including degradation or failure of some part of the network. Berdica (2002, p. 117) offered the following definition of serviceability: "the serviceability of a link/route/road network describes the possibility to use that link/route/network during a given time period," from which she then defined vulnerability in the road transport system as "a susceptibility to incidents that can result in considerable reductions in road network serviceability" (p. 119). Thus two issues arise in considering serviceability: (1) what types of incidents may occur that can reduce serviceability; and (2) what components of a road system likely to be affected by the incidents?

The main focus of this book is on land transport networks, i.e., predominantly roads and railways, and so the following discussion looks at each of these network types.

The types of incidents that can reduce serviceability include road crashes and vehicle breakdowns, which may cause partial or full blockages until cleared, roadwork, traffic snarls from congestion, road closures catering for special events, and weather events and natural hazards that cause road blockages or reduced capacity. Some of these incidents may be of short duration, but others may persist for days, weeks, or longer.

In a road network the roads form the links and the nodes form the intersections and terminal points (e.g., representing a traffic generator, car park, or cul-de-sac). In terms of physical structure, road pavement is the predominant feature, although structures such as bridges and tunnels—to carry the road pavement over physical obstacles such as waterways or through physical barriers such as hills and mountains—are of special interest and may well be strong candidates as critical locations, of which failure could have substantial impacts on network serviceability. Road pavements are designed for finite engineering lives (they are designed to wear out and require rehabilitation or replacement) and their design loads are generally based on the cumulative loading of heavy vehicles traversing the road. The design life of a road pavement is thus based on the expected heavy vehicle traffic usage of the road, with motorways and highways expected to carry larger volumes of heavy vehicles over time, compared to local roads and streets. Incidents requiring detours of heavy vehicle traffic from major roads onto side roads may thus have significant impacts on the condition of the local road pavement, if the detour has to persist for an extended period of time. Taylor and Philp (2015, 2016) described the design process for flexible road pavements, estimation of heavy vehicle (axle) loads, and long-term pavement performance, including the potential impacts of climate change. Bridges and tunnels, as expensive components of road infrastructure, are designed for much longer engineering lives than road pavements (of the order of 80–100 years or more), although a trend for increasing mass of heavy vehicles may require reconsideration of the strength of individual bridges. Bridge failure may occur through weakening of some parts of the bridge such as decks, columns, or abutments, which may occur due to natural disasters (e.g., earthquakes, scouring due to floods, and other extreme weather events). Excessive traffic loads may also play a part, especially for older bridges constructed when design traffic loads were perhaps lower than those generally applied in the present day, and where the materials used for parts of the bridge structure have deteriorated over time (e.g., wooden bridge construction in rural areas). In the past 20 years massive bridge rehabilitation schemes have been undertaken in North America and Europe to increase the structural carrying capacity of older bridges on highway systems. Bridges are generally of major economic importance because they allow easier movement across physical barriers to movement (such as rivers and waterways), but they are also often of considerable social importance too. Bridges can be regional icons, often representing both the culture and history of a region—for instance think of San Francisco's Golden Gate Bridge, Sydney Harbour Bridge, and Tower Bridge, London.

The traffic capacity of a road is the main factor affecting serviceability in terms of traffic operations. The capacity of a road is the maximum number of vehicles that can use the road per unit time. Capacity is often expressed as a flow rate of equivalent passenger car units per hour (pcu/h). Use of this unit enables comparisons of traffic streams containing mixed vehicle types. In mature traffic systems, such as those of North America, Western Europe, and Australasia where "lane discipline" is well established and accepted, traffic capacity of a road is determined in terms of the numbers of lanes available for traffic flow.[4] As a first order approximation for a 3.5–3.7 m wide traffic lane, the capacity would be about 1800 pcu/h, corresponding to a minimum time headway of 2 s between successive vehicles. Narrower lanes would have lower capacities, and the actual number of vehicles at the capacity flow rate would depend on the mix of vehicle types in the traffic (on the open road in level terrain a heavy goods vehicle or bus might be taken as the equivalent of two passenger car units, but when climbing a steep grade a much larger pcu equivalent would apply). Traffic capacity and the methods for estimating the capacity of a specific road section are given in TRB (2016).

At the same time, road capacity is a transient. Complete blockage of one traffic lane would remove its capacity from the overall capacity of the road, but partial blockage of a lane would also result in reduced capacity. In everyday life this is seen when vehicles are parked in a traffic lane; some traffic flow in the lane is still possible, but at a reduced rate. Reduced capacity means reduced serviceability.

Congestion is another factor affecting serviceability. Congestion occurs as traffic volume (the demand) approaches road capacity (the supply), leading to delays and increases in travel time along the road. Increased travel time means reduced serviceability, and so road design is often based on the concept of "level of service" design traffic volumes, which may be much less than the physical capacity of the road but would ensure smooth traffic operations under normal conditions (TRB, 2016). A reduction in road capacity through an incident (e.g., road crash, vehicle breakdown, roadwork, storm, or flooding) will reduce serviceability. Taylor (1999) proposed the following definition for road traffic congestion (see also Taylor, Woolley, & Zito, 2000): "traffic congestion is the phenomenon of increased disruption of traffic movement on an element of the transport system, observed in terms of delays and queuing, that is generated by the interactions amongst the flow units in a traffic stream or in intersecting traffic streams." The phenomenon is most visible when the level of demand for movement approaches or exceeds the present capacity of the element and the best indicator of the occurrence of congestion is the presence of queues.

This definition caters for the occurrence of incidents that may temporarily reduce the capacity of a given road section.

[4] An alternative in less developed traffic systems might be to consider capacity in terms of pcu per meter of road width.

Railway capacity is a key consideration in the planning and operation of railway systems. Capacity of a rail track is dictated by the basic operating rules for trains, which always seek to provide for a fail-safe operation. In the first instance, this means that only one train at a time is allowed on a rail track section (e.g., between stations or, in the case of bidirectional flows on a single track line, between passing loops). Capacity of a rail track is assessed in terms of the number of trains per unit time (hour or day) that can operate on the track without causing the propagation of unnecessary delays. The capacity will depend on the fixed installations on the track, types and power of the locomotives, types of rail cars used, and the way the traffic is organized (e.g., in a system containing mixed passenger and freight trains, with potential short-distance urban operations and long-distance regional operations using the same infrastructure, some trains may receive priority over others). Appendix B provides a short introduction to the analysis of railway capacity.

For road traffic, further consideration of traffic flow, road capacity, and level of congestion is required. The traffic flow on a road can be described in terms of two primary variables, traffic volume (q, vehicles per unit time) and traffic density (k, vehicles per unit distance). For uninterrupted traffic flow (one in which the performance of the traffic stream is affected only by the interactions between vehicle in that stream[5]), volume and density are related by the continuity equation

$$q = k\bar{v} \tag{3.10}$$

where $\bar{v}$ is the space mean speed of the traffic (i.e., the average speed of all vehicles in the road section at a given instant of time[6]). This leads to the "fundamental diagram of traffic flow," the plot of density versus volume. Figure 3.2 provides an archetypal picture of this plot. It shows a k—q curve as an asymmetric curve starting from the origin and rising to a maximum volume ($q_{\max}$) as density increases to k_m, then with decreasing volume with further increases in density until volume is again zero at k_j, the "jam density". A salient feature of this curve is that there may be two possible values of k for

[5] When two or more traffic streams interact, e.g., at an intersection, the traffic flow regime is described as interrupted flow and other methods are required for capacity analysis (e.g., Taylor, Bonsall, & Young, 2000).

[6] Formally, traffic volume is defined as the number of vehicles passing a designated point on a road over a given time interval divided by the duration of that time interval; while traffic density is the number of vehicles on a road section at a given instant of time divided by the length of the road section.

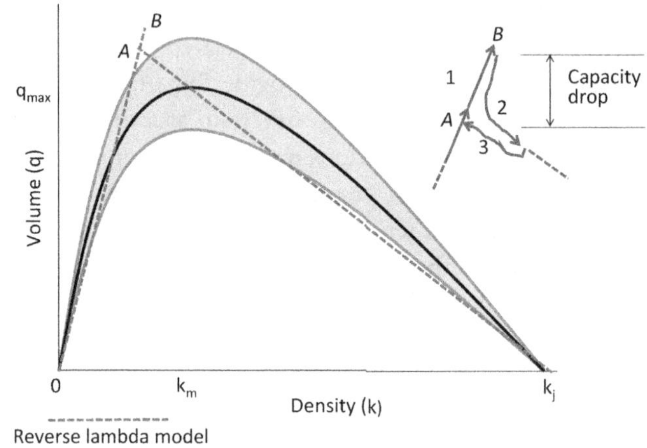

Figure 3.2 The fundamental model of traffic flow, showing "capacity drop" hysteresis effect and the "reverse lambda" model.

a given value of q, representing free-flow traffic on the left arm of the curve and congested ("stop—start") traffic flow on the right arm. Density is therefore a better single descriptor of the state of a traffic stream than volume. The shaded band around the curve represents the typical spread of observed data, which is also part of a further realization about congested traffic flow. There is a hysteresis effect—after an episode in which density has reached or exceeded k_m, a subsequent decrease in density does not lead to a return to volumes of the order of q_{max}, but to a lower value, a "capacity drop." This well-known and commonly recorded effect often leads to the persistence of bottlenecks on highways for long periods after the incident that caused the initial descent into congested flow. One simple descriptor of this effect is the "reverse lambda" model,[7] represented by two dashed lines (OAB and Ak_j) shown in Figure 3.2. The inset in the top right-hand corner of the figure shows the dynamics of the capacity drop. A more detailed account of the fundamental diagram and the models representing it is available in Ni, Li, Wang, and Jia (2016). Modern highway traffic control systems strive to keep volumes below "point A," sometimes through measures to keep the total number of vehicles on the highway system below some supposed value, e.g., by ramp metering to restrict the entry of new vehicles on to the highway network. However, degradation of the highway through a lane blockage or

[7] This model is termed as "reverse lambda" model because its shape is the mirror image of the Greek letter λ.

lane/carriageway closure, from whatever source, would lead to significant restrictions on traffic movement on that road section, which may then spill back on to upstream sections. This situation may continue to exist for some time, until a substantial drop in traffic demand to use the highway occurs, allowing density to decrease well below k_m.

Interrupted traffic flow is different. It applies when two or more traffic streams intersect, and some set of priority rules have to be applied to enable the streams to operate. Traffic signals, e.g., at arterial road intersections, are a widely known case of interrupted traffic flow. While continuity of flow considerations still apply, queuing is expected—indeed is a basic consequence of the control regime—and therefore has to be accounted for. Traffic capacity and delays at traffic signals have been studied extensively and there are highly refined methods for signal design including the optimization of traffic signal timings (e.g., see TRB, 2016). Besides their ongoing use at intersections, temporary installations of traffic signals are often employed at roadwork and road blockage sites where single lane operation for two-way traffic flow has to be imposed. Delay functions for signals and the underlying theory were discussed at length by Akcelik and Rouphail (1993), and interested readers are referred to this work. For the following discussions in this book (e.g., in Chapter 4), the basic variable "degree of saturation" from signalized intersection analysis is important. For a traffic stream this is the ratio of the total number of arrivals at the signal during a nominated time period to the total number of vehicles discharged through the signal in that interval. A degree of saturation less than one means that there should be no residual queue of vehicles waiting for discharge at the end of the time period, whereas a value exceeding one means oversaturated conditions in which there will be a residual queue, and this queue may continue to grow over an extended period as long as that high level of traffic demand persists.

Travel demand of itself is a basic consideration in transportation network analysis. The flows of people, vehicles, and goods on the network stem from and are largely determined by the spatial and temporal patterns of travel demand in the region serviced by the network. The usual representation of travel demand is in the form of the origin–destination (O–D) matrix $[H_{hd}]$, in which the cell value H_{hd} is the number of trips (people, vehicles, or quantity of goods) moving from origin h to destination d. In this description, the row h of the matrix contains all the trips from h traveling to all destinations, and the column d contains all trips destined for d. The row and column sums of the O–D matrix thus define the total trip generation of the region, with rows sums being defined as the trip production of the origins and column sums the trip attraction of the destinations. A trip distribution model can be used to estimate the numbers of trips from each origin to each destination, while a traffic assignment model is used to estimate the anticipated volumes on each part of the network representing the travel demand. Very often there will be a family of O–D matrices applicable to the study region, perhaps accounting for such things as different purposes of travel, different modes of transportation and types of vehicles used, different times of day, and different types of travelers or goods.

A comprehensive account of travel demand modeling is not possible in this book, but there are many excellent texts and references on this subject, see for example de Dios Ortuzar and Willumsen (2011). The equilibrium traffic assignment model is one of particular interest as this impinges on vulnerability analysis (as described in the next chapter). This model also allows some insight into the development of traffic congestion in a network and how congestion levels and patterns may change as network serviceability changes.

Equilibrium assignment can be written as a mathematical programming problem, with a nonlinear objective function (representing the economic, environmental, or social value of travel activity) and a set of linear constraints (which represent conservation of trips and continuity of flow in the network). There are many formulations of traffic assignment models, but these can generally be represented by one of the three commonly used strategies for assignment modeling: Wardrop's principles (Wardrop, 1952) and Jewell's principle (Jewell, 1967). These can be used to define a family of equilibrium assignment models. Different members of this family will have different objective functions in the mathematical programming formulation for the equilibrium assignment problem.

According to *Wardrop's first principle*, the journey times on all of the routes used for travel between an origin and a destination will be equal at the equilibrium point, and will be less than the times which would be experienced on any other route. No individual driver can gain an advantage by a unilateral change of route. This strategy implies that drivers seek a route which minimizes their individual travel times given that all drivers are attempting this strategy for themselves. The strategy is one of individual travel time optimization, and it implies competition between drivers, who are all seeking the best outcomes for themselves independent of each other, and minimal information sharing. However, the resulting pattern of flows on the network represents a stable "Nash" equilibrium, for at the equilibrium solution no driver can gain from a unilateral deviation from that solution. To do so will incur a longer travel time, so no advantage is gained for the individual. The equilibrium assignment problem for Wardrop's first principle is known as *user travel time minimization*.

Wardrop's second principle considers the overall minimization of the travel task represented by the total travel time (vehicle-hours of travel, *VHT*) in the network. In this case drivers select their routes to produce the minimum *VHT* which is necessary for the travel demand to be satisfied, i.e., for all of the trips in the O–D matrices to reach their destinations. This model is described as *system travel time minimization*. The solution to this problem implies a degree of cooperation and information sharing between drivers to attain this result. Although the total *VHT* will be less than that in the user travel time minimization, some individual drivers will encounter much longer travel times than the minimum available to them (for the "greater good"). Should such drivers decide to improve their own situations, then the system-wide optimum solution will be lost, and there is no incentive (other than the ideal of cooperation for the overall gain of the community) for them not to do so. Without external intervention this solution is unstable. It does, however, define a datum in terms of the best distribution of flows that could occur if the overall minimization of "travel effort" (e.g., *VHT*) was to be achieved, and other solutions (e.g., for user travel time minimization) can be compared to it on those grounds.

Jewell's principle is a generalization of the two Wardrop principles, each of which can be seen as a special case of Jewell's principle. Jewell's principle is that the assigned flow pattern should optimize some overall economic objective for the network. This objective can be the minimization of travel time, either by individuals (Wardrop's first principle) or for the system as a whole (Wardrop's second principle). Other definitions of economic objective can be chosen, such as minimum perceived travel times and costs (known as "stochastic user equilibrium assignment"), minimum energy consumption, vehicle operating costs, generalized cost of travel, or pollutant emissions. The optimization problem for any of these objectives may be defined as either a user minimization problem or a system minimization problem.

The basic equilibrium assignment model for fixed (inelastic) travel demand is an expression of Wardrop's first principle. This model formulation provides a useful macroscopic simulation of travel on an urban network. It can be written as the following nonlinear optimization problem, for which a convergent solution can be found (e.g., as described in de Dios Ortuzar & Willumsen, 2011):

$$Z_{W1} = \min\left\{ \sum_a \int_0^{q(a)} T_a(x)dx \right\} \tag{3.11}$$

in which $q(a)$ is the traffic volume on link a, and subject to the continuity of flow constraints

$$H_{hd} = \sum_r X_{rhd} \quad \forall \ h, \ d \tag{3.12}$$

and

$$q(a) = \sum_{hdr} \delta_{ahdr} X_{rhd} \quad \forall \ h, \ d \tag{3.13}$$

$$\text{where } \delta_{ahdr} = 1 \text{ if and only if } a \text{ is in path } r \text{ from } h \text{ to } d, \\ = 0 \text{ otherwise}$$

X_{rhd} is the number of trips using path r between h and d, and the function $T_a(q(a))$ is the congestion function for link a, i.e., the travel time on a when the link traffic volume is $q(a)$. Constraint Equation (3.12) ensures that all of the trips in travel demand are assigned to the network, while Equation (3.13) indicates that the total traffic volume on a link is composed of all of the trips from each O—D pair that take a path that uses that link.

The equivalent system-wide travel time minimization problem (i.e., the assignment flow pattern corresponding to Wardrop's second principle), or "total travel time minimization," can be written as a similar optimization problem, with objective function

$$Z_{W2} = \min\left\{ \sum_a q(a) T(q(a)) \right\} \tag{3.14}$$

with the same conservation of flow constraints (Equations 3.12 and 3.13).

A number of forms exist for congestion functions. A popular form in the academic literature is the "Bureau of Public Roads (BPR)" function, which in general form is written as

$$T(a) = T_0 \left(1 + \beta \left(\frac{q(a)}{Q_a} \right)^n \right) \tag{3.15}$$

in which T_0 is the "free-flow" travel time on the link (i.e., when there is no other traffic on it), Q_a is the representative capacity of the link, β is a constant parameter, and n is an integer exponent (β and n may depend on the link (road) type). While this function is well behaved in algebraic terms, it seldom provides a good representation of link travel times under congested conditions in real world networks, and a variety of alternative functions are used in practice, such as Spiess' conical function (Spiess, 1990) and Akcelik's function (Akcelik, 1991), among others (Davis & Xiong, 2007). Davis and Xiong (2007) and TRB (2012) each provides useful reviews of various forms of the congestion function.

User equilibrium assignment (Wardrop's first principle) can be taken as a reasonable simulation of real world traffic distribution across a network, at least in the absence of travel information. The minimum total travel time assignment of Wardrop's second principle represents a best global solution for that traffic distribution—a planner's ideal—but is unlikely to occur in reality. That said, the user of a good traffic information system might push the traffic pattern from user equilibrium towards something closer to that ideal. The Wardrop principles can be treated as meeting different economic objectives for network travel, if travel time is taken as one possible alternative measure of travel cost. Thus they may be seen as particular cases of Jewell's assignment principle that the ultimate pattern of flow in a network will satisfy some explicit economic objective, for instance minimum generalized travel cost or minimum energy consumption (both either individual or system-wide). For instance, generalized cost functions including travel time, fuel consumption, pollutant emissions, tolls and road user charges, vehicle operating costs etc. could also be used in equilibrium assignment.

The assignment models presented in the above equations assume fixed, "inelastic" travel demand, i.e., the O–D matrix is held constant. In reality, if there are substantial changes in a network then, over time, the travel demand pattern will vary (this is known as "elastic demand"), and there are models, still using the mathematical programming formulation described above, which can account for elastic demands. See, for example, Evans (1976), Taylor (1999), and de Dios Ortuzar and Willumsen (2011).

A simple form of vulnerability analysis using the serviceability approach is to estimate the likely changes in travel times and costs in a network, as indicated by D'Este and Taylor (2003). This approach will identify the network links whose degradation will lead to the largest increases in travel times and costs, but may not provide substantial diagnostic information on network performance. The importance–exposure approach (Jenelius, Mattsson, & Petersen, 2006) described in Chapter 4 provides the basis for the diagnostic treatment of road networks on the basis of serviceability.

3.6 ACCESSIBILITY-BASED METHODS

The serviceability approach offers a powerful method for vulnerability analysis focused on the ability of the transportation system to continue to operate when under stress, and to identify critical locations where incidents and infrastructure degradation may have the most serious impacts on those operations. The broader context, in which the transportation system is a facilitator of economic activity and development, and social interaction, in a region, also requires consideration in network vulnerability analysis. As indicated earlier in this chapter, transport is a derived demand, and travel is undertaken because individuals need to participate in different activities at different locations in an area, and need to send physical goods between places. These requirements lead to the consideration of accessibility for people to facilities, services, and activities, i.e., how readily available are these facilities and services to the inhabitants of a region, and conversely for a facility or service how many people have ready access to it? This is the basis of accessibility theory in transportation planning—the "ease of reaching" from a specific location. Indeed, some planners believe that planning for accessibility is the core transportation planning function.

The notion of accessibility in transportation planning can be illustrated through basic definitions, such as *accessibility is the ease for participation in activities from different specific locations using a transport system* (D'Este & Taylor, 2003) and *accessibility is the ease with which desired destinations may be reached* (Niemeier, 1997). The concept can be applied to different spatial areas and at different levels of regionality, e.g., continental, national, regional, and urban. In particular circumstances, this broad definition can be refined to explicitly include other relevant factors, such as time dependency, which may be an issue in, for instance, assessing accessibility levels for public transport users in urban and suburban areas where the level of service of public transport provision varies widely over hours of the day or days of the week. Thus, for an urban multimodal transport environment, Primerano and Taylor (2005) defined accessibility as the ease for people to participate in activities from specific locations to a destination using a mode of transport at a specific time. In similar vein, Chen, Yang, Kongsomsaksakul, and Lee (2007) defined accessibility as *the quantification of an individual's freedom to participate in activities in the environment.*

Accessibility can be seen as a key driver of regional and urban development using the "wagon wheel" model originally proposed by Wegener (1996) as a model of transport–land use interaction. Figure 3.3 portrays

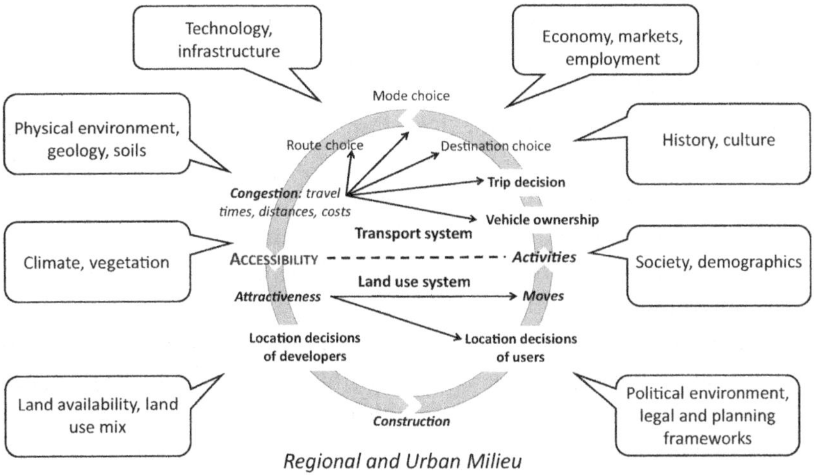

Figure 3.3 Accessibility as a key driver in regional and urban development—the "Wagon Wheel" model.

regional development—indeed the evolution of regional economic and social systems—as a continuous process. The central part of the figure comprises the land-use system and the transportation system, connected through accessibility and the activities undertaken in the region. The wheel includes a number of decisions made by different players and a number of outcomes stemming from those decisions. The outcomes are indicated in italics in Figure 3.3. The basic outcome is the set of activities. Location decisions of developers, businesses, and consumers are made on the basis of the relative accessibility of different areas—outcome "attractiveness"—including their suitability for different activities (services, facilities, production, consumption). The accessibility of a given location is affected by the travel choices of the consumers (when, where, and how to travel, and of course a basic decision about private vehicle ownership and use), which leads to the development of congestion and hence the actual (time, distance and cost) separations between localities. These separations affect the accessibility actually experienced by people, hence the ongoing evolution of the system. Choices of location, vehicle ownership, and travel depend on (or are influenced by) broader characteristics and influences of the urban area, including its physical environment, history and culture, social and economic environment, and available technology. These factors in the regional and urban milieu serve to influence the choices of players in the development system, at macro-, meso-, and microlevels. While subject to external shocks (such as geopolitics, energy prices, and overall economic conditions, including competition between regions and cities, and climate change) the system is effectively closed and is evolutionary.

The original D'Este—Taylor definition of network vulnerability based on the accessibility concept was given in Chapter 1. To reiterate, this two-part definition of vulnerability says:

- A network node is vulnerable if loss (or substantial degradation) of a small number of links significantly diminishes the accessibility of the node, as measured by a standard index of accessibility.
- A network link is critical if loss (or substantial degradation) of the link significantly diminishes the accessibility of the network or of particular nodes, as measured by a standard index of accessibility.

Accessibility is certainly a real concept but does not have a physical unit to represent it, although some measures of accessibility such as "how many jobs are there within a specified travel time of a given location" certainly have a physical representation (e.g., see Farber & Fu, 2017). As a consequence, a number of indices representing accessibility of given locations were proposed. Two dimensions influence accessibility: (1) the degree of separation between the (home) location and the (nearest) location where the required activity can be undertaken, and (2) the size or intensity of that activity at its location. In any region, there may be more than one site where the activity can be found. These will be at different separations (e.g., different travel times or distances) from the individual and also be of different size, intensity, and perhaps quality. The individual may then have a number of alternatives to choose between. Some of the possible representations of accessibility are:

- observed or expected travel cost between two points;
- the opportunity presented to an individual to participate in a given activity or set of activities;
- the number of opportunities reached within a given travel time or distance;
- the ease by which activities can be reached from a given location using a specific transport system; and
- the possibility to reach a given location within an acceptable amount of time, effort, or financial cost with respect to a given policy.

Primerano and Taylor (2005) classified the approaches for the measurement of accessibility as:

- topological accessibility, concerned with connectivity in networks;

- space–time framework, considered the constraints imposed on an individual's movement around a region in terms of available time and the speeds of travel possible given the transport infrastructure, modes, and services available to that individual in the region (i.e., could an individual reach a given location in the time available using a particular form of transport); and
- opportunity (or impedance)-based accessibility, based on the separation between the individual and the activities (s)he wishes to participate in, and the density or intensity of those activities at their different locations.

Formal definition of specific accessibility indicators can be given in terms of a binary classification of the indices, as either *relative accessibility* or *integral accessibility*. Relative accessibility describes the degree of connection between two given points (e.g., a given location and a specific activity), which may be assessed in terms of distance, travel time, or travel cost. It is commonly used, for instance, in determining the locations of emergency services (such as fire, ambulance, or police) where the location of the nearest facility is the first consideration. Then relative accessibility A_{ij} between two points i and j with separation C_{ij} (distance, time or cost) can be given as

$$A_{ij} = C_{ij} \tag{3.16}$$

In terms of network vulnerability, this definition of accessibility under the D'Este–Taylor definition of vulnerability measures a loss of utility of travel between two points as a consequence of network degradation. This connective vulnerability is dealt with as part of serviceability-based vulnerability analysis (Section 3.5).

On the other hand, integral accessibility describes the interconnections between a given point and all other points or activities within a region. An integral accessibility measure gives the overall level of accessibility from a specified location to all defined available destinations. Let A_i be the integral accessibility measure of an object i, for the case when i has a defined spatial location in a study area. The object can be a defined region, a town or city, a subarea or zone within that town or city or defined region, a group of individuals, a household, or indeed an individual. The choice of object-type will depend on the particular application. At the strategic level, object i is likely to be a town or city, at the urban level it may be a zone, household, or individual, and at the regional (rural) level it may be a zone or settlement. Following the definition of Morris, Dumble, and Wigan (1979), an integral accessibility index is a measure of the overall accessibility of object i to all relevant activity locations in a study area. Further, the summation $TA = \sum_i A_i$ provides a measure of the overall accessibility level in the study area. In terms of the definition or choice of a suitable index of accessibility, Weibull (1976) suggested the following desirable properties (or performance criteria) for an accessibility index:

1. The order in which the activities are listed should not affect the value of the measure.
2. The value of the accessibility index should not increase with increasing distance (or travel time or travel cost) and should not decrease with increasing attraction.
3. A single activity with infinite attraction situated at zero distance is better than a pair or activities with finite attractions.
4. Activities with zero attraction should not contribute to the accessibility value.
5. The attraction of any activity should not be influenced by surrounding activities.
6. The attraction of any activity is a continuous and increasing function of the size of that activity.

Morris et al. (1979) provided an additional set of requirements for an accessibility indicator suitable for use by transport planners:

- The indicator should include an element of spatial separation which is responsive to changes in performance of the transport system.
- he indicator should have sound behavioral foundations.
- The indicator should be technically feasible and operationally simple.
- The indicator should be easy to interpret, and preferably be intelligible to lay people.

There are several specific accessibility indices that meet these criteria. Strategic level studies of network vulnerability have found that the classic Hansen integral accessibility index (Hansen, 1959) is one such index that is suitable for use at the level of national and state transport networks, e.g., to consider the accessibility of one city relative to all other cities on the study network. On the other hand, a generalized cost measure alone is an inferior choice as an accessibility index—because it violates Weibull's second criterion. An increase in travel costs would normally be associated with a decrease in accessibility, because travel costs were higher, or congestion levels had increased, or travel separation between origin and destination had increased.

The Hansen integral accessibility index (AH_i) for location (node, town, city) i can be written as

$$AH_i = \sum_j B_j f(C_{ij}) \tag{3.17}$$

where $f(C_{ij})$ is an impedance function involving the travel cost C_{ij} between i and j, and B_j is the attractiveness of the location j, e.g., the number of opportunities available at j. In national and regional studies, the variable B_j is often taken as the population of town/city j. Equation (3.17) is often used in a normalized form, viz.

$$AH_i = \frac{\sum_j B_j f(C_{ij})}{\sum_j B_j} \tag{3.18}$$

which weights the accessibility index value in terms of the population size of the different cities involved. The impedance function $f(C_{ij})$ in Equations (3.17) and (3.18) represents the separation between the two cities and is defined in a way that the higher the cost of travel between the two cities, the lower the accessibility between them. The conventional definition of $f(C_{ij})$ is the reciprocal of network travel distance (d_{ij}), i.e.,

$$f(C_{ij}) = \frac{1}{d_{ij}} \tag{3.19}$$

although sometimes a negative exponential form is used:

$$f(C_{ij}) = \exp(-\beta C_{ij}) \tag{3.20}$$

where β is a positive constant.

As will be discussed in Chapter 5, the Hansen index is used in a number of strategic level network vulnerability analyses.

However, the Hansen index is less useful for in-depth regional or intra-urban studies. The index is a discrete measure, i.e., it assumes that populations can be represented by point locations (i.e., at nodes) in the study network. This is not reasonable inside an urban area, or in a rural region where a sparse population may be distributed widely across that region with few significant "population centers." Other indices are required for these types of applications. For example, Primerano and Taylor (2005) developed an accessibility framework for use in urban areas. This approach was expressly designed for use in detailed urban area analysis, and included behavioral utility (as applied in discrete choice models) and the consumer surplus (CS) value from microeconomic theory. CS is the benefit, in monetary terms, which an individual receives from a consumption choice situation. It can also be seen as a measure of the willingness-to-pay for a commodity as it is the difference between what a person would pay for a commodity and what they actually pay. The extra (or less) value an individual receives above (or below) what they paid is CS. When a change occurs (e.g., a price movement) the margin between what the person is willing to pay and what (s)he actually pays changes. The difference between what (s)he was willing to pay and actual payment under the two scenarios represents the change in CS.

The CS measure of accessibility can be applied at a variety of levels of spatial aggregation in a study region, from the census collector district or traffic activity zone to the municipal or "statistical local area", or aggregations of these zones to regional, sub-metropolitan or whole metropolis levels. In theory—and given the appropriate data—the measures could be applied to individuals or to the households to which they belong. The theoretical background to the CS measure was provided by Ben-Akiva and Lerman (1985) and Train (2009), and their application in the accessibility framework approach was described in Primerano and Taylor (2005). An accessibility metric derived from marginal choice probabilities in logit models of multidimensional choice (see Ben-Akiva & Lerman, 1985), which is also called the *inclusive value* or *logsum*, has the form

$$IV_n = \log \sum_{r \in R_n} \exp(Y_{rn}) \tag{3.21}$$

where IV_n is the deterministic component (observable attributes) of the maximum utility for an individual n and Y_{rn} is the deterministic component of each secondary choice r in the set of choices R_n. This measure, in a single value, represents the overall benefit that an individual obtains from a set of alternatives. When using the multinomial logit model of discrete choice, it is possible to use the inclusive value and a coefficient representing cost to estimate consumer surplus as follows

$$E(CS) = \frac{1}{\alpha} \log\left(\sum_{n=1}^{N} \exp(IV_n) \right) + K \tag{3.22}$$

where the logsum part is equivalent to Equation (3.21), α represents the negative of the coefficient of time or cost from the deterministic part of the utility function, and K is an unknown constant that represents the difference between the actual value of consumer surplus and the estimated value (Train, 2009). The estimated change in consumer surplus is then given as

$$\Delta E\left(CS^{AB}\right) = \frac{1}{\alpha}\left[\log\left(\sum_{n=1}^{N^A}\exp\left(IV_n^A\right)\right) - \log\left(\sum_{n=1}^{N^B}\exp\left(IV_n^B\right)\right)\right] \tag{3.23}$$

where the superscripts B and A represent "before" and "after" scenarios and the two logsum terms represent the inclusive values derived from behavioral models under the two scenarios. Equation (3.23) thus gives an estimated change in consumer surplus with a measurement unit (e.g., hours or dollars) depending on the choice of α (Train, 2009). Thus the change in consumer surplus represents an accessibility metric with a well-known physical unit (money or time), and hence has a useful interpretation.

The Primerano-Taylor accessibility framework, and its use in vulnerability analysis, is described in Section 5.4. The framework was developed to combine the strengths of existing accessibility measures for use in transport and urban planning. The aim was to have a framework where policies related to transport and urban form could be tested and implemented to improve accessibility for all socioeconomic groups in multimodal transportation systems. The method used to develop the framework was activity-based rather than just location-based. This means that the accessibility framework determines the accessibility of an individual to an activity rather than the accessibility between locations. Considering accessibility in this way implies that accessibility is dependent on three components, namely the:

- traveler (individual or group);
- transport system (modes, roads and service, and traffic characteristics); and
- land use (characteristics of land uses at origins and destinations).

In regional and rural areas the basic definition for accessibility is appropriate but given the likely almost-complete reliance on the road network as the infrastructure system providing mobility in these areas, the definition can be refined to say *accessibility is the ease with which services and facilities can be reached while using the road network*. In addition, given the typical sparseness of regional road networks and the dispersed population in rural or remote regions, it may be more useful to consider the inverse of accessibility, which may be termed as *remoteness*. A broad definition in keeping with that for accessibility is that remoteness is measured by the difficulty in accessing services and facilities while using the road network.

The issue of locality-based remoteness (or its inverse, accessibility) is of concern to government agencies responsible for the provision of social, health, and education services for rural regions in Australia and other countries (and likewise for the provision of private sector services and facilities, such as markets, banking and financial, and retail services). In Australia this has led to the development of a locality-based index of remoteness which may be used to indicate the degree of separation or isolation of communities or localities, and the influence of the transport network in the degree of remoteness experienced (DHAC, 2001; GISCA, 2009). The index, known as *ARIA*, the "Accessibility/Remoteness Index of Australia," was developed expressly for use in rural and regional areas in that country and is adopted as a "whole of government" measure of regional accessibility (or, more accurately and in line with the Weibull criteria, given that the larger the value of *ARIA*, the more remote is the location, of regional *remoteness*).

ARIA is a continuous index which is calculated for all locations in a region. This calculation is generally performed on the basis of a 1.0 km^2 grid laid over the region. The index is based on the ratio of the road network distance from the location to the nearest "service center" of a given intensity to the average distance of all locations to that class of service center. Service centers are cities and towns with populations in defined ranges. The index is calculated for all locations, not just population centers, so that it can capture all residents of a region, not just those living in towns and cities. Thus the *ARIA* metric is an index of remoteness derived from measurements of road network distance between localities and service centers. In its current form, the values of *ARIA* range from zero (high accessibility) to 15 (high remoteness), based on road network distance measurements from localities to their nearest service centers, where there are five categories of service centers based on their population. *ARIA* has the following attractive properties for application to sparsely settled regions (GISCA, 2009), as it is:

- a purely geographic measure of remoteness, excluding any consideration of socioeconomic status, rurality, and population size factors (other than the use of natural breaks in the population distribution of urban centers to define the service center categories);
- flexible and can be aggregated to a range of spatial units or used as a continuum; and
- stable over time.

ARIA provides a measure of remoteness (or accessibility) suitable for a broad range of applications including community service planning,

Table 3.1 ARIA Service Center Categories A–E (GISCA, 2009)

Service Center Category	Population	Mean Distance to Service Center (km)
A	≥250,000	413
B	48,000–249,999	239
C	18,000–47,999	139
D	5,000–17,999	88
E	1,000–4,999	43
(F)	(200–999)	(na)

demographic analysis, and resource allocation. Service center destinations are populated localities (towns and cities) with populations exceeding 999 persons. There are five categories of service center used as destinations, as defined in Table 3.1. Each category is assessed as having distinct levels of public and private sector facilities available. Table 3.1 also shows the overall average road distances to the different categories of service center.

The *ARIA* index is calculated by considering the distance by road d_{iL} from location i to the nearest service center in category L, for $L = A$, B, C, D, E, as defined in Table 3.1:

$$ARIA_i = \sum_L \min\left\{3, \frac{d_{iL}}{\overline{d}_L}\right\} \tag{3.24}$$

where $\overline{d}_L$ is the mean road distance of all locations to the nearest category L service center. An upper limit of three on the ratio between d_{iL} and $\overline{d}_L$ is used to remove the effects of any remaining extreme values from the index (GISCA, 2009). The maximum value of *ARIA* as defined in Equation (3.24) is then 15, which represents an extremely remote location. In the calculations, if a higher category service center (say category A) is closer to a given locality than (say) a category B center, then the higher category center takes the place of the lower category center in the calculations. Note that *ARIA* is only intended for regional and remote area analysis—for instance all urban centers with populations of 250,000 or more automatically have $ARIA = 0$. This index does not consider intra-urban accessibility at all—it was neither intended nor designed to.

The explicit inclusion of distance by the road network makes the *ARIA* index attractive for use in accessibility-based vulnerability analysis in rural and remote areas. Chapter 5 includes two case studies using the index.

In general terms, the use of an accessibility index in vulnerability analysis can be summarized as follows. An integral accessibility index A_i for object i

can be represented by a mathematical function in general terms, which includes the accessibility objects to be considered in the analysis, parameters, and variables representing the configuration of the transport network, the operational state of that network, and the facilities and services accessible using the network. Broadly, this can be written as

$$A_i = fn(N; X_i; S_{jk}, j \in J, k \in K) \tag{3.25}$$

where N is the transportation network in a specific state, X_i represents the object i and its location and characteristics, and S_{jk} represents facility type j located at site k, which thus describes the land-use distribution and intensity in the study area. Using this formulation, assume that A_i^0 is the integral accessibility index of object i in the network N^0, where this represents the network in an original state (e.g., a complete, intact network, or one in an uncongested state). Then $TA^0 = \sum_i A_i^0$ is the overall accessibility index for the network N^0. Now assume that the network N^σ is an alteration of the original network, such as one in a degraded state (e.g., because of some link or node failure, full or partial[8]) or one in a congested state. Then $TA^\sigma = \sum_i A_i^\sigma$ is the overall accessibility index for the altered network N^σ. We can then assess the changes in both total overall accessibility and in the accessibility of each object i, and these changes in accessibility can then be used to indicate network vulnerability and to identify critical links (and nodes) in it. Absolute changes in accessibility are given by $\Delta TA = TA^0 - TA^\sigma$ and $\Delta A_i = A_i^0 - A_i^\sigma$ while relative changes in accessibility are given by $\Delta RT = 1 - \frac{TA^\sigma}{TA^0}$ and $\Delta RA_i = 1 - \frac{A_i^\sigma}{A_i^0}$. This approach is an application of the general Equation (2.6) for relative decline in performance of an infrastructure system as outlined in Chapter 2. The use of accessibility metrics in vulnerability analysis is developed in detail in Chapter 5.

3.7 SUMMARY

This chapter has provided an overview of the three broad methods for vulnerability analysis of transportation networks. It also described two of

[8] A partial failure could be modeled by weighting the link distance, to reflect (say) an increased effective distance or increased travel time due to road pavement degradation, delays due to maintenance or construction work, or similar.

these methods; the inventory-based risk-assessment method and topologically based vulnerability analysis. The following chapters describe the serviceability-based methods (Chapter 4) and accessibility-based methods (Chapter 5) in more detail, noting that elements of both risk assessment and topological analysis are found in both of those. Chapter 6 focuses on public transport systems, where both topological and serviceability methods have been employed.

REFERENCES

Akcelik, R. (1991). Travel time functions for transport planning purposes: Davidson's function, its time-dependent form and an alternative travel time function. *Australian Road Research, 21*(3), 49–59.

Akcelik, R., & Rouphail, N. M. (1993). Estimation of delays at traffic signals for variable demand conditions. *Transportation Research Part B, 27B*(2), 109–131.

Beer, A., Tually, S., Kroehn, M., Martin, J., Gerritsen, R., Taylor, M., et al. (2015). Climate change and the future of Australia's country towns. In J. P. Palutikof, S. L. Boulter, J. Barnett, & D. Rissik (Eds.), *Applied studies in climate adaptation* (pp. 332–341). Chichester): John Wiley and Sons.

Ben-Akiva, M. E., & Lerman, S. R. (1985). *Discrete choice analysis: Theory and application to travel demand*. Boston, MA: MIT Press.

Berdica, K. (2002). An introduction to road vulnerability: What has been done, is done and should be done. *Transport Policy, 9*(2), 117–127.

Chen, A., Yang, C., Kongsomsaksakul, S., & Lee, M. (2007). Network-based accessibility measures for vulnerability analysis of degradable transportation networks. *Networks and Spatial Economics*, 7(3), 241–256.

Davis, G. A., & Xiong, H. (2007). *Access to destinations: Travel time estimation on arterials*. Report #3 in the series: Access to destinations study, to Minnesota department of transportation. Department of civil engineering. Minneapolis, MN: University of Minnesota. Retrived from http://www.lrrb.org/PDF/200735.pdf.

D'Este, G. M., & Taylor, M. A. P. (2003). Network vulnerability: An approach to reliability analysis at the level of national strategic transport networks. In M. G. H. Bell, & Y. Iida (Eds.), *The network reliability of transport* (pp. 23–44). Oxford: Elsevier.

DHAC. (2001). *Measuring remoteness: Accessibility/remoteness index of Australia (ARIA) (revised edition)*. Occasional Paper, new series no 14. Department of health and aged care, DHAC 2001., measuring remoteness: Accessibility/remoteness index of Australia (ARIA) (revised edition). Occasional Paper, new series no 14. Canberra, ACT: Department of health and aged care.

de Dios Ortuzar, J., & Willumsen, L. G. (2011). *Modelling transport* (4th ed.). New York: John Wiley and Sons.

Evans, S. P. (1976). Derivation and analysis of some models for combining trip distribution and assignment. *Transportation Research, 10*(1), 37–57.

Farber, S., & Fu, L. (2017). Dynamic public transit accessibility using travel time cubes: Comparing the effects of infrastructure (dis)investments over time. *Computers, Environment and Urban Systems, 62*, 30–40.

FHWA. (2016). *FHWA climate resilience pilot program*. Washington, DC: Federal Highways Administration, US Department of Transportation. Retrived from http://www.fhwa.dot.gov/environment/climate_change/adaptation/.

Freeman, L. C. (1979). Centrality in social networks: Conceptual clarification. *Social Networks, 1*, 215–239.

GISCA. (2009). *Centre for the social applications of geographic information systems*. Adelaide, Australia: University of Adelaide. Retrived from http://www.gisca.adelaide.edu.au/products_services/ariav2_about.html.

Hansen, W. G. (1959). How accessibility shapes land use. *Journal of the American Institute of Planners, 25*, 73–76.

Jenelius, E., Petersen, T., & Mattsson, L.-G. (2006). Importance and exposure in road network vulnerability analysis. *Transportation Research Part A: Policy and Practice, 40*(7), 537–560.

Jewell, W. S. (1967). Models for traffic assignment. *Transportation Research, 1*, 31–46.

Latora, V., & Marchiori, M. (2001). Efficient behavior of small-world networks. *Physical Review Letters, 87*(19), 198701.

Mattsson, L.-G., & Jenelius, E. (2015). Vulnerability and resilience of transport systems – a discussion of recent research. *Transportation Research Part A: Policy and Practice, 81*, 16–34.

Morris, J. M., Dumble, P. L., & Wigan, M. R. (1979). Accessibility indicators for transport planning. *Transportation Research Part A: General, 13A*, 91–109.

Ni, D., Li, L., Wang, H., & Jia, C. (2016). Observations on the fundamental diagram and their interpretation from the human factors perspective. *Transportmetrica B: Transport Dynamics*. http://dx.doi.org/10.1080/21680566.2016.1190673.

Niemeier, D. (1997). Accessibility: An evaluation using social welfare. *Transportation, 24*, 377–396.

Pokharel, R., & Ieda, H. (2016). Reliability and vulnerability of road network: An accessibility and network closure vulnerability approach. *Asian Transport Studies, 4*(1), 37–56.

Porta, S., Crucitti, P., & Latora, V. (2006). The network analysis of urban streets: A primal approach. *Environment and Planning B: Planning and Design, 33*(5), 705–725.

Primerano, F., & Taylor, M. A. P. (2005). An accessibility framework for evaluating transport policies. In D. M. Levinson, & K. J. Krizek (Eds.), *Access to destinations* (pp. 325–346). Oxford: Elsevier.

Scott, V., & Dunn, R. (2015). A prototype method to rate the link vulnerability of strategic rural roads. *Road and Transport Research, 24*(2), 3–12.

Spiess, H. (1990). Conical volume-delay functions. *Transportation Science, 24*(2), 153–158.

Taylor, M. A. P. (1999). An extended family of traffic network equilibria and its implications for land use and transport policies. In H. Meersman, E. Van Der Voorde, & W. Winkelmans (Eds.), *World transport research. Selected proceedings from the eighth world conference on transport research* (Vol. 4, pp. 29–42). Oxford: Elsevier. Transport Policy.

Taylor, M. A. P., Bonsall, P. W., & Young, W. (2000). *Understanding traffic systems: Data, analysis and presentation* (2nd ed.). Aldershot: Ashgate Publishing Ltd.

Taylor, M. A. P., & Philp, M. L. (2015). Investigating the impact of maintenance regimes on the design life of road pavements in a changing climate and the implications for transport policy. *Transport Policy, 41*, 117–135.

Taylor, M. A. P., & Philp, M. L. (2016). Beyond agriculture – a review of the Thornthwaite Moisture Index with respect to road pavements and other infrastructure applications. *International Journal of Sustainable Transportation, 10*(6), 528–540.

Taylor, M. A. P., Woolley, J. E., & Zito, R. (2000). Integration of the global positioning system and geographical information systems for traffic congestion studies. *Transportation Research C, 8*(1–6), 257–285.

Train, K. (2009). *Discrete choice methods with simulation* (2nd ed.). Cambridge: Cambridge University Press:

TRB. (2012). *Metropolitan travel forecasting: Current practice and future direction*. Special Report 288. Washington, DC: Transportation Research Board.

TRB. (2016). *Highway capacity manual* (6th ed.). Washington, DC: Transportation Research Board.

Vragovic, I., Louis, E., & Diaz-Guilera, A. (2005). Efficiency of informational transfer in regular and complex networks. *Physical Review E, 71*, 036122.

Wardrop, J. G. (1952). Some theoretical aspects of road traffic research. *Proc Institution of Civil Engineers, 1*(2), 325–378.

Wegener, M. (1996). Reduction of CO_2 emissions of transport by reorganisation of urban activities. In Y. Hayashi, & J. R. Roy (Eds.), *Transport, land-use and the environment* (pp. 103–124). Dordrecht: Kluwer Academic Publishers.

Weibull, J. W. (1976). Axiomatic approach to the measurement of accessibility. *Regional Science and Urban Economics, 6*, 357–379.

CHAPTER FOUR

Serviceability Methods

Serviceability methods examine the performance of a transportation network in different operating states, such as congestion or degradation of some part of the network, and allow an assessment of performance in terms of some presupposed acceptable level. Performance relates to the operating characteristics of the transport system, such as delays and route diversions in the face of network closures. The performance of a road traffic system can be indicated in terms of "level of service" for uninterrupted traffic flow streams or degree of saturation for traffic at signals, or other traffic control devices that arrange priorities between intersecting traffic streams (interrupted flow). In both cases the performance variable is basically a ratio of the traffic demand to use a facility (e.g., link) to the traffic carrying capacity of that facility in that time period. TRB (2016) describes the various methods for determining level of service or degree of saturation. In general vulnerability analysis is concerned with transportation networks that have some reduced operating functionality rather than complete shutdown, and the general question for the planner or analyst is to determine those locations where degradation will have the major effects. Vulnerability analysis is then used as a diagnostic tool for testing alternative scenarios for the network. Some researchers also consider it as an important tool for "congestion auditing," which involves testing scenarios of network failure or network incident locations which would have the most severe effects on network operations, and thus identify locations that may need additional traffic engineering treatments to ensure that the impacts of incidents or congestion at those locations can be minimized.

Berdica (2002) provided an introduction to vulnerability analysis based on serviceability considerations. She considered road network serviceability as an opportunity to use a link, route, or road network, during a specified time period, so that vulnerability of the network is then "the susceptibility to incidents that can result in considerable reductions in road network serviceability" (Berdica, 2002, p. 119, see also Section 3.5). This definition stresses the importance of risk—probability times consequence—through its statement on *considerable reductions* in performance, and on capacity, through its notion of a *specified time period* applied to the incident. The general

Vulnerability Analysis for Transportation Networks
ISBN: 978-0-12-811010-2
http://dx.doi.org/10.1016/B978-0-12-811010-2.00004-6

manifestation of reduced serviceability is in extended travel times and delays. Extended travel times occur in an uncongested network when a link is broken, and so travelers need to find alternative paths which avoid that link. Extra travel time is then incurred along the alternative path. Delay is generally defined as travel time above the free-flow travel time on a link or route, so that some delay is a natural and expected consequence of an increase in traffic volume on the road. However, further additional travel time can occur due to incidents such as crashes or vehicle breakdowns, roadwork, and full or partial road closures. Traffic engineers recognize this additional travel time as unacceptable delay, thus recognizing that some delay (regular increases in travel time at busy times of day, for instance) is expected and anticipated by travelers. Unacceptable delay and additional travel time due to route diversions are by nature unpredictable and are generally due to unusual events. These events relate to reductions in road capacity or deterioration in road operating characteristics and occasionally to abnormally high levels of traffic demand. Extended travel times and unacceptable levels of delay are therefore of primary concern in vulnerability analysis for serviceability. In addition, the incidence of queuing and stop—start traffic movement is also important.

The measurement of traffic performance on a network or components of it (e.g., routes and links) is therefore important for considering the level of serviceability available under a given traffic state and for comparing serviceability levels between different traffic states (including network degradations). The basic variables to be considered in performance assessment include travel time and traffic volume, but these are not sufficient on their own for comparisons between traffic states or between different parts of a network, so measures derived from these variables are required. Table 4.1 sets out a list of traffic performance measures, the relationships between them, and the potential applications of the measures.

The performance measures in Table 4.1 generally concern travel time and delay, expressed in terms of vehicles or people using a component of the network. Taylor, Woolley, and Zito (2000) described the use of the performance measures in assessing congestion levels in an urban highway corridor and discussed methods for estimating the performance measures from traffic data, including GPS data from probe vehicles. There are further performance measures that can also be considered. These include:

- Volume—capacity ratio (VCR)—the ratio of the traffic volume (vehicles) using the component (or attempting to use it) to the capacity of the component over a specified time period

Table 4.1 Performance Measures for Road Transportation Systems

Measure	Definition	Unit	Comment
Travel time, T	Actual time taken to traverse a section	Time	
Free-flow travel time, T_0	Minimum time required to traverse a section, when unimpeded by other traffic	Time	
Total delay, d	$d = T - T_0$	Time	Basic definition of delay from transport economics, sometimes referred to as "system delay."
Space speed, v	$v = X/T$	Distance/time	Space speed is the average travel speed on a section of length X.
Unit travel time (UTT)	$\text{UTT} = T/X$	Time/distance	Unit travel time is the inverse of travel speed, but is easier to use in traffic analysis and statistical analysis. May be used for comparison of sections of different lengths.
Running time, T_r	Time spent moving along the section	Time	
Stopped time, T_s	Time spent stationary (or with instantaneous speed less than a small amount, e.g., 2 km/h) on the section	Time	Travel time is $T = T_r + T_s$. Stopped time is also known as stopped delay (d_s), noting that $d \geq d_s$.
Delay rate (DR)	$\text{DR} = d/X$	Time/distance	Similar to UTT but for delay time only
Proportion stopped time (PST)	$\text{PST} = T_s/T$		Dimensionless. Can be used to compare performance on different sections.
Congestion index (CI)	$\text{CI} = (T - T_o)/T_0$		Dimensionless. Indicates ratio of delay time to free-flow travel time. Can be used to compare performance on different sections.

(Continued)

Table 4.1 Performance Measures for Road Transportation Systems—cont'd

Measure	Definition	Unit	Comment
Total vehicle delay (TVD)	$\mathrm{TVD} = dqt_r$	Vehicle-time	Total delay time for all vehicles using the section in specified time period t_r.
Total person delay (TPD)	$\mathrm{TPD} = \mathrm{TVD}\bar{n}$	Person-time	Total delay time for all people using the section in the specified time period, with average vehicle occupancy $\bar{n}$.
Vehicle-kilometer of travel (VKT)	$\mathrm{VKT} = qX$	Vehicle-km	Total traffic load (traffic activity) on section, in terms of vehicular traffic (VMT, vehicle-miles of travel, is equivalent).
Person-kilometer of travel (PKT)	$\mathrm{PKT} = q\bar{n}X$	Person-km	Total traffic load (traffic activity) on section, in terms of person movement (person-miles of travel is equivalent).
Congested travel (CT)	$\mathrm{CT} = \sum_i q_i \bar{n}_i X_i$	Person-km	Person-km of travel on congested sections (i) of a route, $\mathrm{CT} \leq \mathrm{PKT}$.
Acceleration noise (AN)	$\mathrm{AN} = \sqrt{\frac{1}{t_r} \sum_j \frac{\Delta v_j^2}{\Delta t_j}}$	Distance/time^2	Δt_j is time taken for change of speed Δv_j in traveling along section. AN is a measure of the quality of traffic progression, reflecting the incidence of stop–start traffic.

- System reliability—defined by Taylor (2013) as the proportion of journeys undertaken on the network that can be successfully completed within a specified time period. This time period can be related to the expected travel time for the particular journeys. If personal travel is the prime interest, then the proportion of journeys completed within the acceptable time limits can be weighted in terms of the total numbers of travelers attempting the journeys
- Generalized cost of travel—which recognizes that travel time alone may not fully reflect the impedance experienced by travelers or the concerns of travelers when making travel decisions. Generalized cost is usually a weighted sum of factors such as distance, money cost, and travel time associated with a journey.

  A general formulation of generalized travel cost (c) is

$$c = \omega_x x + \omega_m m + \omega_T \sum_i \lambda_i \Delta T_i + \sum_j \omega_j X_j \tag{4.1}$$

In this equation, x is travel distance, m is money cost, $T = \sum_i \Delta T_i$ is total travel time (which can be composed of a number of different components ΔT_i), and other factors X_j. Each factor in the equation has a weight (w_k) which reflects the relative importance of that factor in the total travel cost (and can be used, for instance, to determine a money-cost equivalent of travel time). Total travel time may be split into different components, with each component having a different weight. For example:

- for road traffic on a link different weights can be associated with running time (T_r) and stopped time (T_s), reflecting different levels of tolerance of drivers to time spent moving and time spent in queues, and
- for travel by public transport, travelers may associate different weights with time spent walking to the transit stop and waiting at the stop as opposed to time spent in the transit vehicle.[1]

El-Rashidy and Grant-Muller (2014) identified six attributes of vulnerability and related these to link characteristics and traffic volumes. These attributes are as follows:

1. The link VCR, defined as $\text{VCR}^i_{ia} = q^i_a / Q^i_a$, where q^i_a is the volume on link a in time period i and Q^i_a is the capacity of the link at that time. VCR reflects local values of volume and capacity pertaining to the given link.

[1] A useful rule of thumb is that 1 min spent waiting at a stop or walking to the stop is valued at 2 min of time in the transit vehicle. i.e., is twice as valuable as that.

2. A scaled traffic volume $sq_a^i = q_a^i / \left(1 - \mathrm{VCR}_a^i\right)$ which reflects the relationship between q_a^i and Q_a^i for each link with respect to the full network.
3. The time needed for the tail of a queue to reach the upstream junction (t_L) and thus to completely block the link, estimated by $t_{La} = \frac{x_a}{q_a^i\left(n_a k_{ja} - q_a^i / v_{0a}\right)}$ where x_a is the link length, n_a is the number of lanes available on the link, k_{ja} is the jam density of a lane on the link, and v_{0a} is the free-flow travel speed.
4. Link capacity relative to the maximum capacity of links in the network, given by $RQ_a = \frac{Q_a}{\max_a\{Q_a\}}$. This value reflects the relative importance of the link in the network in terms of traffic carrying capability.
5. Link length (x_a) as a physical property reflecting relative importance of a link.
6. The number of the shortest paths using a link, $ns(a) = \sum_{ij} \delta_{ij}$ where $\delta_{ij} = 1$ if a is on a shortest path from i to j, or zero if it is not. This attribute is a measure of the centrality of the link, as discussed in Chapters 3 and 6, and is thus another measure of link importance.

Dehghani, Flintsch, and McNeil (2014) proposed the use of changes in vehicle-kilometer of travel (VKT)[2] in disrupted networks as a simple measure of network vulnerability which could include road conditions as well as link closures. They did so by considering a set of alternative scenarios σ for network degradation, allowing for potential multiple link failures in each scenario. If p_a is the probability that a link can fail and A_S is the set of links failing in scenario σ, then the probability $\Pr\{\sigma\}$ of that scenario occurring is

$$\Pr\{\sigma\} = \prod_{a \in A_\sigma} p_a \prod_{a \notin A_\sigma} (1 - p_a) \tag{4.2}$$

The total VKT in the network under scenario σ is VKT(σ), given by

$$\mathrm{VKT}(\sigma) = \sum_{i \neq j} \mathrm{VKT}_{ij}(\sigma) = \sum_{i \neq j} H_{ij} d_{ij}(\sigma) \tag{4.3}$$

where H_{ij} is the travel demand between origin—destination pair ij and $d_{ij}(\sigma)$ is the network travel distance between i and j under scenario S.

The expected network performance (ENP) under all scenarios is then

$$\mathrm{ENP} = \sum_{\sigma} \mathrm{PR}\{\sigma\} \mathrm{VKT}(\sigma) \tag{4.4}$$

[2] See Table 4.1.

and vulnerability metric V for the network under the set of scenarios is

$$V = \frac{\text{ENP} - \text{VKT}(0)}{\text{VKT}(0)} \tag{4.5}$$

where VKT(0) is the vehicle-km of travel in the intact network.

D'Este and Taylor (2003) used a similar approach based on changes in generalized cost of travel as a measure of changes in vulnerability introduced in Section 2.4. This work has led to the accessibility-based measures of vulnerability described in Chapter 5.

The remainder of this chapter considers serviceability-based methods, starting with considerations of traffic operations and traffic management before moving to network-wide methods and concerns in strategic planning.

4.1 NETWORK OPERATIONS MANAGEMENT

The primary objective for transportation systems managers is to provide and maintain acceptable levels of service of their systems under normal and abnormal operating conditions. For highway and main road networks, the management task is concerned with maintaining throughput of traffic between origin–destination pairs efficiently and safely. Normal conditions include the cyclical fluctuations in travel demand over hours of the day, days of the week, and seasons of the year as well as potential trend growth in average demand levels (e.g., in response to population growth, economic development, and demographic change). These factors provide challenges in both the provision of infrastructure and the use of existing infrastructure (e.g., parking restrictions on arterial roads and traffic management plans) but represent known (or anticipated) circumstances, and hence can be managed effectively. Abnormal conditions include the range of phenomena that may lead to network disruption and are largely unknown in occurrence, magnitude, and duration—until a specific event occurs. Disruptions may occur from traffic incidents, vehicle breakdowns, road crashes, lane and road blockages, extreme weather events (including rain, blizzards, hurricanes, dust storms, and even heat waves), natural disasters (e.g., flooding, wildfires, and earthquakes), roadwork, reallocation of road space (sometimes temporary, e.g., for special events), and additional traffic demand due to special events. In the main—and apart from the potential long-term consequences of some natural disasters—the abnormal conditions will exist for relatively short time periods, from few hours to perhaps 1 or 2 days, therefore a permanent change in travel demand patterns would not take place. In addition, the disruption event may be quite minor, such as a need for emergency braking by one or a few vehicles, so that the effect is short term (even if such events can lead to flow breakdown on a highway link that may persist for some hours, or until demand to use the facility decreases substantially).

Vulnerability analysis for network operations is mainly concerned with the occurrence of abnormal situations and the use of scenario planning to develop suitable traffic management plans to cope with those situations, perhaps at a lower service level than normal but still with acceptable serviceability. The general consequence of "abnormality" is the loss of capacity on one or more links for the duration of the incident or event and perhaps for some time afterwards. There is also a process of restoration of normal conditions. The ability of a link to return to normal conditions is an indication of its resilience, as defined in Section 2.5 (see also Bhavathrathan & Patil, 2015).

Figure 4.1 presents a process model for network operations management when abnormal traffic conditions may occur. This model is an extension of an earlier version, directed at travel time reliability assessment, suggested by Snelder, Van Zuylen, and Immers (2012).

The first part of the model in Figure 4.1 is for normal operating conditions, in which there is an assumed long-run equilibrium between the travel demand pattern and the network operating state, with operating conditions

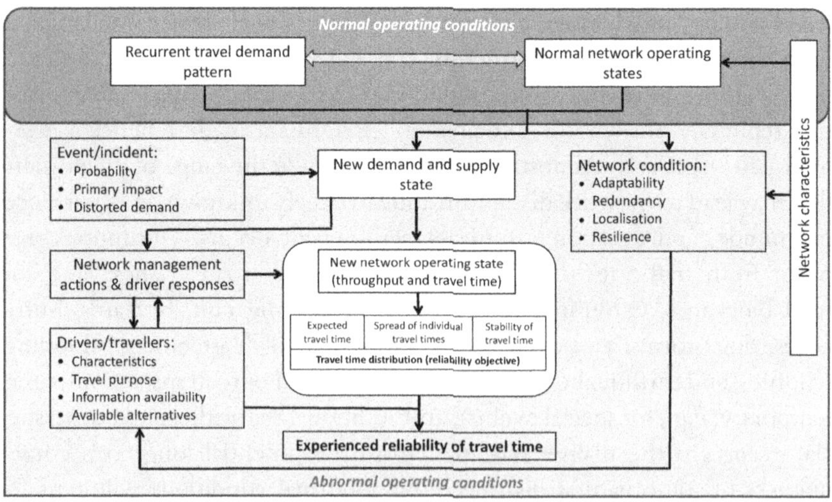

Figure 4.1 Process model for network operations management including the occurrence of abnormal traffic conditions.

thus depending on the physical characteristics of the network and its components, and the levels of demand and their variations over time. A disrupting event or incident, of sufficient impact, may lead to the creation of a new demand–supply situation under which network operating conditions may change substantially. Changes in the level of throughput and travel times, and delays may then occur, first at the local level but potentially permeating further across the network. Substantial changes in delay and travel time, and in the development of standing queues on highway facilities, will be the symptoms of system breakdown in the network. Thus observations of changes in expected (average) travel times and in the spread of individual travel times provide useful information about the operating state. Stability in travel times (under a given level of demand) would be the basic objective of network managers. Drivers using the network will also respond to signals about traffic conditions in downstream parts of the network, in the absence of definite information on those conditions probably on the basis of previous experiences and perceptions. Thus the success of incident mitigation action plans implemented by system managers will depend on driver responses as well as the necessary traffic management implementations. Vulnerability analysis in these circumstances needs to include characteristics of driver behavior as well as the characteristics of the network. This requires the use of suitably calibrated traffic models in scenario planning aimed at designing appropriate incident management plans for different types of incidents at different locations on the network.

An example of the application of the process model of Figure 4.1 for highway networks was provided by Calvert and Snelder (2015). As discussed in Section 3.5, highway networks are examples of uninterrupted traffic flow, in which the flow characteristics are determined internally by the interactions between the vehicles in the traffic stream. While an external phenomenon, e.g., a weather event or a lane blockage through vehicle breakdown, may lead to a disturbance of the traffic stream, the resultant operating state of the traffic stream (and hence the road link on which the flow occurs) is due to the internal interactions within the stream. Under these conditions the macroscopic fundamental diagram (MFD) of traffic flow (see Figure 3.2) provides the underlying traffic performance model. Calvert and Snelder developed a method using the MFD to examine the resilience of a given highway section to flow disturbances, yielding a "Link Performance Index for Resilience" (LPIR), as a quantitative measure of the ability of the section to recover from a flow disturbance and return to continuous traffic flow within a reasonable time after the disturbance. Calvert and Snelder adopted the definition of resilience as provided by Snelder et al. (2012), i.e., "the ability of a system to cope with disturbances and recover its original function after a loss of function".

The method starts with the concept of resistance, taken to be as the ability of a traffic system to resist a disturbance. This is taken in terms of the ability of a road section to maintain a density (k) lower than the critical density (k_m), with an index expressed as the ratio k/k_m. Density k relates to traffic volume (q), speed (v), as discussed in Section 3.5, and the volatility of flow (ψ_q). Critical density, as shown in Figure 3.2, is the density above which flow breakdown and loss of capacity (traffic throughput) can occur. It depends on road capacity (Q), road characteristics (g), such as road geometry and physical condition, traffic/driver characteristics (h), volatility of capacity (ψ_{cap}), and temporal capacity reductions (i.e., incidents or events), designated as f in the following equations.

The LPIR is developed as follows. Consider Resistance (RS) and Recovery (RT) for the highway section as indices based on Equations (4.6) and (4.7). These can then be expressed in terms of the continuity of flow Equation (3.10) for uninterrupted traffic streams, allowing for flow volatility. First,

$$\mathrm{RS} = \frac{\left[\dfrac{q + \psi_q}{v}\right]}{\dfrac{q_{cap}(g, h)f + \psi_{cap}}{v_m}} \tag{4.6}$$

where v_m is the mean space speed at density k_m ($= q_{\max}/k_m$, see Equation 3.10), the volatility of traffic flow over a defined period Δt is given by $\psi_q(\Delta t) = (q_{\max}(\Delta t) - q_{\min}(\Delta t))/2$, and the volatility of capacity is given by $\psi_{cap}(\Delta t) = (Q_{\max}(\Delta t) - Q_{\min}(\Delta t))/2$.

Recovery is the ability to come out of a state of congestion, i.e., the ability of a road section to regain a density lower than the critical density from its current (congested) state $k > k_{crit}$. The two main variables influencing recovery are the capacity drop experienced in the section and the difference between the inflow and outflow of traffic on the section, so that

$$\mathrm{RT} = \frac{\left[\dfrac{q + \Delta q}{v_{eq}(q)}\right]}{\dfrac{q_{cap}(g, h) - q_{cd}}{v_m}} \tag{4.7}$$

In this equation, $\Delta q = q_{in} - q_{out}$, q_{cd} is the capacity drop and $v_{eq}(q)$ is the speed corresponding to volume q in the fundamental diagram (Figure 3.2), given by

$$v_{eq}(q) = \frac{q}{k_{crit} + \left(1 - \frac{q}{q_{cap} - q_{cd}}\right)(k_{jam} - k_m)}$$

Then LPIR is defined in terms of RS and RT, depending on the density:

$$\mathrm{LPIR} = \frac{1}{N_t} \sum_{t=1}^{N_t} (\mathrm{RS}(t)\delta_t + \mathrm{RT}(t)(1 - \delta_t)) \tag{4.8}$$

where $\delta t = 1$ if $k(t) \leq k_m$ and $\delta t = 0$ if $k(t) > k_m$. Total LPIR on a road section is thus the average overall considered time interval in the specified time period. The interpretation of LPIR is as follows. If LPIR ≤ 1 then the link can resist a significant drop in level of service and thus remains uncongested. It is therefore resilient and robust. However, a link that does suffer a drop in level of service but can recover quickly should also be considered resilient, although it may not be robust. It is not necessarily the case that LPIR > 1 means that the link is always non-resilient.

Calvert and Snelder (2015) used LPIR in a case study of two interconnecting highways near Rotterdam, Holland, and were able to demonstrate that the method provided a useful tool[3] for analysis of highway networks and the identification of critical links. It could thus be used in deciding on priorities for highway improvements. An important feature of the method is that it is aimed specifically at the local level in a network, rather than treating the network as a whole. It expressly considers resistance and resilience for traffic flow on specified road sections and the ability of those sections to maintain their designated purpose of traffic movement while minimizing the occurrence or impact of traffic congestion. The method also accounts for the observed volatility of traffic flow. Calvert and Snelder argue that the LPIR method is preferable to alternative approaches such as "recovery time" and "total delay." The former is a component of LPIR. It indicates the ability of the section to recover from a congestion episode but does not account for the frequency of occurrence of congestion. The latter is a

[3] Knoop and Daamen (2016) describe useful methods for collecting the required data to apply the LPIR model. Kim and Yeo (2016) provide an alternative description of the use of the MFD in determining vulnerability to congestion episodes in highway networks.

symptom of flow breakdown, but cannot necessarily define the location of the cause of congestion. Congestion on one road section may be due to failure on a downstream section. LPIR can help to determine the trigger point of the congestion and so identify the specific weak link or bottleneck location.

The situation for arterial roads, i.e., roads with at-grade intersections, is more complicated than that for highways. The main reason for this is that stop–start traffic (interrupted traffic flow), e.g., for traffic streams at a signalized intersection, is an inherent part of the traffic control system. Observing stationary vehicles thus does not necessarily mean that an incident has occurred. Urban arterial roads feature interrupted traffic flow, turning movements, and a variety of traffic controls, and therefore provide a more challenging environment for incident detection. A further difference with highway networks is that arterial roads are open systems with vehicles able to enter or leave the road at many locations, whereas highway networks are essentially closed systems, with limited points of access or egress. One approach to incident detection on urban arterial roads under signalized traffic control was provided by Zhang and Taylor (2006) for arterial roads, who applied Bayesian networks in an automatic incident detection (AID) tool to model causal dependencies between traffic events (e.g., incidents) and observed real-time traffic parameters. The incidents under examination were lane-blocking, and another that blocked an entire carriageway (a link-blocking incident) was defined as an extreme case of the lane-blocking incidents. The typical traffic situation for application of the AID tool is illustrated in Figure 4.2, as a road section between two signalized intersections and the upstream and downstream connections of the section. The major traffic stream on the road was considered, with traffic data processing focused on extracting traffic information (volume and occupancy[4]) for the traffic stream and converting this information into traffic states.

Figure 4.2 shows the detector configuration for the AID tool, based on the presence of stop line detectors [S12 and S22, corresponding to the usual Sydney Coordinated Adaptive Traffic System (SCATS) traffic control system configuration] and detectors (S3) on the exit link from an intersection [as in the Split Cycle Offset Optimization Technique (SCOOT) system], see Zhang and Taylor (2006) for full details. In this case the major traffic stream

[4] Traffic occupancy is the proportion of time that a given point on a road (e.g., a vehicle detector) is covered by vehicles (moving or stationary). Under certain assumptions (e.g., that vehicle speed is independent of vehicle length) occupancy is directly proportional to density.

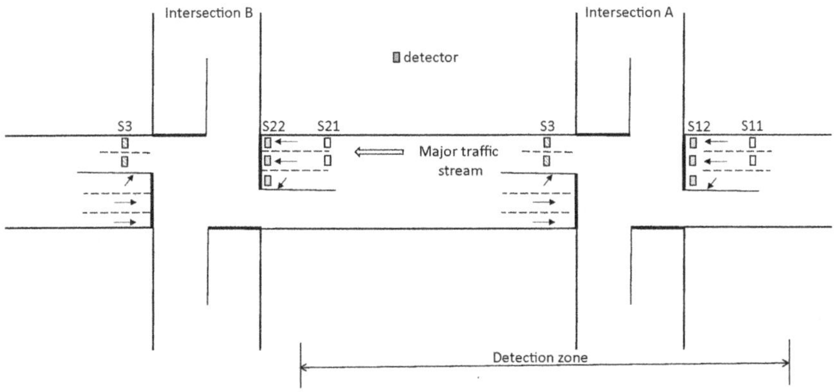

Figure 4.2 Detector configuration for arterial road incident detection.

is flowing from upstream intersection A to downstream intersection B. The AID tool requires further detectors (S11 and S21) for incident detection, located about 50 m upstream of the intersection stop line. These detectors are used to monitor queue evolution during each signal cycle and provide a better indication of traffic demand than the stop-line detectors. The use of modern video detectors means that each detector pair (S11 and S12, S21 and S22) can generally be serviced simultaneously. S12 data provides the upstream traffic volume data, while S11 data from the same signal cycle provides the occupancy data. S21 data provides downstream volume and occupancy values and corresponds to the same traffic stream from the upstream intersection. The starting time for the relevant S21 data is determined:

1. if the signals are coordinated, by using the offset time for the downstream signals, or
2. otherwise, using an empirical average travel time between the two intersections for the specific time of day.

The phase-specific lane volume and occupancy data for both upstream and downstream of each signal cycle are then averaged over the number of lanes. This processed lane average data is then compared to predetermined thresholds to determine the traffic state. The incident detection interval is then dependent on the upstream signal cycle time.

The traffic state data then provide the input to a Bayesian network, in which the nodes represent the variables of interest (each variable has a finite set of mutually exclusive states, hence the estimation of traffic states from the observed traffic data) and the directed links reflect causal relationships between the variables. An important observation is that congestion on arterial road network tends to be initiated at the intersections (nodes) rather

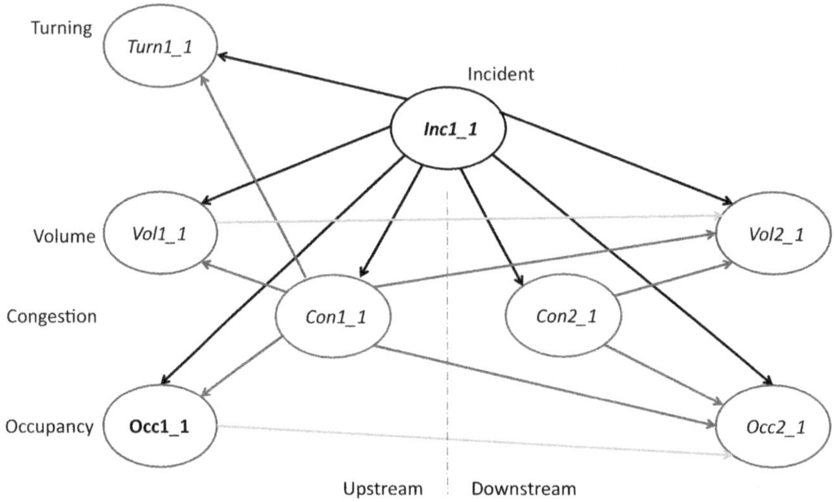

Figure 4.3 A Bayesian network for arterial road incident detection using the method of Zhang and Taylor (2006).

than midblock (i.e., on links) Thus the concept of "node congestion" is used to develop the Bayesian network. Figure 4.3 shows the Bayesian network for the AID tool. Any node in the Bayesian network that has no parents (i.e., there are no links pointing to it, such as node *Inc1_1* in Figure 4.3) contains a marginal probability table (a probability distribution over the states of the variable that it represents). If a node has parents (such as *Occ1_1*) then it contains a conditional probability table (CPT)—each cell of the CPT holds a conditional probability for the variables being in a specific state given the configuration of states of its parents. The CPTs of the Bayesian network may then be used to quantify the causal relationships described in the Bayesian network. Table 4.2 illustrates a CPT, in this case for variable *Occ1_1* (the upstream occupancy of the major traffic stream) and its relationship to variable *Con1_1* (the upstream congestion state), in which *Occ1_1* has two possible states (Yes, there is an incident, and No, there is no incident) and *Con1_1* has three states (high, medium, and low) with base probabilities as shown in the table. The Bayesian network may then be used to update the probability distributions of the variables whenever information on other variables becomes available. This is done by inference, using Bayes theorem, which is expressed as

$$\Pr\{B|A\} = \frac{\Pr\{A|B\}\Pr\{B\}}{\Pr\{A\}} \tag{4.9}$$

Table 4.2 Example Conditional Probability Table (CPT) for the Bayesian Network Arterial Road Incident Detection Method of Zhang and Taylor (2006) (See Figure 4.3 for Variables)

Variable	**State**			
Inc1_1	Yes		No	
Con1_1	Yes	No	Yes	No
High	0.85	0.2	0.8	0.1
Medium	0.15	0.6	0.15	0.5
Low	0.0	0.2	0.05	0.4

where $\Pr\{A\}$ and $\Pr\{B\}$ are the prior probabilities of events A and B, $\Pr\{A|B\}$ is the conditional probability of A given B (e.g., expert knowledge about the domain of interest), and $\Pr\{B|A\}$ is the posterior probability of B given that information on A is available. The probability of an event (e.g., B) can then be refined by obtaining new information about event A, and this provides the basic inferential mechanism for the Bayesian network. Zhang and Taylor (2006) described the application of this method to incident detection on arterial roads, and concluded that the method could provide rapid notification of the occurrence of an incident with a false alarm rate well below 1%. The method can be used to assess the impact of blockage incidents on links in an arterial road network, and thus to determine critical locations for congestion management plans.

The methods discussed in this section relate to traffic operations, and the impacts of blockages and restrictions on traffic movement, largely concerned with events of relatively short duration (perhaps hours) and probably of localized impact. After a review of the spectrum of blockage-causing events, largely traffic incidents and severe weather, the remainder of this chapter is concerned with larger events, which may have impacts across a significant part of a network and perhaps last for longer periods, possibly even days or weeks.

4.2 INCIDENTS AND SEVERE WEATHER

At this point there is value in considering the potential causes of blockage in a network. Section 2.4 (see especially Figure 2.5) illustrated the broad spectrum of causes of blockages and disruption. These included traffic incidents, severe weather events, natural disasters, human errors, sabotages, acts of terrorism, and warfare. Of these, the most common causes are traffic incidents and severe weather events, noting that some natural disasters such as landslides, floods, dust storms, and wildfires are often caused or strongly affected by severe weather.

Traffic incidents can range from minor events such as a vehicle illegally parked on the roadside, vehicle breakdowns, traffic signal failures, road crashes, roadwork, and even special events (which lead to temporary road closures and traffic diversions). Most traffic incidents are generally resolved within a matter of minutes or hours, although special events may have effects for days (installation and removal of traffic barriers, etc.) and major roadwork projects may persist for months. Generally no lasting change in travel demand patterns would be expected as a result, although perhaps with the exception of special events (see for example Berdica & Mattsson, 2007). Most severe weather events have similar durations, with gales and rainstorms perhaps only affecting network operations while the event persists. Other events such as blizzards may have longer impacts, and of course extreme weather may lead to natural disasters, e.g., landslides or washouts that may disrupt network operations for some time until repairs can be completed. Other natural events such as earthquakes may also induce long-term disruptions depending on the level and extent of damage to transportation infrastructure and the need for structural safety checks followed by repair or reconstruction as necessary before roads or rail lines can be reopened.

Taylor (2008) reviewed the research on the impacts of traffic incidents and extreme weather on traffic systems performance and concluded that these can be responsible for a considerable part of the delay time and costs associated with urban congestion. This review found that about 55% of the $67.5 billion costs of congestion in US cities could be attributed to vehicle breakdowns and traffic accidents. Traffic incidents accounted for 25% of the congestion on British highways, while about 50% of traffic congestion in Australia's major cities could be attributed to traffic incidents, including planned roadwork, maintenance activities, and special events (Charles, 2005). The random occurrence in space and time of incident-based congestion (also known as nonrecurrent congestion) is particularly disruptive, and so accentuates the operational impacts of the congestion on social and economic activities through higher travel costs and increased uncertainties. During periods of high travel demand, nonrecurrent congestion due to incidents can cause significant impacts on total delay and the variability of travel times experienced by travelers. The amount of delay experienced in an incident depends on three main factors: the nature of the incident, the ambient traffic conditions at the time of the incident, and the subsequent duration of the incident. Consideration of traffic conditions includes both the level of travel demand and the location within the network, in terms of the potential spill-back of incident-induced delay to other parts of the network. The relative impacts of similar incidents occurring at different locations then becomes of interest. Vulnerability analysis may be used to assess these impacts and to indicate more critical locations.

Natural phenomena, especially climate and weather, are also a major potential source of network failures. Severe weather can test the long-term integrity of transport infrastructure, although design and maintenance practices are generally devised to account for the climate and expected variations in a specific region. Climate change may, however, disturb the balance in this regard—see for example Taylor and Philp (2015) for a discussion of the potential impacts of alternative climate change scenarios on road infrastructure in different environments. Severe weather events and their consequences can cause substantial, and sometimes sustained, disruptions to transportation networks. Fog, dust storms, and heavy rainfall may cause loss of visibility, bringing traffic to near standstill. Snow may completely block some roads and leave others impassable. Rainstorms may lead to flooding, which may cut roads and railways, and perhaps isolate some areas, may be for days on end. Hurricanes may lead to a shutdown of transport services and restrict use of infrastructure for several days, as well as requiring the imposition of special traffic management plans to handle evacuations.

The physical components of transport infrastructure include bridges, tunnels, pavements, rail tracks, culverts, wharfs, aprons, and pipes. These elements are located on the ground, or above or below ground level—but are always associated with or attached to the ground. They may exist in cuttings or embankments, or on the natural surface. Thus transport infrastructure is directly affected by local environmental and climate conditions.

Water in its many manifestations, e.g., sea-level rise, tidal surge, flooding, rainstorms and wash outs, scouring, ponding, seepage, freezing, thawing, corrosion, and drying, is the major natural element that degrades the performance and integrity of transport assets. While natural disasters such as earthquakes can have immediate and serious local impacts on the assets, the insidious impacts of water in inappropriate locations over time is an ongoing universal threat to transport infrastructure. This is of particular concern for road pavements, which form the major part of the transport infrastructure asset. Water penetration into and under road pavements has serious impacts on the structural integrity (and hence usability) of pavements and can significantly decrease the engineering life of the asset.

In the main, extreme weather events may lead to network disruptions for periods of hours or days, perhaps longer if the consequences of the weather include landslides, rock falls, or washouts when significant repairs are required before the facility can be reopened.

A comprehensive review of the impacts of climate and extreme weather on the condition and use of transportation infrastructure is given in ITF (2016).

Other phenomena, such as earthquakes, can have devastating effects including total collapse of some facilities and infrastructure. In these situations considerable repair, if not reconstruction, may be required before system operation can be reinstated. Methods for network design to cope with earthquake potential, including the use of vulnerability analysis, are described in Nagae, Fujihara, and Asakura (2012). Flooding is perhaps the most widespread natural disaster, likely to reduce the serviceability of transportation networks. Accessibility-based vulnerability methods specifically intended for applications for flooded roads were reported by Sohn (2006), Chen, Lu, Peng, and Ash (2015), and Bil, Vodak, Kubecek, Bilova, and Sedonik (2015), and are described in Chapter 5.

4.3 NETWORK DEGRADATION AND FAILURE

Given a disruption that leads to blockage of one or more links, a network-wide perspective is required for vulnerability analysis. Link blockages will lead to redistribution of traffic flow as travelers seek (or are compelled to use) alternative routes for their journeys. This will lead to a redistribution of link volumes on the network—and if the blockage continues for a considerable period of time then perhaps also a redistribution of travel demand across the region as travelers seek alternative destinations which remain accessible to them.

Network analysis of the types indicated in Chapter 3 then becomes important. The key variables for consideration are:

- for each link a in the network, its length x_a, the link traffic volume q_a, travel time $T(q_a)$, and (generalized) travel cost $c(q_a)$, and
- for each origin–destination pair i-j, the travel demand (number of trips from i to j) H_{ij}, and the average trip travel distance d_{ij}, travel time T_{ij}, and travel cost C_{ij}.

The link variables are related to the origin–destination variables through the continuity of flow constraint Equations (3.12) and (3.13) introduced in Chapter 3. These equations ensure that (1) all trips from an origin make their way along paths r through the network to a destination (X_{rij} is the number of trips i-j using path r), and (2) the link volumes are compatible with (in fact are the aggregates of) the path volumes between the origin—destination pairs. Any set of link volumes meeting the requirements of Equations (3.12) and (3.13) is a feasible set of volumes on the network. Three system-wide measures of network activity can then be formulated. The first of these, VKT (i.e., the total distance traveled by all flow units, e.g., vehicles, in the network) was encountered earlier in this chapter, as Equation (4.3) and changes in VKT were proposed by Dehghani et al. (2014) as a simple measure of network vulnerability. VKT can also be expressed in terms of link volumes, as the summation of the product of link volume and link length over all the links in the network, i.e.,

$$\text{VKT} = \sum_a q_a x_a \tag{4.10}$$

and under the conservation of flow constraint equations this is equivalent to Equation (4.3). The other network-wide performance (or usage) measures are the total travel time experienced (total vehicle-hours of travel, VHT) and total cost of travel (vehicle-cost of travel, VCT, expressed in money units). Travel cost is represented by Equation (4.1), in which the generalized cost of travel is given as a weighted sum of different aspects of a journey, such as travel time, distance traveled, and money costs incurred.

VHT is given by

$$\text{VHT} = \sum_a q_a T(q_a) \tag{4.11}$$

VCT is given by

$$\text{VCT} = \sum_a q_a c(q_a) \tag{4.12}$$

VHT and VCT include the possible effects of traffic congestion because of the dependency of both travel time and travel cost on traffic activity (link volumes), and these effects are included in the expressions of Equations (4.11) and (4.12). While it is possible to observe (average) travel times on network links, travel times (and travel costs) would be more commonly estimated using a traffic assignment model as previously discussed in Section 3.5. A number of vulnerability indices are based on the difference between VHT or VCT in networks with disruptions and the full, intact network, as described below. Note that the user equilibrium traffic assignment flow distribution defined by Equation (3.11) is one formulation of VHT, as is the system optimization assignment flow distribution of Equation (3.14). Both of these solutions feature in particular models for vulnerability analysis.

Rupi, Bernardi, Rossi, and Danesi (2015) provided one example of a vulnerability index developed to assist in the identification of critical links in a road network. Their link importance (LI_a) index contains elements of both generalized cost and transport network flows. The index for link a is defined as

$$LI_a = \beta\phi_1(q_a) + (1-\beta)\phi_2(\Delta VCT)_a \tag{4.13}$$

In this equation, ϕ_1 is a normalized function of the average daily traffic volume on link a, while ϕ_2 is a function of ΔC_a, the increase in total vehicle-cost caused by disruption on link a, and $0 \le \beta \le 1$ is a weighting factor. ϕ_1 represents the local importance of the link, while ϕ_2 represents its global importance across the network. The equation enables the two functions for local and global importance to be weighted differently. Rupi et al. (2015) also allowed for the use of observed link traffic volumes (expressed as AADT, i.e., Annual Average daily Traffic) as an alternative to the use of volumes estimated by a traffic assignment model.

Local importance depends on link volume (locally, a link with higher volume is more vulnerable). The local importance indicator ϕ_1 is given by

$$\phi_1(q_a) = \frac{q_a - \min_a\{q_a\}}{\max_a\{q_a\} - \min_a\{q_a\}} \tag{4.14}$$

The global importance function ϕ_2 is defined as follows. The variation in total trip cost for the network due to the closure/disruption of link is given in terms of VCT_0, the total vehicle-cost in the intact network and VCT_a, the total vehicle-cost in the network with link a disrupted:

$$\Delta VCT_a = VCT_a - VCT_0 \tag{4.15}$$

This result does not fully account for the existence of cut links, for which the network would be divided into two or more separate subnetworks. This is a likely scenario in mountainous terrain where there are few alternative routes for origin–destination pairs. This situation leads to unsatisfied demand, and it is likely that the cut links may be seen as more important at the global (societal) level. To include the cut links, the global importance index (g_a) of a link for the operation of the whole network is defined as

$$g_a = \begin{cases} \Delta VCT_a & \text{if } a \in A_{nc}, \text{ the set of non} - \text{cut links} \\ \Delta VCT_a + \sum_{ij,a\in r} \alpha_{ij} X^a_{rij} & \text{if } a \in A_c, \text{ the set of cut links} \end{cases} \tag{4.16}$$

In Equation (4.16) α_{ij} is equal to the cost of a missing trip between origin i and generic destination j due to closure of link a, and X^{a}_{rij} is the trip demand i-j using path r that includes link a and hence cannot be satisfied. To combine global importance with local importance, the indicator g_a must be normalized, i.e.,

$$\phi_2(\Delta\mathrm{VCT_a}) = \frac{g_a - g_{\min}}{g_{\max} - g_{\min}} \tag{4.17}$$

in which $g_{\min}$ and $g_{\max}$ are the minimum and maximum values of g for the set of links considered. Rupi et al. (2015) applied the index in a study to rank importance for the links of the road network of the Province of Bolzano, a highly mountainous area in the Italian Alps. A value of $\beta = 0.5$ was chosen in this study, on the basis of a sensitivity analysis of the effects on the ranking of critical links for different values of β.

A similar index, the network robustness index (NRI), was proposed by Scott, Novak, Aultman-Hall, and Guo (2006), which then led to the formulation of the network trip robustness index (NTR) (Sullivan, Novak, Aultman-Hall, & Scott, 2010). NRI for link a is defined as the difference in total travel time between the network without that link and the base case of the intact network. It uses user equilibrium assignment to estimate link travel times. If VHT_0 is the total VHT in the full network and VHT_a is that in the network when link a fails (VHT as defined by Equation 4.11) then

$$\mathrm{NRI}_a = \mathrm{VHT}_a - \mathrm{VHT}_0 \tag{4.18}$$

NRI was originally proposed as an alternative to link-based VCR for identifying critical links because it provided a relative value of each link in the network, whereas VCR is only a local measure. While it is a useful method for comparing links in a given network, the index is scaled and cannot be readily used in making comparisons between networks. The NTR was thus proposed for this purpose. It provides a summary index for the network and can be used for comparisons between networks. Computation of NTR requires the summation of all travel demands in the network, i.e., $\sum_{ij} H_{ij}$ for origin—destination pairs i-j, which is the total number of trips using the network. Then, for network n,

$$\mathrm{NTR}_n = \frac{\sum_{a \in A_n} \mathrm{NRI}_a}{\sum_{ij} H_{ij}} \tag{4.19}$$

The units of NTR are (excess travel) time per trip, a measure which is comprehendible and intuitive, and therefore may be suitable for use in policy formulation. Total travel demand may be used as a measure of network size, and thus NTR can be used for comparisons between networks. One deficiency of the index is that it may not allow for cut links, but this was not seen as a problem in the dense highway networks for which it was proposed, where it could be assumed that alternative paths were always available to all destinations. While Scott et al. (2006) and Sullivan et al. (2010) used travel times (VHT) in their vulnerability calculations, equivalent indices using travel costs (VCT) could equally be used.

As described in de Oliveira, Da Silva Portugal, and Porto (2016), the analytical procedure common to the calculation of network vulnerability indicators, such as LI, NRI, and NTR, is the comparison of traffic volumes and travel times or costs on a network in its full intact state, and in a degraded state. The common procedure can be shown diagrammatically as in Figure 4.4. The network characteristics (nodes, links, link lengths, etc.)

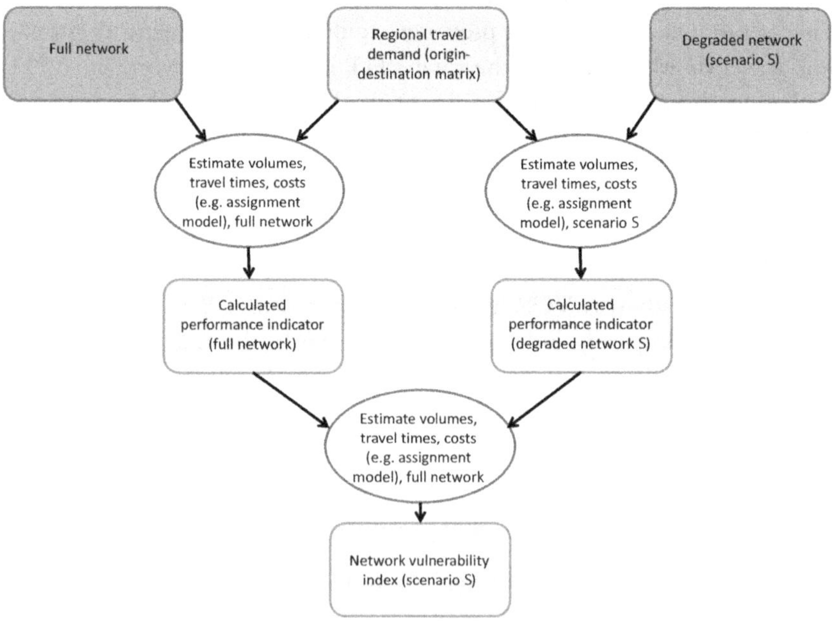

Figure 4.4 Network-based flow-travel cost procedure for estimating vulnerability indices. *Derived from de Oliveira, E. L., Da Silva Portugal, L., & Porto, W., Jr. (2016). Indicators of reliability and vulnerability: Similarities and differences in ranking links of a complex road system.* Transportation Research Part A: Policy and Practice, 88, *195–208.*

and the regional travel demand pattern (represented by an origin–destination trip matrix) provide the basic inputs. Link volumes and travel times or costs are modeled for the full network and for alternative scenarios involving link or node blockages. Network performance indicators (e.g., VKT, VHT, or VCT) are then determined, and the indicators for the degraded scenarios are compared to that of the full network, to provide a vulnerability index. The index values for the degradation scenarios may then be compared and used to identify critical locations in the network and perhaps to rank these locations in terms of importance.

Nagurney and Qiang (2008) also developed a vulnerability index (the NQ index) on the basis of the outputs of a user equilibrium assignment model for a network and by consideration of the Latori-Marchiori index (see Section 3.4). The index is defined in terms of the number of origin–destination pairs (N_{ij}), travel demand, and cost of travel between the pairs, and is given by

$$NQ = \frac{1}{N_{ij}} \sum_{ij} \frac{H_{ij}}{C_{ij}} \tag{4.20}$$

It may be used as an alternative to the LI and NRI/NTR indices discussed above. Other researchers have also reported vulnerability analysis using equilibrium assignment results. These include Murray-Tuite and Mahmassani (2004), Chen, Lam, Sumalee, Li, and Li (2012), and Connors and Watling (2015).

In the context of urban road network modeling, Balijepalli and Oppong (2014) considered the vulnerability of urban road networks, serviceability and identification of critical links. They identified three specific factors for urban networks that required a different perspective. The first was that urban networks are dense networks, often possessing a large number of alternative routes between origin–destination pairs. The second was that urban networks can be prone to chronic congestion. Finally, urban roads are often subject to partial closures—lane blockages rather than link blockages—whereas the studies of highway and regional networks tend to focus on link blockages. Lane blockages (from roadwork, vehicle breakdowns, queuing to enter off-street car parks, etc.) lead to reductions in capacity and increases in delays and congestion, although the link is still available for travel. Thus they proposed a new vulnerability index (the network vulnerability index, NVI) which accounted for lane blockage and link capacity decreases. NVI considers both the serviceability and the importance of each link in the network. This index requires calculation of a serviceability index r_a for link a. The serviceability index is defined as the total available capacity of the link divided by the standard hourly link capacity per lane for the given type of road (reflecting the road's traffic importance in a hierarchy of roads). Total available capacity is the sum of the capacities of all available operational traffic lanes. The value of r decreases when a road link is impacted by an event, such as a road crash or flood, because the effective capacity after the event is lowered.

$$\text{NVI} = \sum_{a \in A} \frac{q_a^0 t_a^0}{r_a^0} - \sum_{a \in A-AC} \frac{q_a^\sigma t_a^\sigma}{r_a^\sigma} \tag{4.21}$$

In this equation, superscript 0 means the full network in its normal operating state, superscript σ is for scenario σ where one or more links have been degraded, A is the set of all links in the network, $A-AC$ is the set of links excluding any cut link (i.e., blocked links are excluded from the summation, and would have $r_a^\sigma = 0$), and the variables are:

- q_a^0 (Directional) link volume on link a in the normal network
- t_a^0 Travel time on link a in the normal network
- r_a^0 Serviceability index on link a in the normal network
- q_a^σ (Directional) link volume on link a in the degraded network of scenario σ
- t_a^σ Travel time on link a in the degraded network of scenario σ
- r_a^σ Serviceability index on link a in the degraded network of scenario σ

The formulation of NVI means that a higher loss of capacity on a major (dual carriageway) arterial road is likely to have higher impact on the index, as would a loss of capacity on a two-way-two-lane road. Balijepalli and Oppong (2014) applied NVI to the arterial road network of the center of York, UK, an area that is prone to flooding. They concluded that (1) travel time was the appropriate variable to use in urban networks as opposed to regional networks where travel distance is generally chosen, and (2) the NVI index could be used in the development of a traffic management and diversion plan for York when its road network was affected by flooding.

A major advance in serviceability-based vulnerability analysis that focuses on criticality through the consideration of link importance and node exposure was introduced by Jenelius, Petersen, and Mattsson (2006). This method has been developed significantly since its introduction (e.g., see Jenelius, 2009, 2010; Jenelius and Mattsson, 2012), and is discussed in detail in the next section.

4.4 EXPOSURE AND IMPORTANCE

Jenelius, Mattsson, and their colleagues at the Royal Institute of Technology, Stockholm, developed the exposure-importance method of vulnerability analysis for road networks over the last decade. They argued that vulnerability is divided into two parts: first, the probability of a hazardous event and, second, the consequences of that event at a given location. This latter part is the exposure and is site-dependent. The consequences for a set of locations (e.g., nodes) of a failed link (or a network component[5]) indicate the importance of the network component. In addition, consequences may be viewed in terms of social equity or social efficiency. The consequences of network degradation are measured by increases in travel costs. Social equity considers all roads to be of equal significance, irrespective of how much they are used, and that each trip is of equal importance. Social efficiency implies that those roads that have maximum use should be considered more significant, because the serve more people, more businesses, and more social and economic activity. To consider social efficiency, increases in travel costs can be weighted by travel demand. Criticality of a network component involves both probability of failure and the consequences of that failure. If probability of failure of the component is high, the component is weak. If consequences are great, the component is important. If it is both weak and important, the component is critical.

Jenelius et al. (2006) used Berdica's definition of vulnerability in terms of loss of serviceability and, in keeping with D'Este and Taylor (2003), considered an increase in generalized travel cost as a measure of reduced serviceability. Considering a single origin–destination pair *i*-*j*, given C_{ij}^0 as the travel cost between *i* and *j* in the full network and C_{ij}^a as the travel cost if link *a* has failed, the basic measure of change in serviceability is the cost difference

$$\Delta C_{ij}^a = C_{ij}^a - C_{ij}^0 \tag{4.22}$$

However, there is a further, and perhaps more serious, consequence to be considered. Failure of a network component may mean that the network splits into two or more separate parts (subnetworks), and is thus disconnected. In this situation the travel costs between some origin–destination

[5] A network component could be a link, a set of links, a node or a set of nodes. Under failure of a node, all the links starting or finishing at that node are deemed to have failed.

pairs are then infinite. To account for this situation but still maintain computational realism, Jenelius et al. (2006) defined unsatisfied demand u_{ij}^{a} as

$$u_{ij}^{a} = \begin{cases} H_{ij} & \text{if } C_{ij}^{a} = \infty \\ 0 & \text{if } C_{ij}^{a} < \infty \end{cases} \tag{4.23}$$

Thus a link closure results in finite increases in travel cost (possibly zero) or a level of unsatisfied demand. A link (component) causing finite increases in travel cost when closed is a *non-cut link*. Let the set of all links be A, the set of non-cut links be A^{nc}, and the set of cut links be $A^{c} = A \backslash A^{nc}$ (the set of A outside of A^{nc}). Measures based on increased travel cost must be limited to non-cut links, but measures based on unsatisfied demand apply to, are well defined for, all links.

Importance of a link applies to a single demand node, a group of demand nodes (e.g., a municipality), or the whole network. The importance $I_{net}(a)$ of link a is then

$$I_{net}(a) = \begin{cases} \dfrac{\sum_{i}\sum_{j \neq i} w_{ij}\left(C_{ij}^{a} - C_{ij}^{0}\right)}{\sum_{i}\sum_{j \neq i} w_{ij}} & \text{for } a \in A^{nc} \\ \infty & \text{for } a \in A^{c} \end{cases} \tag{4.24}$$

The weights w_{ij} reflect the significance of each origin–destination pair. If $w_{ij} = 1$ (are equal) for all origin–destination pairs, then all origins and destinations are equally important. This is the case for social equity. If travel demand H_{ij} is used as the weight, the severity of increased travel cost depends on the traffic between the zones, i.e., the capability of network to provide socially and economically efficient transport (demand-weighted importance).

The importance in terms of unsatisfied demand of any link a for the whole network is

$$I_{net}^{uns}(a) = \frac{\sum_{i}\sum_{j \neq i} u_{ij}^{a}}{\sum_{i}\sum_{j \neq i} H_{ij}} \quad \text{for } a \in A \tag{4.25}$$

which is a proportion of the total demand that is unsatisfied. Note that, for $a \in A^{nc}$, $I_{net}^{uns} = 0$.

Exposure to an event can be calculated for a single demand node, a group of demand nodes, or whole network. Consider a "municipality" m, a subset of origin—destination pairs. Then ΔC_{ij}^{a} is aggregated over all origins i in the municipality and all destinations j in the network. For failure of random link $a \in A^{nc}$ the exposure can be written as the expected increase in travel cost:

$$Ex = \frac{\sum\limits_{a \in A^{nc}} \sum\limits_{i \in M_m^d} \sum\limits_{j \neq i} w_{ij} \Delta C_{ij}^{a}}{N^{nc} \sum\limits_{i \in M_m^d} \sum\limits_{j \neq i} w_{ij}} \quad \text{for } a \in A^{nc} \tag{4.26}$$

where N^{nc} is the number of non-cut links and M_m^d is the set of demand nodes in m. This is the simple model of failures that have some probability distribution in the region. Another event is the failure of the most important link for m. The exposure of m is then the maximum value over all non-cut links, i.e.,

$$Ex_{\max}(m) = \max_{a \in A^{nc}} \left\{ \frac{\sum\limits_{i \in M_m^d} \sum\limits_{j \neq i} w_{ij} \Delta C_{ij}^{a}}{\sum\limits_{i \in M_m^d} \sum\limits_{j \neq i} w_{ij}} \right\} \quad \text{for } a \in A^{nc} \tag{4.27}$$

For cut links i.e., $a \in A^c$ the exposure is defined in terms of the proportion of unsatisfied demand:

$$Ex^{uns} = \frac{\sum\limits_{a \in A} \sum\limits_{i \in M_m^d} \sum\limits_{j \neq i} u_{ij}^{a}}{n_L \sum\limits_{i \in M_m^d} \sum\limits_{j \neq i} H_{ij}} \tag{4.28}$$

where n_L is the number of links in the network.

These equations are for inelastic demand, i.e., for closures that are long enough to develop a new user equilibrium assignment (route choice) but short enough not to affect travel demand patterns (destination, mode, and trip-timing choices) significantly. Thus they would apply generally to events that last for a few hours or days. Jenelius et al. (2006) decided that travel time was a reasonable representation of travel cost. While a more general definition of travel cost (e.g., including distance and/or money cost) might be seen as more rigorous, this would require detailed data on the value of time for different people under different conditions. In addition, the choice of travel time has some further advantages when the duration of a link-blocking incident is taken into account.

The issue of event duration was considered by Jenelius (2009, 2010). During a closure of link a for duration τ, say due to a flood, blizzard, or fire, there may still be an alternative route from i to j or there may be no available alternative. In the former case, a traveler will be faced with an increase in travel time on the alternative route, say ΔT_{ij}^{a}. In the latter case, which is for a cut link, the traveler will have to wait for a period before being able to undertake or resume the journey. Assuming that the travel demand rate is constant over time (at $h_{ij} = H_{ij}/\tau$ trips per unit time) then on average a traveler wanting to depart during the closure will be delayed for a period of $\tau/2$. The total demand during the closure is $h_{ij}\tau$, so that the additional VHT is

$$\Delta \mathrm{VHT}_{ij}^{a}(\tau) = \frac{h_{ij}\tau^2}{2} \quad \text{for } a \in A^c \tag{4.29}$$

When an alternative route is available, the traveler can weigh up the alternatives of using the new route (with additional travel time ΔT_{ij}^{a}) or waiting for the link to reopen—if this provides an earlier arrival time. Then the additional VHT is

$$\Delta \mathrm{VHT}_{ij}^{a}(\tau) = \begin{cases} \dfrac{h_{ij}\tau^2}{2} & \text{if } \Delta T_{ij}^{a} \geq \tau \\ h_{ij}\Delta T_{ij}^{a}\left(\tau - \dfrac{\Delta T_{ij}^{a}}{2}\right) & \text{if } \Delta T_{ij}^{a} < \tau \end{cases} \quad \text{for } a \in A^{nc} \tag{4.30}$$

This is an important result, for it provides a firm connection between the modeling of vulnerability and the real world situation for travelers facing a network disruption. The traveler needs to consider whether there is a time advantage or disadvantage in using a detour, should this be available, to complete the journey. If there is no advantage then the traveler can decide to wait *en route*, or if still planning the journey to delay departure time. If there is no detour then the traveler also has that latter choice.

Jenelius and Mattsson (2012) extended the exposure-importance method to consider area-wide network disruptions, in which multiple elements of a network in the same vicinity fail together. This scenario is likely in the event of severe weather in a region, under flood and fire conditions, and in the aftermath of natural disasters such as earthquakes. The approach adopted by Jenelius and Mattsson was to superimpose a rectangular grid of cells across the study region, where each cell represents the spatial coverage of a given disruptive event. The links covered by a given cell are then taken as having failed simultaneously. The use of grids of different sizes enables the analyst to study the impacts of events of different spatial extents. Figure 4.5 provides a schematic view of the grid-based approach. All links intersected by the "closed cell"—representing the area covered by the disruptive event—are deemed to have failed and be no longer available for use.

Extending the concept of link importance, as summarized in Equations (4.24) and (4.25), leads to the definition of cell importance, as the total impact for network users if all links intersecting the cell are closed for a given duration. Let $\Delta C_{ij}^{k}(\tau)$ be the total impact for travelers from i to j when all links in cell k are closed for duration τ. This impact may be a change in generalized travel cost (ΔVCT) or in total travel time (ΔVHT). Cell importance is then

$$I_{net}(k|\tau) = \sum_{i} \sum_{j} \Delta C_{ij}^{k}(\tau) \tag{4.31}$$

Given that i and j may represent aggregated zones, then j may equal i in the summation.

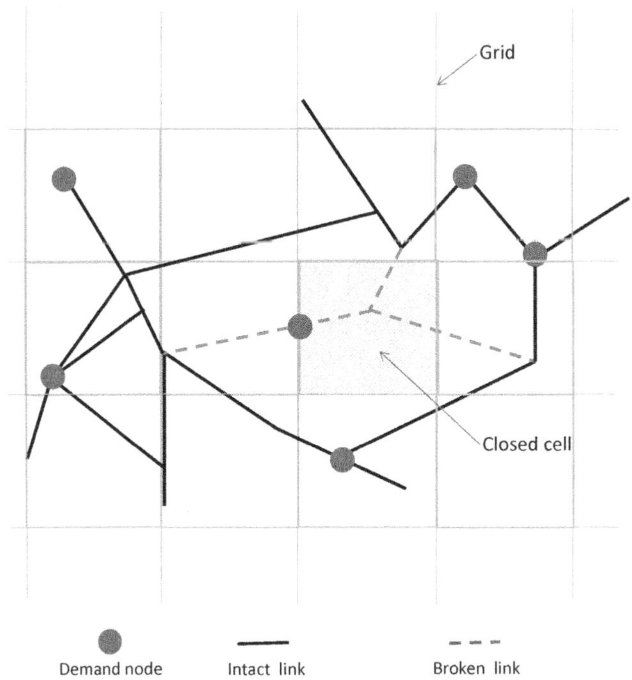

Figure 4.5 Schematic of the Jenelius-Mattsson grid-based method for area-wide disruption events.

In terms of exposure, for this grid-based analysis Jenelius and Mattson used a measure of user exposure, the average impact per traveler, and took the worst case scenario, where the cell having the most severe impact for each region (r) in the study area is closed. Then $i \in r$ indicates that origin i is in region r. If the collection of all cells is K, then the traveler exposure of region r is given by

$$Ex(r|\tau, K) = \max_{k \in K} \left\{ \frac{\sum_{i \in r} \sum_{j} \Delta C_{ij}^{k}(\tau)}{\sum_{i \in r} \sum_{j} h_{ij}\tau} \right\} \tag{4.32}$$

Jenelius and Mattsson (2012) explained how the size of grid cells and the model used to evaluate the impacts of disruptions should be chosen to meet the characteristics of the event under consideration. In a case study application to the road network of Sweden—with a focus on regional and rural roads, i.e., those outside the major cities—they considered disruptions of relatively short durations (hours to days), and considered delays as the indicator of disruption (delays included both increases in travel times and waiting time for facilities to reopen). Figure 4.6 shows the Swedish national road network, population density, and travel demand. Figure 4.7 indicates the computed cell importance values for two different grid cell scales (12.5 and 25 km), for incidents involving link closures for a 12 h period.

This case study suggested that the factors determining the more severe consequences of area-wide disruptions may be quite different from those for single link failures. Network vulnerability for these two types of degradation may therefore show quite different geographical distributions. Jenelius and Mattsson concluded that, whereas for single link failures vulnerability can depend on the degree of local redundancy in the network, network redundancy had a smaller effect for disruptions covering wide areas, generally because the alternative routes were also disabled. The unsatisfied demand inside, into and out of the affected area tended to determine the magnitude of the impact. Given that travel demand and population are closely correlated, regions with population concentrated in a few central locations were likely to be more exposed to area-wide disruptions.

4.5 IDENTIFICATION OF CRITICAL LOCATIONS

The identification of critical locations is a key outcome of a vulnerability analysis. de Oliveira et al. (2016) argue that the ranking of links and locations according to their impact on the performance of a network is a vital

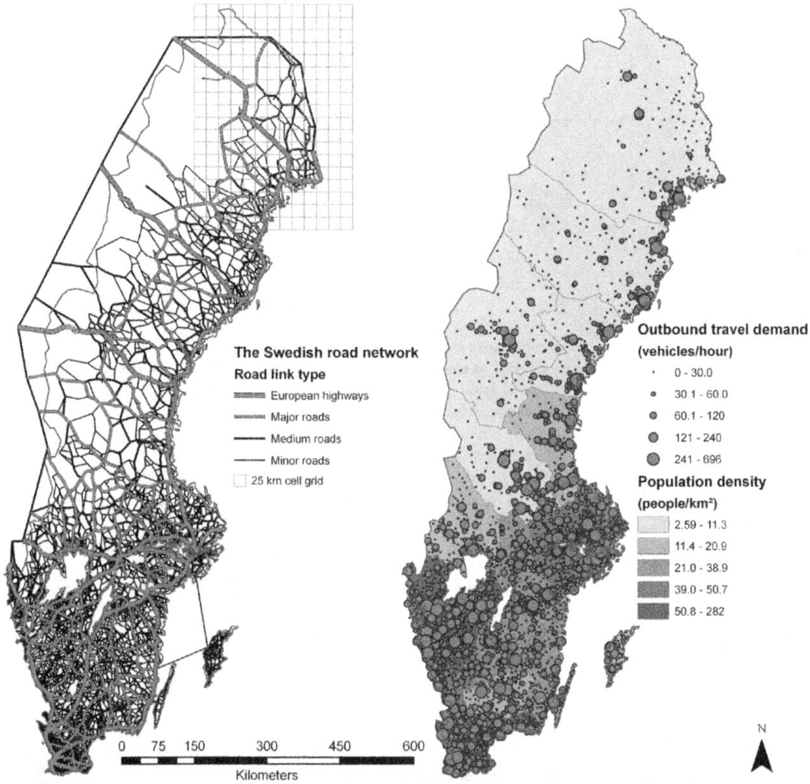

Figure 4.6 The road network of Sweden with portion of a 25 km cell grid (left) and total outbound travel demand (veh/h) for each demand node and county population densities (right). *Reproduced with permission from Jenelius, E., & Mattsson, L.-G. (2012). Road network vulnerability analysis of area-covering disruptions: A grid-based approach with case study.* Transportation Research Part A: Policy and Practice, *46(5), 746–760, Figure 2, p.752.*

task in the planning and management of transportation systems. This chapter has identified a large set of similar indices that have been proposed as indicators of that importance. In general terms, a network scanning approach may be used to determine critical locations. The basic process of the network vulnerability scan for a network may be seen as follows:

Step 1: Compute the network performance indices for the original network.

Step 2: Identify candidate critical links, route sections or grid cells.

Step 3: Fail or degrade these candidate links, route sections or grid cells in turn, and determine the new performance indices for the degraded network.

Step 4: Determine the resulting changes in performance and identify the most critical links or route sections.

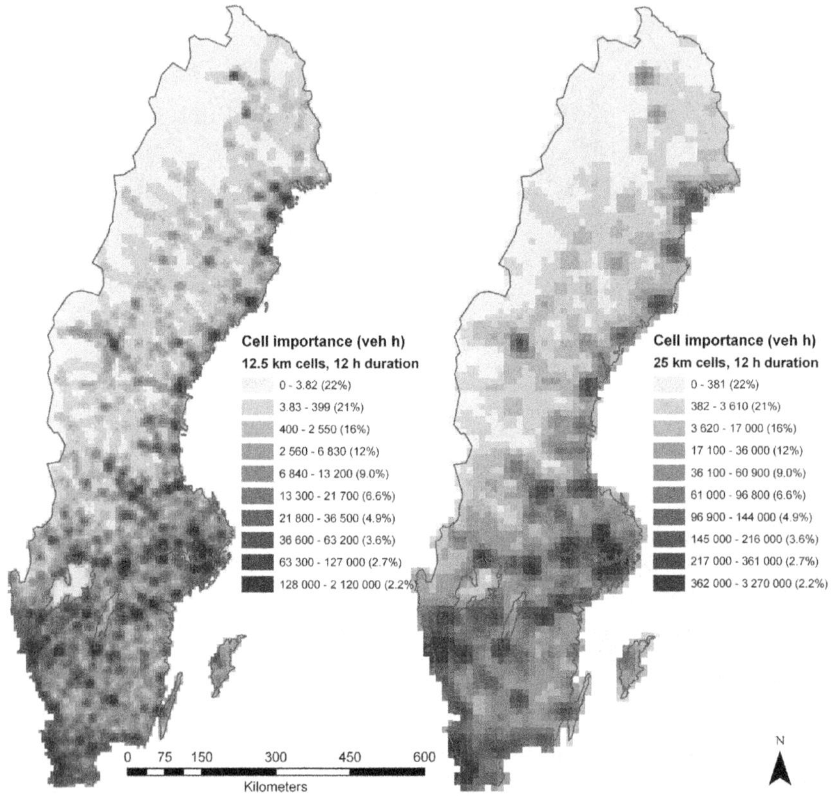

Figure 4.7 Local cell importance (veh-h of travel) for 12.5 km grid cells (left) and 25 km grid cells (right) for incident closure duration 12 h. *Reproduced with permission from Jenelius, E., & Mattsson, L.-G. (2012). Road network vulnerability analysis of area-covering disruptions: A grid-based approach with case study.* Transportation Research Part A: Policy and Practice, *46(5), 746–760, Figure 4, p.755.*

This is a simple strategy which may be adopted readily for small networks. However, it may quickly become a substantial if not impossible computational task in large and dense networks. The network of Figure 4.6 would be a good example. According to Jenelius and Mattsson (2012) this network has more than 32,000 nodes (including 8764 demand nodes) and nearly 87,000 directional links. Failing each link in turn requires the network performance model to be rerun each time, a substantial and largely fruitless task. Failing combinations of links, even if using a regular grid system as proposed earlier is still an enormous task. Thus researchers and analysts continue to seek more efficient methods to reduce the size of the computational effort.

One practical approach is to use expert judgment and considered selection of candidate links, as done by Peterson and Church (2008) and Taylor and Susilawati (2012), but this process is open to errors of omission. It can work quite well in sparse regional networks of the type in the studies reported by those authors, or in highway networks with limited access and egress points—as shown by Kurauchi, Uno, Sumalee, and Seto (2009) in their case study of the Kansai regional road network in Japan, where the critical links were shown to be the set of cut links in that network. However, a method based on judgment may miss potential vital locations in a network. Another alternative was suggested by D'Este and Taylor (2003). In this case the suggested procedure was to compute probabilities of use of different links or route sections (link sequences or even paths) in the full network, using a multipath traffic assignment procedure, and then select those links with probability of use exceeding some threshold value. They reasoned that, in general, the higher the link probability, the greater the adverse impact if that link is broken, so that candidates for the source of network vulnerability could be identified by setting a probability threshold of 0.5 or greater and then selecting those links with probability higher than this threshold as candidates. However, this procedure again only works well in networks with relatively small numbers of demand nodes (origin–destination pairs).

In their study of a regional road network in the Italian Alps—and thus a sparse network with limited alternative routes for much of the travel demand—Rupi et al. (2015) adopted the basic network scanning procedure adopted above, using the LI_a index defined in Equation (4.14). This index has two components, one related to local link importance (expressed in terms of link traffic volume) and the other in terms of changes in vehicle operating costs (and thus representing global importance). While Equation (4.13) presents a weighted sum of normalized values of these two components, Rupi et al. did consider each component in its own right, and formulated ranked lists of critical links for both components. They concluded that there were statistically significant differences in the rankings using the two components separately. In particular, heavily trafficked links usually had viable alternative routes, specifically to account for potential flow disruptions. Thus while their local importance was high, there global importance was often not as high as that for links with lower utilization. On the basis of a sensitivity test of the weighting factor (β) in Equation (4.13), Rupi et al. decided to use equal weights ($\beta = 0.5$) for final determination of critical links. In similar vein, after testing a number of alternative indices, Nicholson, Barker, and Ramirez-Marquez (2016) concluded that a weighted volume-based importance measure was the most successful indicator if a policy of minimum overall network vulnerability was adopted.

Wang, Liu, Szeto, and Chow (2016) concluded that the set of most critical links determined under single link failure scenarios was not the set determined when simultaneous link failures were considered. They also found that critical links under simultaneous failure scenarios were not necessarily connected or even in proximity to each other. This result builds on that provided by Jenelius and Mattsson (2012) for their cell-grid model.

The final conclusion of de Oliveira et al. (2016) was that vulnerability analysis needs to be viewed from the perspective of strategic policy. This issue is discussed in the next section.

4.6 STRATEGIC PLANNING CONSIDERATIONS

The main thrust of de Oliveira et al. (2016) was that reliability and vulnerability need to be considered as separate although related performance attributes of transportation networks in the development of strategic policies for network planning and management. They suggested that vulnerability was more strongly influenced by the characteristics of alternative routes while reliability was more sensitive to levels of congestion. Nicholson et al. (2016), whose main objective concerned network resilience, supported this point of view but noted that planning for network resilience, for which vulnerability is one potential cause of difficulty, required consideration of vulnerability in a multifaceted way. Therefore, in general, topological indicators of vulnerability should also be considered alongside the flow-based measures which they found to be the most informative for the networks they had studied. In particular, they were concerned that individual vulnerability indicators could affect an impact analysis to the extent that the analysis might not be able to represent a wide range of alternative disruption events. Further research was needed to explore how different vulnerability indicators performed under a wide range of different events, especially in the context of informing tactical policies (for operational recovery from incidents) and strategic policies concerned with network design and the provision of infrastructure and facilities.

One method for addressing this need was suggested by Erath, Löchl, and Axhausen (2009) as a result of their study of the road and railway networks of Switzerland. They developed a framework for vulnerability analysis using both topological and volume-based indicators for classifying the transportation network and for assisting in the planning of future network upgrades. This required consideration of both local and global impacts.

Balijepalli and Oppong (2014) applied their NVI (see Equation 4.21) to situations involving traffic management plans to deal with a natural disaster (in this case chronic flooding in an urban area). They concluded that vulnerability analysis for urban traffic networks needed to focus on travel time and delay, as opposed to the travel distance and generalized cost factors widely applied in regional road networks. Further, all network link characteristics were of interest in urban areas, because drivers often knew and made use of alternative routes in the dense networks characteristic of urban areas. Tu, Yang, Chen, and Chen (2012) also considered the situation of congested networks, and as a result devised an urban transportation vulnerability analysis framework for use in the development of transport policies and traffic management plans. This framework is shown in Figure 4.8. It shows the dimensions of performance assessment (connectivity, accessibility, and delays

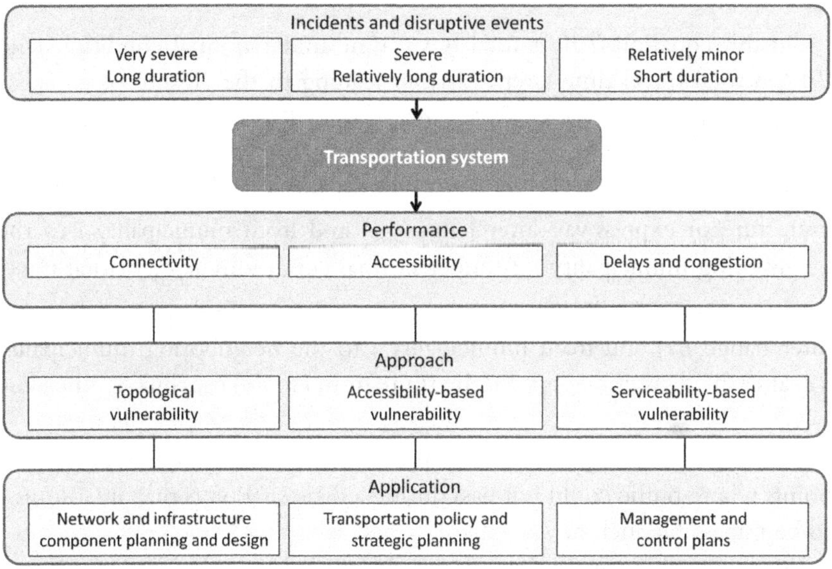

Figure 4.8 Framework connecting vulnerability analysis to transportation policy making and systems planning. *Derived from Tu, Y., Yang, C., Chen, A., & Chen, X. (2012). A framework of transportation network vulnerability analysis for different administrative prospects. In W. H. K. Lam, H. K. Lo, & S.C. Wong (Eds.),* Proceedings 5th international symposium on transport network reliability, Hong Kong, December 18–19 *(pp. 27–49). Hong Kong Polytechnic University and Hong Kong Society for Transportation Studies.*

and congestion) and indicates how these may be handled in terms of topological analysis, accessibility-based vulnerability, and serviceability-based vulnerability. The framework then provides for applications in network and infrastructure component design, policy setting, and management and control plans.

One indication of the approach taken for vulnerability analysis by transportation agencies is provided by Pokharel and Ieda (2016). In their review of methods for vulnerability analysis in terms of accessibility analysis and generalized cost analysis they identified three main approaches: (1) serviceability methods (as described in this chapter), accessibility methods (the subject of Chapter 5), and a disaster prevention approach, as currently adopted by the Japanese Ministry of Land, Infrastructure and Transport (MLIT). The MLIT method is based on an inventory-based risk assessment (Section 3.3). It considers the evaluation of road networks under emergency conditions and defines an index known as the "degree of weakness" (DW) of a link (a) as:

$$\mathrm{DW}(a) = \frac{TT_D^a}{TT_0} \tag{4.33}$$

In this equation TT_0 is total travel time under normal conditions and TT_D^a is total travel time after a disaster leading to the closure of a. These are defined as $TT_0 = \sum_i \sum_j T_{ij(n)}^0 \delta_{ij(n)}$ and $TT_D^a = \sum_i \sum_j T_{ij(n)}^{Da} \delta_{ij(n)}$ in which $T_{ij(n)}^0$ = total travel time from municipality i to the nearest capital of prefecture or expressway interchange $j(1)$ and from municipality i to the neighboring municipality $j(2)$ under normal conditions. $T_{ij(n)}^{Da}$ = total travel time from municipality i to the nearest capital of prefecture or expressway interchange $j(1)$ and from municipality i to the neighboring municipality $j(2)$ after the disaster. $\delta_{ij(n)} = 1$ if the route from i to $j(n)$ uses link a, otherwise zero.

This measure does not include a probability of link failure, but identifies points where traffic could not pass during a disaster. Points that are assumed to be impassable include:

- locations where an earthquake would cause damage
- road sections within a designated tsunami inundation zone
- road sections prone to landslides, rock fall or avalanches
- any bridge constructed before 1980
- locations where smooth traffic flow is difficult (defined as locations with road pavement width < 5.5 m).

While the DW method only considers route travel times, which is very uncertain after a disaster and other parameters such as area population and link lengths are important, it provides a practical method for use in disaster scenario planning.

4.7 SUMMARY

This chapter has provided a comprehensive review of the definition, development, and application of a number of approaches to vulnerability analysis with a focus on the serviceability of a transportation network and the transport consequences of network failure and degradation under different conditions, including traffic congestion and incidents, severe weather, and natural disasters. The methods cover a range of different intensities and extensions of disruptive incidents, from link-specific incidents and incident durations of a few hours, to area-wide disruptions and consequences lasting for days or weeks. Most of these methods require consideration of adverse changes in travel costs, notably as increases in travel times and delays as a consequence of network failure, blockages or service disruption. The performance indices and metrics invoked in these methods often bear directly on the performance measures commonly employed by transportation system planners and managers, and relate directly to system performance and diagnostics for improved performance.

Serviceability is a vital and important performance characteristic for transportation systems and vulnerability analysis rightly focuses on this. There is a still wider context of network vulnerability which incorporates much of the work on serviceability but attempts to extend the impacts of network degradations and failures to the broader socioeconomic systems served by transportation. Bil et al. (2015) considered the link between network vulnerability and the regional economic systems in their analysis of the regional road network in the Czech Republic, and in doing so provided a strong link to the next area of attention, accessibility-based network vulnerability analysis.

REFERENCES

Balijepalli, C., & Oppong, O. (2014). Measuring vulnerability of road network considering the extent of serviceability of critical road links in urban areas. *Journal of Transport Geography, 39*, 145–155.

Berdica, K. (2002). An introduction to road vulnerability: What has been done, is done and should be done. *Transport Policy, 9*(2), 117–127.

Berdica, K., & Mattsson, L.-G. (2007). Vulnerability: A model-based case study of the road network in Stockholm. In A. T. Murray, & H. Grubesic (Eds.), *Critical infrastructure: Reliability and vulnerability* (pp. 81–106). New York): Springer.

Bhavathrathan, B. K., & Patil, G. R. (2015). Quantifying resilience using a unique critical cost on road networks subject to recurring capacity disruptions. *Transportmetrica A: Transport Science, 11*(9), 836–855.

Bil, M., Vodak, R., Kubecek, J., Bilova, M., & Sedonik, J. (2015). Evaluating road network damage caused by natural disasters in the Czech Republic between 1997 and 2010. *Transportation Research Part A: Policy and Practice, 81*, 90–103.

Calvert, S. C., & Snelder, M. (2015). A methodology for road traffic resilience analysis and review of related concepts. In *Proceedings 6th international symposium on transport network reliability, Nara, Japan, August 1–2, Kyoto University*.

Charles, P. (2005). Effective implementation of regional transport strategy: Traffic incident management case study. *WIT Transactions on the Built Environment, 77*, 609–618.

Chen, B. Y., Lam, W. H. K., Sumalee, A., Li, Q., & Li, Z.-C. (2012). Vulnerability analysis for large-scale and congested road networks with demand uncertainty. *Transportation Research Part A: Policy and Practice, 46*(3), 501–516.

Chen, X.-Z., Lu, Q.-C., Peng, Z.-R., & Ash, J. E. (2015). Analysis of transportation network vulnerability under flooding disasters. *Transportation Research Record, 2532*, 37–44.

Connors, R. D., & Watling, D. P. (2015). Assessing the demand vulnerability of equilibrium traffic networks via network aggregation. *Networks and Spatial Economics, 15*(2), 367–395.

Dehghani, M., Flintsch, G., & McNeil, S. (2014). Impact of road conditions and disruption uncertainties on network vulnerability. *Journal of Infrastructure Systems, 20*(3). Retrieved from http://dx.doi.org/10.1061/(ASCE)IS.1943-555X.0000205.

D'Este, G. M., & Taylor, M. A. P. (2003). Network vulnerability: An approach to reliability analysis at the level of national strategic transport networks. In M. G. H. Bell, & Y. Iida (Eds.), *The network reliability of transport* (pp. 23–44). London: Emerald Publishing.

El-Rashidy, R. A., & Grant-Muller, S. M. (2014). An assessment method for highway network vulnerability. *Journal of Transport Geography, 34*, 34–43.

Erath, A., Löchl, M., & Axhausen, K. W. (2009). Graph-theoretical analysis of the Swiss road and railway networks over time. *Networks and Spatial Economics, 9*(3), 379–400.

ITF. (2016). *Adapting transport to climate change and extreme weather: Implications for infrastructure owners and network managers*. International Transport Forum, ITF Research Reports. Paris: OECD Publishing. Retrieved from http://dx.doi.org/10.1787/9789282108079-en.

Jenelius, E. (2009). Network structure and travel patterns: Explaining the geographical disparities of road network vulnerability. *Journal of Transport Geography, 17*(3), 234–244.

Jenelius, E. (2010). User inequity implications of road network vulnerability. *Journal of Transport and Land Use, 2*(3), 57–73. Retrieved from http://dx.doi.org/10.5198/jtlu.v2i3.16.

Jenelius, E., & Mattsson, L.-G. (2012). Road network vulnerability analysis of area-covering disruptions: A grid-based approach with case study. *Transportation Research Part A: Policy and Practice, 46*(5), 746–760.

Jenelius, E., Petersen, T., & Mattsson, L.-G. (2006). Importance and exposure in road network vulnerability analysis. *Transportation Research Part A: Policy and Practice, 40*(7), 537–560.

Kim, S., & Yeo, H. (2016). A flow-based vulnerability measure for the resilience of urban road network. *Procedia – Social and Behavioral Sciences, 218*, 13–23.

Knoop, V. L., & Daamen, W. (2016). Automatic fitting procedure for the fundamental diagram. *Transportmetrica B: Transport Dynamics*. Retrieved from http://dx.doi.org/10.1080/21680566.2016.1256239.

Kurauchi, F., Uno, N., Sumalee, A., & Seto, Y. (2009). Network evaluation based on connectivity vulnerability. In W. H. K. Lam, S. C. Wong, & H. K. Lo (Eds.), *Transportation and traffic theory 2009: Golden jubilee* (pp. 637–649). New York): Springer.

Murray-Tuite, P., & Mahmassani, H. (2004). Methodology for determining vulnerable links in a transportation network. *Transportation Research Record, 1882*, 88–96.

Nagae, T., Fujihara, T., & Asakura, Y. (2012). Anti-seismic reinforcement strategy for an urban road network. *Transportation Research Part A: Policy and Practice, 46*(5), 813–827.

Nagurney, A., & Qiang, Q. (2008). A network efficiency measure with application to critical infrastructure networks. *Journal of Global Optimization, 40*, 261–275.

Nicholson, C. D., Barker, K., & Ramirez-Marquez, J. E. (2016). Flow-based vulnerability measures for network component importance: Experimentation with preparedness planning. *Reliability Engineering and System Safety, 145*, 62–73.

de Oliveira, E. L., Da Silva Portugal, L., & Porto, W., Jr. (2016). Indicators of reliability and vulnerability: Similarities and differences in ranking links of a complex road system. *Transportation Research Part A: Policy and Practice, 88*, 195–208.

Peterson, S. K., & Church, R. L. (2008). A framework for modeling rail transport vulnerability. *Growth and Change, 39*(4), 617–641.

Pokharel, R., & Ieda, H. (2016). Reliability and vulnerability of road network: An accessibility and network closure vulnerability approach. *Asian Transport Studies, 4*(1), 37–56.

Rupi, F., Bernardi, S., Rossi, G., & Danesi, A. (2015). The evaluation of road network vulnerability in mountainous areas: A case study. *Networks and Spatial Economics, 15*(2), 397–411.

Scott, D. M., Novak, D. C., Aultman-Hall, L., & Guo, F. (2006). Network robustness index: A new method for identifying critical links and evaluating the performance of transportation networks. *Journal of Transport Geography, 14*, 215–227.

Snelder, M., Van Zuylen, H. J., & Immers, L. H. (2012). A framework for robustness analysis of road networks for short term variations in supply. *Transportation Research Part A: Policy and Practice, 46*(5), 813–827.

Sohn, J. (2006). Evaluating the significance of highway network links under the flood damage: An accessibility approach. *Transportation Research Part A: Policy and Practice, 40*(6), 491–506.

Sullivan, J. L., Novak, D. C., Aultman-Hall, L., & Scott, D. M. (2010). Identifying critical road segments and measuring system-wide robustness in transportation networks with isolating links: A link-based capacity-reduction approach. *Transportation Research Part A: Policy and Practice, 44*(5), 323–336.

Taylor, M. A. P. (2008). Critical transport infrastructure in urban areas: Impacts of traffic incidents assessed using accessibility-based network vulnerability analysis. *Growth and Change, 39*(4), 593–616.

Taylor, M. A. P. (2013). Travel through time: The story of research on travel time reliability. *Transportmetrica B: Transport Dynamics, 1*(3), 174–194.

Taylor, M. A. P., & Philp, M. L. (2015). Investigating the impact of maintenance regimes on the design life of road pavements in a changing climate and the implications for transport policy. *Transport Policy, 41*, 117–135.

Taylor, M. A. P., & Susilawati. (2012). Remoteness and accessibility in the vulnerability analysis of regional road networks. *Transportation Research Part A: Policy and Practice, 46*(5), 761–771.

Taylor, M. A. P., Woolley, J. E., & Zito, R. (2000). Integration of the global positioning system and geographical information systems for traffic congestion studies. *Transportation Research C, 8C*(1–6), 257–285.

TRB. (2016). *Highway capacity manual* (6th ed.). Washington, DC: Transportation Research Board.

Tu, Y., Yang, C., Chen, A., & Chen, X. (2012). A framework of transportation network vulnerability analysis for different administrative prospects. In W. H. K. Lam, H. K. Lo, & S. C. Wong (Eds.), *Proceedings 5th international symposium on transport network reliability, Hong Kong, December 18–19* (pp. 27–49). Hong Kong Polytechnic University and Hong Kong Society for Transportation Studies.

Wang, D. Z. W., Liu, H., Szeto, W. Y., & Chow, A. H. F. (2016). Identification of critical combination of vulnerable links in transportation networks – A global optimisation approach. *Transportmetrica A: Transport Science, 12*(4), 346–365.

Zhang, K., & Taylor, M. A. P. (2006). Effective arterial road incident detection: A Bayesian network based algorithm. *Transportation Research C, 14*(6), 403–417.

CHAPTER FIVE

Accessibility Methods

As introduced in Chapter 3, widening the scope of vulnerability analysis to include potential economic and social impacts of network disruption involves consideration of the accessibility to services and facilities provided by the transport system in a region. The D'Este–Taylor definition of network vulnerability as introduced in Section 1.6, states that

- a network *node is vulnerable* if loss (or substantial degradation) of a small number of links significantly diminishes the accessibility of the node, as measured by a standard index of accessibility.
- a network *link is critical* if loss (or substantial degradation) of the link significantly diminishes the accessibility of the network or of particular nodes, as measured by a standard index of accessibility.

Accessibility-based vulnerability analysis examines the changes in the levels of accessibility across a disrupted network; and it uses these changes to indicate overall impacts. Serviceability considerations will also be a part of this, for the operating state of the degraded network can be different to that of the full network, which will lead to the changes in accessibility seen in different locations. A common application is to consider the performance of a road network affected by events such as floods or landslides, other natural disasters, or network failures such as a bridge collapse. Then some links will be unusable and some communities or subregions served by the network may then be inaccessible. Vulnerability analysis can then assist indicating the level of separation or severance to be expected by a flood of a given size in a designated location. Network disruptions are likely to affect accessibility, and thus economic and social activities include rerouting due to road closures (additional travel distance), increased congestion (increased travel time and costs), and service cancellations or disruptions. These issues were also discussed in Chapter 4 and form a part of serviceability analysis.

A useful example of vulnerability analysis expressly including elements of serviceability and accessibility is that given by Bil, Vodak, Kubecek, Bilova, and Sedonik (2015), who considered the expected road damage to be caused

Vulnerability Analysis for Transportation Networks
ISBN: 978-0-12-811010-2
http://dx.doi.org/10.1016/B978-0-12-811010-2.00005-8

by natural disasters, especially floods, landslides, and extreme rain and snow events, in the Czech Republic. This study can be seen as providing a bridge between the serviceability and accessibility analyses. The authors took Berdica's definition of vulnerability (see Chapter 1 and Section 3.1) and therefore considered vulnerability in terms of consequences rather than probability of failure. The analysis included multiple link failures—an expected situation in the event of a flood—and looked at several metrics, covering both the state of the road network and the impacts on populations served by the network. These metrics are as follows:

1. Number of damaged and severed links. The total number of cut and damaged road links is generally well known and can be presented as the actual number or as the proportion of links in the network. This provides a means for indicating the relative scale of the event and can be used to compare the impacts of different events in a given network, or for different networks.
2. Ratio of network lengths before and after a disaster. In this calculation a severed link is taken as no longer available and thus its length is not included.
3. Potential disintegration of the network into separate components. If the network is split into two or more separate components then the number of separate subnetworks and the size of each of these is a measure of the extent of the natural disaster.
4. Change in global efficiency $\eta(G)$ between the intact network and the degraded network, using the definition of global efficiency given in Equation (3.4)—which considered the network minimum path distances between origin–destination pairs. If the global efficiencies of the intact network is $\eta(G^0)$ and the degraded network is $\eta(G^\sigma)$, then the relative network efficiency index $NER(\sigma)$ is given by $NER(\sigma) = 1-\eta(G^\sigma)/\eta(G^0)$, which is a specific form of the performance degradation Equation (2.6).
5. Number of people cut off from the main network by disintegration of network into two or more components, based on the population of each node in full network, which is a first measure of human impact of the disaster.
6. Weighted network efficiency index $WNER(\sigma)$, which includes the population of each node as a measure of the node's importance and so provides a quantitative measure of the impact of network degradation and provides an initial representation of accessibility change in the vulnerability analysis.

The weighted network efficiency index is given as

$$WNER(\sigma) = \frac{\eta(G^{0P}) - \eta(G^{\sigma P})}{\eta(G^{0P})} \tag{5.1}$$

where $\eta(G^{0P})$ and $\eta(G^{\sigma P})$ are the population-weighted global efficiencies of the intact network and degraded network, respectively, and are given by

$$\eta(G^{0P}) = \frac{1}{N(N-1)} \sum_{i \neq j} \frac{P_i P_j}{d_{ij}}$$

and

$$\eta(G^{\sigma P}) = \frac{1}{N(N-1)} \sum_{i \neq j} \frac{P_i P_j}{d_{ij}^{\sigma}}$$

where P_i and P_j are the populations of centers i and j, respectively; N is the number of population centers; d_{ij} is the distance between the centers in the intact network; and d_{ij}^{σ} is the distance in the degraded network. This index reflects the degree of interaction between communities, and the likely change in degree as a result of disaster.

Bil et al. (2015) used their method to compare the impacts of several natural disaster events which occurred in various regions of the Czech Republic over the period of 1997–2010. They concluded that the multidimensional approach offered by their set of vulnerability metrics provided a strong basis for comparing the impacts of the different events, and they were able to rank the events in order of severity as a result. An interesting conclusion, which came up in other studies and is considered in Section 5.3, was that the boundaries of the study area networks had to be selected with care and attention, as an arbitrary choice of network boundary could affect the results of the computations. The authors accounted for this by selecting an overall region that included all of the affected areas in its road network, and recommended that this should be regarded as best practice.

An early study which expressly used an accessibility metric to determine critical road links in road networks subject to flooding was that of Sohn (2006), who considered the arterial road network of the state of Maryland. This analysis was performed by considering all of the counties in the state, with each county represented by a node in the network (at which the county population was assumed to be located). The composite accessibility index adopted in the study was a weighted sum of a modified Hansen-type accessibility index (e.g., Equation 3.18) and a link importance index based on traffic volumes between counties (in similar vein to the link importance index of Rupi, Bernardi, Rossi, & Danesi 2015) discussed in Chapter 4 (see Equation 4.13). Sohn's accessibility index AS_i for county i is then given by

$$AS_i = \kappa\left[\omega\frac{P_i}{PT}\sum_{j\neq i}\frac{P_j}{PT}\frac{\left(d_{ij}^{\sigma}\right)^{-\beta}}{\sum_k\left(d_{ik}\right)^{-\beta}} + (1-\omega)\frac{P_i}{PT}\sum_{j\neq i}\frac{P_j}{PT}\frac{q_{ij}}{\sum_k q_{ik}}\right] \tag{5.2}$$

In this equation, ω is a weighting factor, $0 \leq \omega \leq 1$, so that the computed accessibility index can be proportioned in terms of its two components (population and link traffic volumes); P_k is the population of county k; $PT = \sum_k P_k$ is the total population of the study region; d_{ij}^{σ} is the shortest road distance between counties i and j in the (possibly degraded) network under study (case σ), where d_{ij} is the shortest road distance in the full, intact network, β is a distance decay factor for which Sohn calculated the value β to be 0.446632 for the Maryland network, and

$$q_{ik} = \frac{\sum_{m=1}^{n} AADT_m d_m}{d_{ik}}$$

is the average traffic volume between i and k on the shortest path, which consists of n segments each of length d_m and $AADT_m$ is the annual average daily traffic on the segment. κ is the normalizing factor, to scale the value of AS_i to the range [0, 1], for which Sohn's value was $\kappa = 4$.

Sohn's composite accessibility index thus includes the two factors of distance and traffic volume. The first term is simple distance-based accessibility in which the population and distance terms are standardized. The second term includes the traffic importance of the link. Traffic volume is represented as a standardized value. The explicit inclusion of volume was seen as necessary because not all traffic on the network is local, there is a considerable portion of external traffic and through traffic on the network—but, as indicated earlier, choice of the value of the weighting factor ω would determine the relative importance of the traffic volume term in the calculation of accessibility.

Critical links are found by failing each link in turn and computing the overall change in accessibility (ΔAS), given by

$$\Delta AS^a = \sum_i AS_i^0 - \sum_i AS_i^a = \sum_i\left(AS_i^0 - AS_i^a\right)$$

where AS_i^0 is the accessibility of county i in the intact network and AS_i^a is the accessibility after failure of link a. The focus of Sohn's study was the effects on network state of flood events. Thus in terms of the risk of flooding, given the probability $\Pr_t^a$ that link a is damaged in a t-year flood event (e.g., $t = 100$), the risk-based expected value of the change in accessibility is

$$E(\Delta AS^a, t) = \Pr_t^a \sum_i \left(AS_i^0 - AS_i^a\right) \tag{5.3}$$

This is an important result in terms of risk because it correlates the consequence of link failure and the probability of that failure for a specified natural disaster. Figure 5.1 displays the framework for link priority assessment for flood protection upgrade including network performance and flooding scenario. The framework considers the structure of the network and the connections between population centers under network analysis. It then computes accessibility values using population, network distance, and traffic volume data and considers different flood scenarios. This allows computation of the risk-based change in accessibility for the scenarios from which a priority link for link upgrades (through flood protection or mitigation works) can be determined.

Sohn ascertained the weighting factor ω to be important. His results showed that critical links identified on the basis of population and distance separation were quite different to only those found using the distance-traffic volume component alone. Thus the priorities for network upgrades would depend on the value chosen for ω. The relative decrease in accessibility of a link closure was generally larger for the distance—volume component

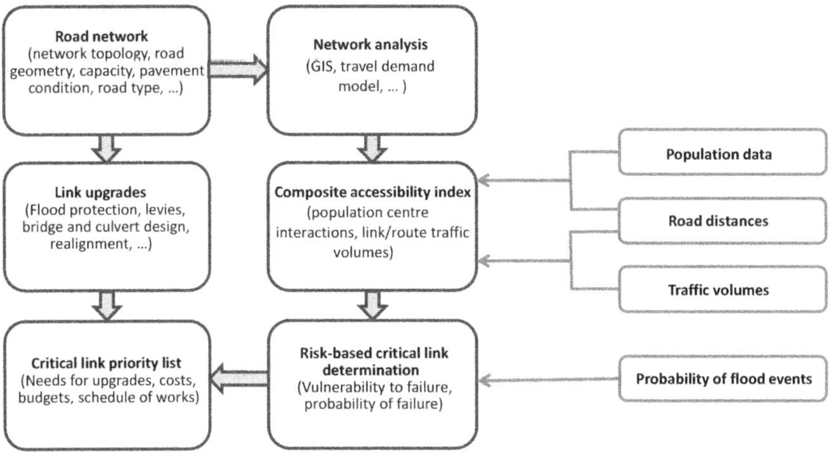

Figure 5.1 Framework for risk-based network upgrade using accessibility model and flood event probabilities. *Developed from the original in Sohn, J. (2006). Evaluating the significance of highway network links under the flood damage: An accessibility approach.* Transportation Research Part A: Policy and Practice, 40*(6), 491–506.*

than for the population–distance component; however, the latter tended to show a broader spatial pattern of links causing accessibility decreases. Some links were prominent in both cases, and in situations where a given link was the only access to a population center then the two components produced similar outcomes.

A similar model to Sohn's work with an extension to multimodal travel was provided by Chen, Lu, Peng, and Ash (2015). In addition to the population as a generator of travel to other centers, this model also considered the trip attraction of each population center (i.e., the attractiveness of the center as a destination), measured as the total employment and student enrolment (G_i) in each center i, with the total employment and student enrolment for the region then given by $GT = \sum_i G_i$. The accessibility index AK_i^a for population center i under network state a (e.g., link a closed, $a = 0$ intact network) used by Chen et al. (2015) was

$$AK_i^a = \frac{G_i}{GT} \sum_{j \neq i} \frac{P_j}{PT} \left(\sum_k \frac{q_{kij}}{Q_{ij}} \frac{C_{kij}^a}{C_{kij}^0} \right)^{-\beta} \tag{5.4}$$

in which β is a distance decay factor, q_{kij} is the traffic volume using mode k to travel between i and j, $Q_{ij} = \sum_k q_{kij}$ is the total traffic volume between i and j, and C_{kij}^a is the travel cost by mode k for network state a. The model can then be used in the framework of Figure 5.1.

These models all provide a representation of accessibility through population and distance separation, with links to the serviceability methods discussed in Chapter 4. A greater use of accessibility metrics can be used in vulnerability analysis at a number of scales of spatial aggregation. The remainder of this chapter considers these applications, using the following spatial scales:

- National road networks
- State/provincial road networks
- Regional (rural) networks
- Urban road networks.

Case studies from the author's previous work in these network types are presented for each spatial scale.

5.1 NATIONAL NETWORKS

Taylor, Sekhar, and D'Este (2006) outlined a procedure for the application of accessibility-based methods to the vulnerability analysis of strategic road networks. Strategic road networks represent the main road network for a region, generally comprising motorways, highways, and main arterial roads. They would not include secondary arterial roads or local roads. The Australian main road network was chosen as strategic network for this application Figure 5.2. This network comprises three road types, based on the administrative agency responsible for each type:

1. The Australian national transport network (NTN), the major trunk roads across the nation, and including major transport terminals (ports and airports). The NTN is the direct responsibility of the Australian federal government, though state and territory government transport agencies are contracted to maintain those parts of the network in their jurisdictions.
2. Designated highways, which are the responsibility of the state or territory where they are located.
3. Other main roads, which are administered by state, territory, or local government agencies.

Figure 5.2 shows the NTN and designated highways as subnetworks forming a skeleton within the matrix of the full main road network. The

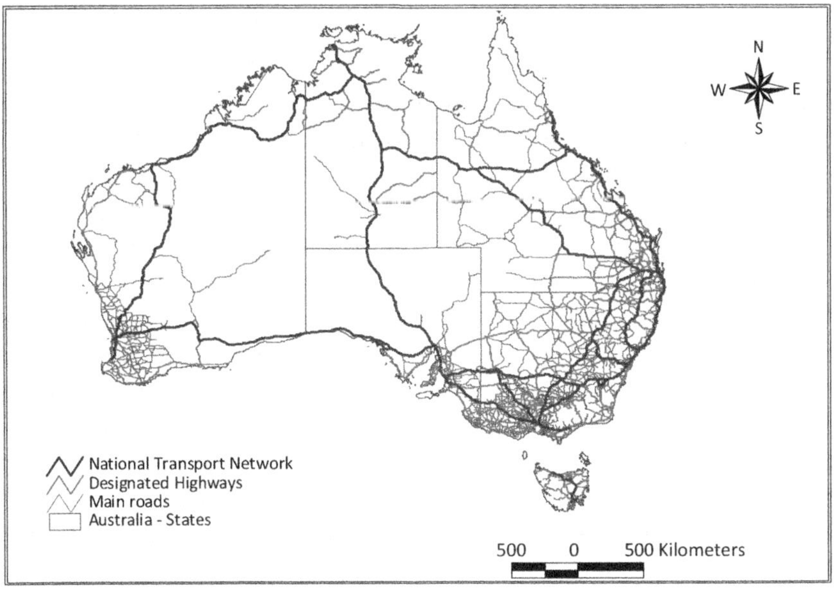

Figure 5.2 The Australian main road network showing all main roads, designated state highways and the NTN subnetworks. *Reproduced with permission from Taylor, M. A. P., Sekhar, S. V. C., & D'Este, G. M. (2006). Application of accessibility based methods for vulnerability analysis of strategic road networks.* Networks and Spatial Economics, *6(3), 267–291.*

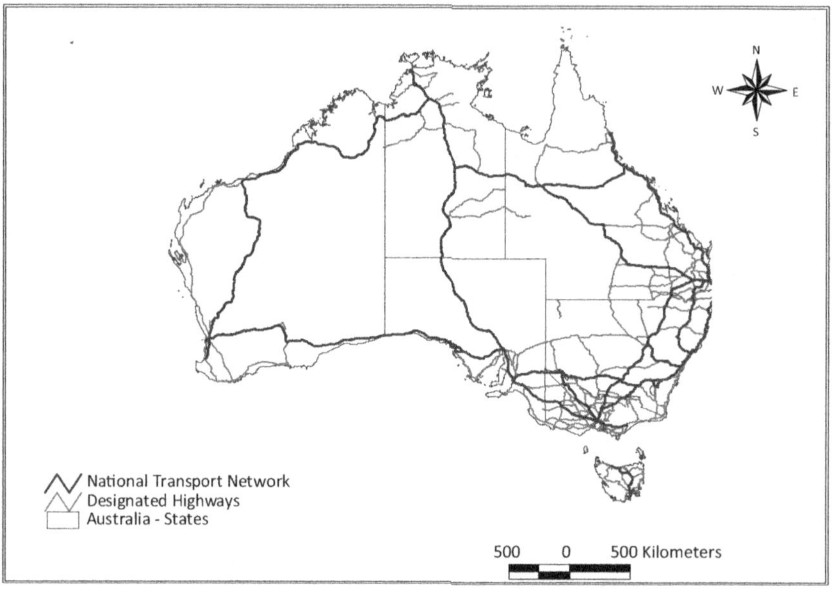

Figure 5.3 The Australian NTN road network and designated highways network, which form a subnetwork within the overall strategic road network subnetworks. *Reproduced with permission from Taylor, M. A. P., Sekhar, S. V. C., & D'Este, G. M. (2006). Application of accessibility based methods for vulnerability analysis of strategic road networks.* Networks and Spatial Economics, *6(3), 267–291.*

density of the full network is a strong indicator of the national population distribution, with the densest development found in the south-east corner of the nation. In the less settled parts the road network is much sparser and the displayed main roads represent almost all of the navigable through road system. Figure 5.3 displays the subnetwork of NTN roads and designated highways, which indicates this dispersion effect.

A critical link scan of the road network in Figure 5.3 was undertaken to locate the most critical links in this network, measured in terms of the disruptive effects of link closure on accessibility between major cities at the national scale. The Hansen integral accessibility index defined by Equation (3.18) was used in this analysis, with city population representing the number of opportunities (B_i) available in city i and with travel impedance function f_{ij} represented by the reciprocal of the road network distance (d_{ij}) between the cities i and j, i.e.,

$$AH_i = \frac{1}{\sum_i P_i} \sum_{j \neq i} \frac{P_j}{d_{ij}} \tag{5.5}$$

where P_i is the population of city i. Table 5.1 provides the population data and intercity road distances for the mainland capital cities of Adelaide, Brisbane, Canberra, Darwin, Melbourne, Perth, and Sydney, as well as the computed values of the Hansen index for each city.

In the link scan each link on the minimum path tree from each city was broken in turn, new minimum path distances determined for the degraded networks, and new values computed for the Hansen accessibility index for each degraded network. Five road sections[1] were determined as critical, on the basis that severance of each section reduced the overall accessibility in the network by 5% or more, as measured by the changes in the Hansen index. The percentage differences for total accessibility changes were computed using the equation

$$\Delta AH = \frac{AH^0 - AH^\sigma}{AH^0} \tag{5.6}$$

in which AH^σ in the Hansen accessibility index in the degraded network and AH^0 is the index for the complete network. This equation is an alternative form of Equations (2.6) (for general relative decline in performance) and Equation (5.1) for the weighted network efficiency index. The five critical road sections were:

1. Hume Freeway, section between Sydney and Goulburn,
2. Hume Freeway, section between Seymour and Melbourne,
3. Hume Freeway, section from the Sturt Highway to Yass,
4. Stuart Highway, section between Katherine and Pine Creek (near Darwin), and
5. Federal Highway, section from Canberra to Goulburn.

It is to note that three of these critical sections lie on the Hume Freeway, the major road link between Sydney and Melbourne, while a fourth critical link is the Federal Highway, which intersects the Hume Freeway near Goulburn and connects to the national capital, Canberra. This indicates the importance of this corridor to national economic and social activity. The fifth critical link is isolated in the far north of Australia, but a cut to this link would mean that Darwin would have no road connection to the rest of the network. Figure 5.4 identifies the critical road sections. Table 5.2 shows the percentage reductions in accessibility for each city and the total

[1] A road section comprises several connected network links in the GIS model used for the study, because the network under study is the NTN roads and designated highways only, with other main roads—which intersect with that subnetwork—discarded from the strategic level analysis.

Table 5.1 City Population, Intercity Road Distances and Computed Hansen Accessibility Indices for the Australian Mainland Capital Cities and the National Strategic Road Network

	Adelaide	**Brisbane**	**Canberra**	**Darwin**	**Melbourne**	**Perth**	**Sydney**
Population (2001)	1,002,127	1,508,161	339,727	71,347	3,160,171	1,176,542	3,502,301
Travel Distances via Australian Strategic Road Network:							
Adelaide	—	1985.7	1167.5	2622.9	722.5	2691.7	1341.9
Brisbane		—	1004.6	3103.0	1536.1	4643.3	796.1
Canberra			—	3765.3	636.2	3828.6	235.5
Darwin				—	3345.5	3465.8	3873.2
Melbourne					—	3414.3	810.6
Perth						—	3999.5
Sydney							—
Hansen accessibility index	0.871	0.836	2.161	0.294	0.999	0.272	1.152

Total Hansen index summed over all cities = 6.585.

Reproduced with permission from Taylor, M. A. P., Sekhar, S. V. C., & D'Este, G. M. (2006). Application of accessibility based methods for vulnerability analysis of strategic road networks. *Networks and Spatial Economics, 6*(3), 267–291.

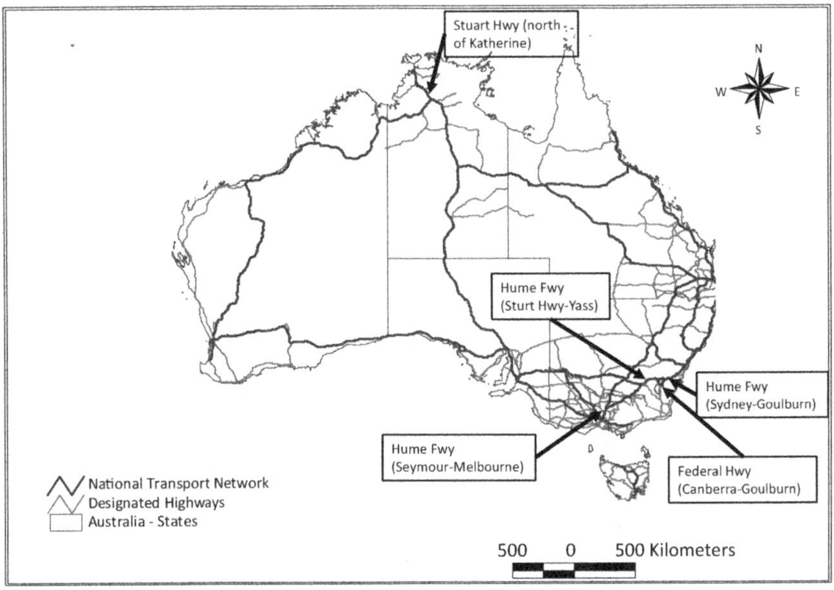

Figure 5.4 Critical road sections identified in the Australian NTN-designated highways road network on the basis of changes in accessibility under network degradation subnetworks. *Reproduced with permission from Taylor, M. A. P., Sekhar, S. V. C., & D'Este, G. M. (2006). Application of accessibility based methods for vulnerability analysis of strategic road networks.* Networks and Spatial Economics, *6(3), 267–291.*

network with cuts to the five critical sections. The impacts of the severance are then illustrated in the radar plots shown in Figure 5.5. The Hume Freeway between Sydney and Goulburn is the most critical link by some measure in terms of accessibility change, as severance of it reduces the overall accessibility by more than a quarter ($\Delta AH = -25.4\%$), and this impact is almost twice that of the second most critical section (Hume Freeway, Seymour–Melbourne, $\Delta AH = -13.6\%$). The accessibility by road of the national capital, Canberra, is more than halved by closure of the Goulburn–Sydney section. These are profound impacts.

This case study indicates that the accessibility index method using defined population centers, and when applied at the strategic levels, can provide a vulnerability metric which, due to obscure formal physical dimension, is widely used in transport planning and is capable of useful interpretation in relative terms—the relative change in the accessibility index between the full and degraded networks. This metric also reveals useful information about relative changes in accessibility for individual cities as well as for the whole system of cities. The data used to compute accessibility index values (populations and

Table 5.2 Percentage Decreases in the Hansen Accessibility Index in Degraded NTN-Designated Highways Road Network for the Five Critical Road Sections

	Adelaide	Brisbane	Canberra	Darwin	Melbourne	Perth	Sydney	All Network
Hume freeway (Sydney–Goulburn)	−4.2%	−1.4%	−53.3%	0%	−15.2%	−1.7%	−27.2%	−25.4%
Hume freeway (Seymour–Melbourne)	0%	−7.5%	−11.5%	0%	−33.4%	0%	−21.4%	−13.6%
Hume freeway (Sturt Highway–Goulburn)	−5.4%	0%	−13.1%	−0.2%	−18.9%	−2.2%	−13.8%	−10.4%
Stuart Highway (Katherine–Pine Creek)	−3.0%	−0.3%	−0.6%	−100%	−0.3%	−0.8%	−0.2%	−5.2%
Federal Highway (Canberra–Goulburn)	0%	−0.2%	−13.6%	0%	0%	0%	−3.5%	−5.1%

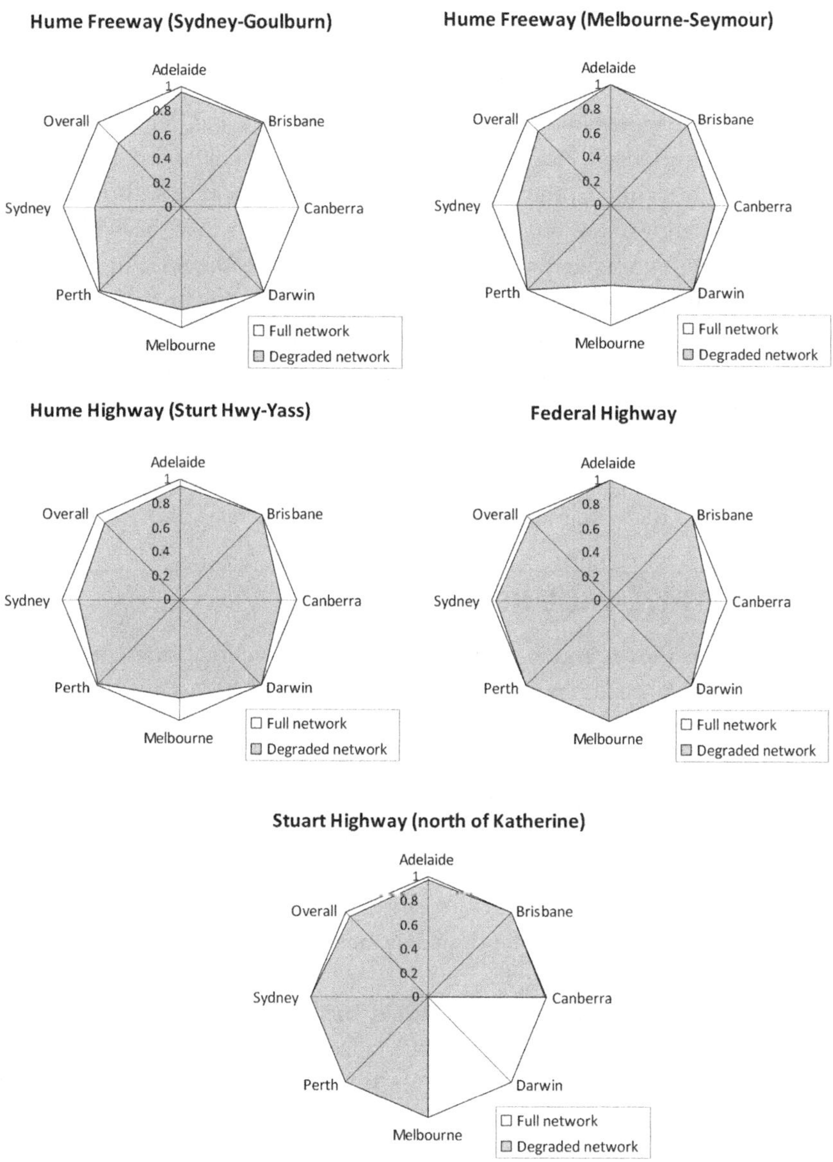

Figure 5.5 Radar plots showing impacts of closures in the critical road sections identified in the Australian NTN-designated highways road network. *Reproduced with permission from Taylor, M. A. P., Sekhar, S. V. C., & D'Este, G. M. (2006). Application of accessibility based methods for vulnerability analysis of strategic road networks.* Networks and Spatial Economics, *6(3), 267–291.*

minimum path distances) are widely available (population) or easily computed (travel distances). Thus the accessibility index method shows considerable utility as vulnerability metric when applied at the strategic level.

At more disaggregated levels of network coverage and detail the usefulness of a point-based accessibility index such as the Hansen index may decrease. The Hansen index is best applied when there are distinct, large population centers well separated from each other, so that the designation of each center as a separate and significant node is reasonable. In situations such as an urban area where the population is spread across the area in a continuum or in rural areas where there are many small communities but few, if any, large population centers, this designation can break down. The following sections of this chapter explore vulnerability analyses applied to such cases, using alternative accessibility indices. The general approach to the analysis was discussed in Chapter 3—see Equation (3.25) and the discussion related to that equation.

5.2 STATE-WIDE NETWORKS

The next level under the national strategic level road network would include the main road network for a large region such as a state or province, as was shown in Figure 5.1. This network is still a small fraction of the total road network in built up areas, but provides substantial coverage of rural areas. The distribution of population in the region, especially the existence or otherwise of multiple large population centers, would determine the suitability of an accessibility index for use in analysis of the network vulnerability. When there is an absence of large population centers or where the population is spread thinly and widely across the region then an index such as Hansen is of less merit.

Vulnerability of the road network in the state of South Australia was studied by Taylor (2008a), using the accessibility/remoteness index of Australia (*ARIA*) introduced in Chapter 3. South Australia lies in the central southern part of mainland Australia (see Figure 5.2). While the state is geographically large, covering an area of 984,377 km^2 (or 13% of the mainland) its population of 1.677 M is only 7% of the national total. Further, 1.25 M of its inhabitants live in metropolitan Adelaide and there are no other urban centers with more than 50,000 people in the state (the largest provincial city is Mount Gambier, with 24,000 people). Thus there is a widely dispersed rural and remote region population spread across the state, for which the road network provides the main transportation system.

ARIA is a continuous index applied to all locations in a region. It was devised expressly for use in rural and remote areas where population density is low, and few large population centers are available, as a metric indicating the degree of separation of any location from government and private-sector services and facilities (e.g., medical, financial, educational, postal, and social-welfare services) as a response to the continuing trend for those services to retreat to larger regional centers (DHAC, 2001; GISCA, 2009). The index is now used on a "whole-of-government" basis, and residents of locations deemed as remote in terms of *ARIA* (score > 7.0) are entitled to taxation concessions and other benefits.

The basic idea behind the development of *ARIA* was that compared to small centers larger population centers have both a wider range of services and facilities and more services. Given that population data are commonly available, population can then be used as a proxy for service availability—thus the hierarchy of service centers [category *A*, *B*, *C*, *D*, *E* (and *F*)[2]] used in *ARIA* is based on population size. The population ranges were set by correlation with the availability of services (GISCA, 2009). Table 5.3 indicates the population ranges for each of these center types and the mean travel distances to each center category in the state. For South Australia, Adelaide is the only category *A* service center, there are no category *B* centers, and only two category *C* centers (Mount Gambier and Whyalla).

The *ARIA* used in the South Australian road network study was defined by the equation

$$ARIA_i = \sum_{L=A,B,C,D,E} \min\left\{3, \frac{d_{iL}}{\overline{d}_L}\right\} \tag{5.7}$$

which is the version of the index given in Equation (3.24). In this equation $ARIA_i$ is the accessibility index for a given location i, d_{iL} is the road network distance from i to the nearest category L service center, and $\overline{d}_L$ is the average distance of all locations to their nearest category L center, i.e.,

$$\overline{d}_L = \frac{1}{N}\sum_{i=1}^{N} d_{iL} \tag{5.8}$$

where N is the number of locations considered. In the South Australian study there were 161 locations defined, being all of the population centers

[2] Service center category F was introduced into the *ARIA* + index by GISCA (2009), and this is the index used in the state-wide analysis.

Table 5.3 ARIA + Service Center Categories A–F, With Mean Distance to Service Center as Computed for South Australia

Service Center Category	Population	Mean Distance to Service Center (km)
A	≥250,000	218.1
B	48,000–249,999	218.1
C	18,000–47,999	126.7
D	5,000–17,999	90.7
E	1,000–4,999	28.2
F	200–999	na

in categories $A-F$ in the state. These average distances are shown in Table 5.3.

Equation (5.7) requires some further attention. An upper limit of three on the ratio between d_{iL} and $\bar{d}_L$ is used to remove potential distortion effects of any remaining extreme values from the index, i.e., a location more than three times the average distance from a given service center category is taken to be remote from that center type. With this upper limit, the maximum value of $ARIA_i$ is 15, and this represents an extremely remote location. A location which is itself a designated service center has an index component value of zero for that category. Values of $ARIA_i$ are thus in the range [0, 15]. In the calculations, if a higher category service center (say category A) is closer to a given locality than (say) a category B center, then the category A takes the place of the category B in the calculations. This situation applied in South Australia, where, as noted earlier, there was no category B center; hence the value of $\bar{d}_B$ in Table 5.3 is the same as $\bar{d}_A$ in compliance with this rule. Note that $ARIA$ is intended only for regional and remote area analysis, for instance, all urban centers with populations of 250,000 or more automatically have a zero value of their $ARIA$. The index does not consider intraurban accessibility at all—it was not intended nor designed to. Section 5.5 considers some suitable accessibility indices for use inside large urban areas.

In addition, the location i can be classified into one of the five remoteness levels. This is done, for instance, in determining eligibility for taxation or other concessions for residents of locations found to be remote. The five remoteness levels adopted are "highly accessible," "accessible," "moderately accessible," "remote," and "very remote." The $ARIA$ score bands corresponding to these levels are shown in Table 5.4. One test of vulnerability would be when a given location moves into a higher level of remoteness as a consequence of network degradation.

Figure 5.6 shows the South Australian road network used in the statewide vulnerability scan. This network contains some 1220 nodes and about

Table 5.4 Location Remoteness Classification Based on *ARIA* Values

Remoteness Class	*ARIA* Value Minimum	*ARIA* Value Maximum
Highly accessible	0	0.80
Accessible	0.81	2.70
Moderately accessible	2.71	7.00
Remote	7.01	11.70
Very remote	11.71	15

3150 one-way links, including population centers. The studied network includes NTN highways, designated state highways, and regional main roads in South Australia. A number of ferry services, including sea ferries from the mainland to Kangaroo Island and between the Yorke and Eyre Peninsulas, and five river ferries along the Murray River are included in

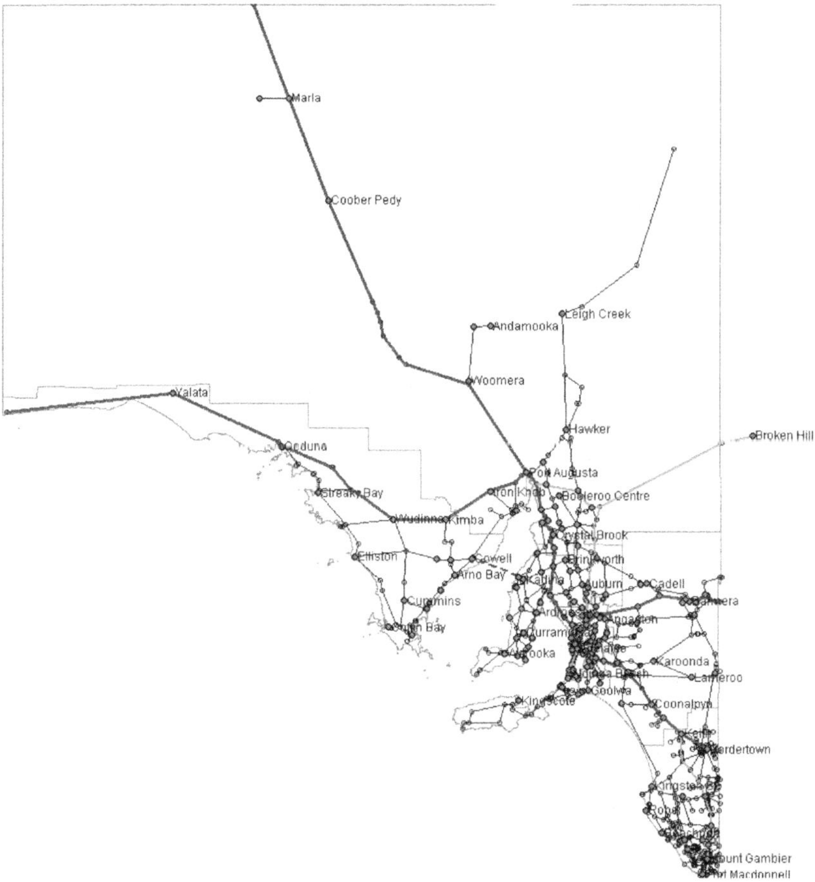

Figure 5.6 The main road network of South Australia, for use in vulnerability analysis (links in green (*dark gray in print versions*) are part of the NTN road network, those in purple (*light gray in print versions*) are designated state highways). The designated population centers (ARIA service categories A–E) are also identified.

Figure 5.7 The South Australian regional road network in the vicinity of Adelaide—approximate 200 km radius [links in green (*light gray in print versions*) are part of the NTN road network; purple (*gray in print versions*) are state highways; blue (*drak gray in print versions*) dashed lines are ferry services; and road bridges across the Murray River are identified].

the network.[3] The network includes 161 population centers, with cities, towns, and villages in the state that had a population of at least 200 people (i.e., *ARIA* class A–F population centers) in the Australian 2001 population census. Figure 5.7 shows more detail in the network, for the region of South Australia within 200 km of Adelaide. It also shows the locations of the two seagoing ferry services and the three road bridges across the Murray River.

Figure 5.8 outlines the vulnerability scan method used to determine critical locations and links in the network. This flowchart has two main arms: first, for a baseline analysis of the full network including calculation of the accessibility indices for designated centers, and second, a set of scenarios ("Scenario X") of network degradation, covering different links or combinations of links set to fail. New accessibility indices are computed for each

[3] Note that there are only three bridges crossing the Murray River in South Australia, one at Swanport on the South Eastern Freeway, one on the Sturt Highway at Blanchetown, and one in the city of Murray Bridge. The last of these three bridges is not regarded as suitable for use by heavy goods vehicles. See Fig. 5.7 for location of the bridges.

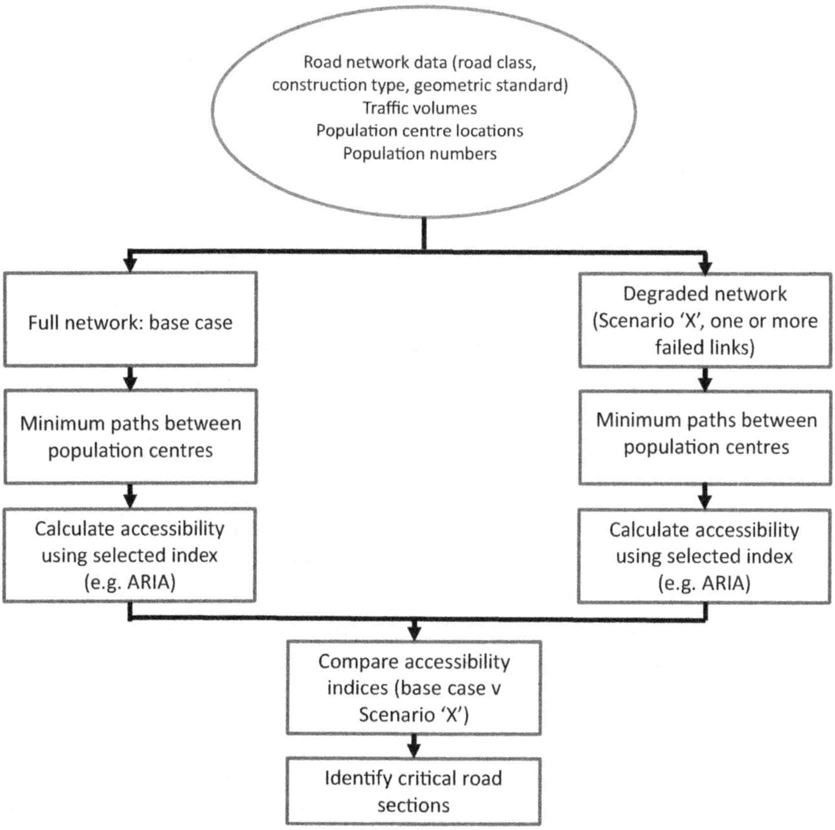

Figure 5.8 Basic process of the network vulnerability scan of alternative network scenarios, as used in the study of the South Australian main road network.

scenario, and compared to each other and to the base case, leading to the identification of the most critical locations or links in the network. The basic process of the network vulnerability scan for a network is as follows:

Step 1: Compute the accessibility indices for the defined objects *i* in the original network.

Step 2: Compute probabilities of use of different links or route sections (link sequences) in the network, using a multipath traffic assignment procedure.

Step 3: Identify candidate critical links/route sections for which there are "reasonable" finite probabilities of use—link failure scenarios.

Step 4: Fail or degrade these candidate links/route sections in each scenario and determine the new accessibility indices for the defined objects in the degraded network.

Step 5: Determine the resulting changes in accessibility values and identify the most critical links or route sections from the scenarios.

The method can also be applied to scans of network nodes as well as links, by examining the effects of node failure instead of link failure. A node failure will remove or degrade all of the links connected to that node.

Note that *ARIA* is used simply as an example of an established accessibility/remoteness index that has found widespread use at the "whole of government" level. Other, similar indices, reflecting factors such as traffic conditions, travel times, and road network conditions, would also be of specific interest in regional transport planning and could be used within the network vulnerability analysis framework outlined in this paper. The advantages of *ARIA* are that (1) it is accepted for use by all levels of government in Australia; (2) it requires only widely available population data; and (3) it uses road network distances, making it a good choice for road network studies. The index is, however, expressly set for conditions in Australia and so other formulations or indices would be required in other countries.

A vulnerability scan of the regional road network using the flowchart of Figure 5.8 with *ARIA* as the accessibility indicator identified a "top 10" list of critical links, being those 10 (representative) links which had the largest effects on the overall (total) accessibility of all of the 161 (*A*−*F*) population centers in the network. Figure 5.9 shows the locations of these "top 10"

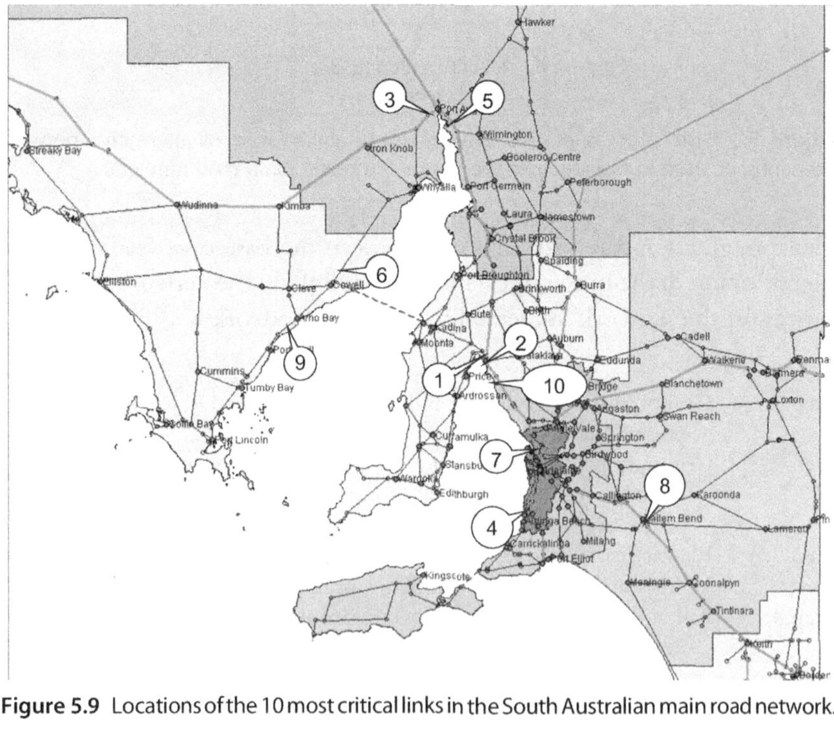

Figure 5.9 Locations of the 10 most critical links in the South Australian main road network.

links, and Table 5.5 shows the impacts on the computed overall *ARIA* score for the network. Together Table 5.5 and Figure 5.10 show the impact of each of the top 10 critical links on the overall level of accessibility in the network, i.e., the effects of these 10 links on *overall regional accessibility* as assessed using *ARIA* values. In terms of the consequences of failure of the most critical links, Figure 5.11 shows bar charts for the effects of the closure of each of the five most critical links, as measured by the switch of population centers between the different *ARIA* remoteness classes (as defined in Table 5.4). This chart provides indication of particular local and regional effects as well as changes across the whole state. The main tendency shown in this chart, especially for the first three critical links, is a degradation of status for some population centers from "moderately accessible" to "remote," which is an important change in remoteness class. The fourth critical link, Main South Road, lies just outside the environs of metropolitan Adelaide. The effect of this closure is a small shift from the more accessible classes for one or two centers south of Adelaide, but as seen in Figure 5.12 there is a doubling of the *ARIA* scores for the centers in this region so that, even with small changes in remoteness class, there are substantial changes in

Table 5.5 "Top Ten" Critical Links in the SA Regional Road Network, Assessed on the Basis of Changes in Total ARIA Values for the 161 Population Centers in the Network—See Figure 5.9 for Link Locations (Overall Average ARIA Value in Full Network is 4.551)

Link	Degraded Network Accessibility (Percentage of Full Network)	Computed Overall Average *ARIA* Value in Degraded Network
1. Copper Coast Highway	97.04	4.690
2. Princes Highway (1) 279–293	97.08	4.688
3. Eyre Highway	97.10	4.687
4. Main south road	98.17	4.636
5. Princes Highway (1) 55–57	98.27	4.631
6. Lincoln Highway 113–1212	98.57	4.617
7. Port Wakefield Road	98.85	4.604
8. Dukes Highway	98.87	4.603
9. Lincoln highway 207–1239	98.96	4.599
10. Port Wakefield Road	99.02	4.596

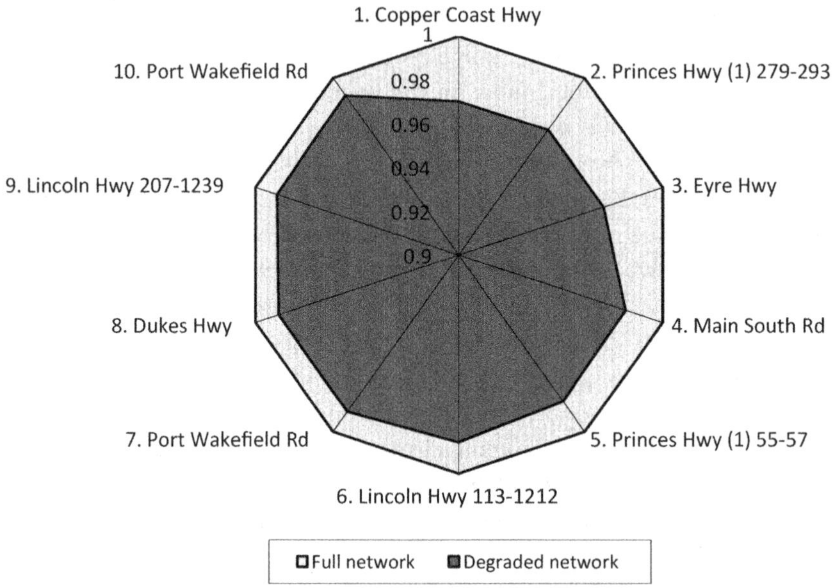

Figure 5.10 Radar plot of the changes in overall accessibility (total *ARIA* value) for each of the top 10 critical links in the South Australian main road network.

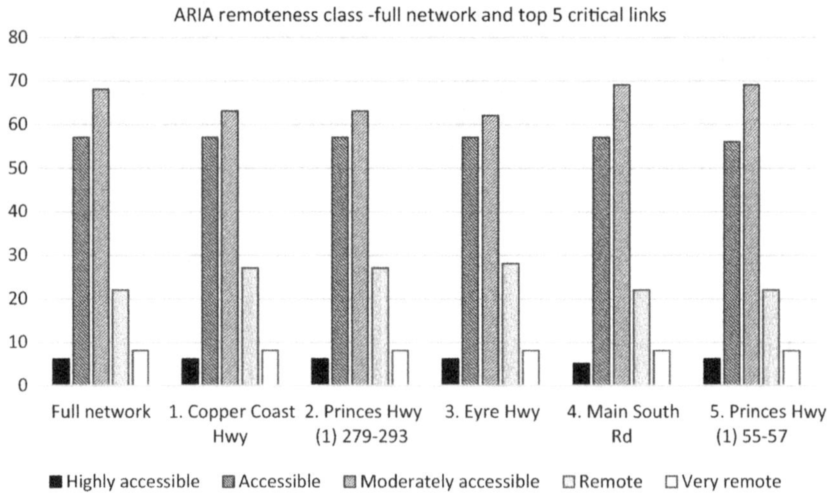

Figure 5.11 Bar charts showing the impacts of closure of each of the five most critical links in the South Australian main road network, in terms of the switch of population centers between the ARIA remoteness classes (highly accessible, accessible, moderately accessible, remote, very remote). See Table 5.4 for the *ARIA* remoteness classification system.

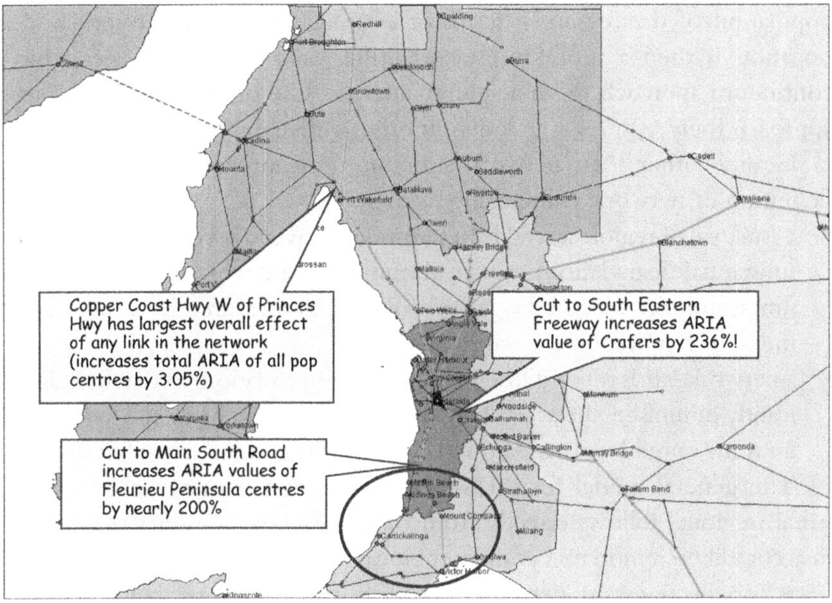

Figure 5.12 The effects of link closures in the environs of metropolitan Adelaide.

accessibility. Figure 5.12 also shows the impact of the closure of the Copper Coast Highway, identified as the most critical link in the main road network in terms of its impact on overall accessibility in the state network—a decrease in total accessible of just over 3%. The figure also shows the modeled decrease in accessibility for the towns in the Adelaide Hills by closure of the South Eastern Freeway. These towns are dormitory settlements for Adelaide. While closure of this freeway did not qualify in the top 10 critical links, the local effect is significant. Road access still exists on other roads, but none of these are of comparable standard to the freeway and all involve some substantial detours for access to the metropolitan area even if these cannot lead to a change in remoteness class.

5.3 REGIONAL NETWORKS

The next level of detail for a network vulnerability scan is the regional network, in which local roads are added to the spine network provided by the main roads. This introduces other issues regarding the representation of population and locations. In regional areas, especially those that are sparsely settled, the representation of the region solely in terms of a network of nodes and links can become unrealistic. It may not be feasible to fully represent the population of the region in terms of assumed clusters at network nodes. Location is then a more realistic identifier, and implies the need for a continuum approach to vulnerability analysis. Use of an accessibility-based approach then requires a new definition of vulnerability, couched in terms of locality rather than network structure. An appropriate locality-based definition of network vulnerability is then:

- a *locality* in a region served by a transport network is vulnerable if loss (or substantial degradation) of a small number of network links significantly diminishes the accessibility of the locality, as measured by a standard index of remoteness (or accessibility), and
- a network *link* is *critical* if loss (or substantial degradation) of that link significantly diminishes the accessibility of the region or of particular locations in it, as measured by a standard index of remoteness (or accessibility).

The general model for accessibility-based vulnerability analysis at the (rural) regional follows directly from this definition. Consider the changes in accessibility/remoteness of different locations in the region under different states for the transport network, e.g., the intact network and a degraded network. This can be done for specified locations and for the entire region. The conceptual models that follow use both accessibility (A) and remoteness (R) indices, presented as continuous variables for a given region.

An accessibility index $A(x,y)$ for location (x,y) in a region Φ can be represented in general terms by a mathematical function which includes the location itself and the activities associated with it, parameters and variables representing the configuration and state of the transport network, and the facilities and services accessible using the network. A remoteness index $R(x,y)$ can be similarly represented, and for immediate purposes we assume that $R(x,y) = A^{-1}(x,y)$. Broadly then,

$$A(x,y) = f(N_\Phi;\ X(x,y);\ d_k(x,y);\ S_{jk}) \quad (x,y)\in\Phi,\ j\in J,\ k\in K \tag{5.9}$$

$$R(x,y) = f^{-1}(N_\Phi;\ X(x,y);\ dk(x,y);\ S_{jk}) \tag{5.10}$$

where N_Φ is the transport network of the region in a given operating state; $X(x,y)$ represents the locality and its characteristics; S_{jk} represents the facility/service type j located at site (service center) k; and $d_k(x,y)$ represents the separation between locality (x,y) and service center k. Different facilities and services (j) can exist at the different service centers (k), e.g., larger service centers can be expected to have a wider range of services available; hence, the use of the facility/service type index j. $A(x,y)$ thus represents an accessibility surface for the region. Then

$$TA(\Phi) = \iint_{xy\in\Phi} A(x, y)dxdy \tag{5.11}$$

is the total accessibility index for the region, and can be described as the "accessibility volume." Similarly,

$$TR(\Phi) = \iint_{xy\in\Phi} R(x, y)dxdy \tag{5.12}$$

is the total remoteness index, or remoteness volume, for the region.

Given the close connection—the reciprocal relationship—between the remoteness index and the accessibility index, it is sufficient to consider remoteness alone. Thus if $R^0(x,y)$ is the remoteness surface for the region for network N^0 (the original network, i.e., a complete, intact network, or one in an uncongested state), then the overall remoteness volume for the region and that network is given by

$$TR^0(\Phi) = \iint_{xy\in\Phi} R^0(x, y)dxdy \tag{5.13}$$

Now assume that the network N^σ is an alteration of the original network, such as one that is in a degraded state (e.g., because of some link or node failure, full or partial) or one in a congested state. Then

$$TR^\sigma(\Phi) = \iint_{xy\in\Phi} R^\sigma(x, y)dxdy \tag{5.14}$$

Absolute changes and relative changes in accessibility/remoteness of specific localities and for the entire region can then be computed. In terms of remoteness, the absolute changes in the remoteness indices are $\Delta TR(\Phi) = TR^\sigma(\Phi) - TR^0(\Phi)$ and $\Delta R(x,y) = R^\sigma(x,y) - R^0(x,y)$. These definitions are chosen so that increases in remoteness from network degradation are expressed as positive values. The corresponding relative changes in local and overall remoteness are

$$\Delta PTR(\Phi) = \frac{TR^\sigma(\Phi)}{TR^0(\Phi)} - 1 \text{ and } \Delta PR(x, y) = \frac{R^\sigma(x, y)}{R^0(x, y)} - 1$$

To cater for the locality-based approach and break the previous representation of location as applying only to network nodes, a modified form of the *ARIA* is introduced by considering the distance by road $d_L(x, y)$ from a locality (x, y) to the nearest service center in category L, for $L = A, B, C, D, E$, as defined in Table 3.1:

$$ARIA(x, y) = \sum_L \min\left\{3, \frac{d_L(x, y)}{\overline{d}_L}\right\} \tag{5.15}$$

where $\overline{d}_L$ is the mean road distance of all localities to the nearest category L service center. This equation may be applied in the same way as Equation (5.7). Again an upper limit of three on the ratio between $d_L(x,y)$ and $\overline{d}_L$ is used to remove the effects of any remaining extreme values from the index. In terms of the grid analysis for the computation of *ARIA*, for each grid cell not including or bordering a road section in the defined road network, a perpendicular line is constructed from the centroid of the cell to the nearest road link. The length of this line is then added to the computed road distance from the point of intersection on that road link to the nearest service centers in each class for the computation of the *ARIA* value for the cell. In terms of real world interpretation, this perpendicular line represents a "driveway" from the cell centroid connecting it to the road network. Contouring for determination of the overall remoteness surface for the region is done by interpolation given the set of computed *ARIA* values across the grid.[4]

More flexibility in an analysis is provided by defining the remoteness index for a region to be

$$R(x, y) = w(x, y)ARIA(x, y) \quad \text{for all } (x, y) \in \phi \tag{5.16}$$

where $w(x, y) \geq 0$ is a weight function. In this way, an analysis can be performed for all locations in the region $[w(x, y) = 1]$ or for selected locations, e.g., populated areas and areas under productive use, such as farmland, mining sites, or industrial or recreational facilities, through the choice of suitable values for the weights (see also Jenelius, Petersen, & Mattsson 2006).

In a degraded network it is then possible to study both the vulnerability of individual locations and the entire region resulting from failure or degradation of a specific link or set of links in the road network, by considering changes in individual *ARIA* values and in the region's total remoteness

[4] This task can be accomplished using a Geographic Information Systems software package such as ArcGIS.

volume. Thus the most vulnerable sites can be determined, and the most critical links identified.

A case study area for application of the above method was the "Green Triangle" region in south-east Australia, reported by Taylor and Susilawati (2012). The region lies midway between the metropolitan cities of Adelaide and Melbourne, covers an area of approximately 70,000 km^2, occupies two time zones, and straddles the state border between South Australia and Victoria. While the region sees itself as a single social and economic entity, given that it lies under the jurisdiction of two different states there are major issues for planning and service provision. Figure 5.13 provides a map of the region and its road network, and identifies its towns and cities. Mount Gambier (South Australia) is the major regional center, with a population of 24,000. It lies almost equidistant by road (about 350 km) from Adelaide (capital of South Australia, population 1.1 M) and Melbourne (capital of Victoria, population 3.5 M). Under the *ARIA* classification (Table 3.1), Mount Gambier and Warrnambool (Victoria) are "C" class service centers, while Adelaide and Melbourne are "A" class centers. All other towns in the region are "D" or "E" class, and there are also a number of smaller settlements (population 200–999), the class "F" service centers in the *ARIA*

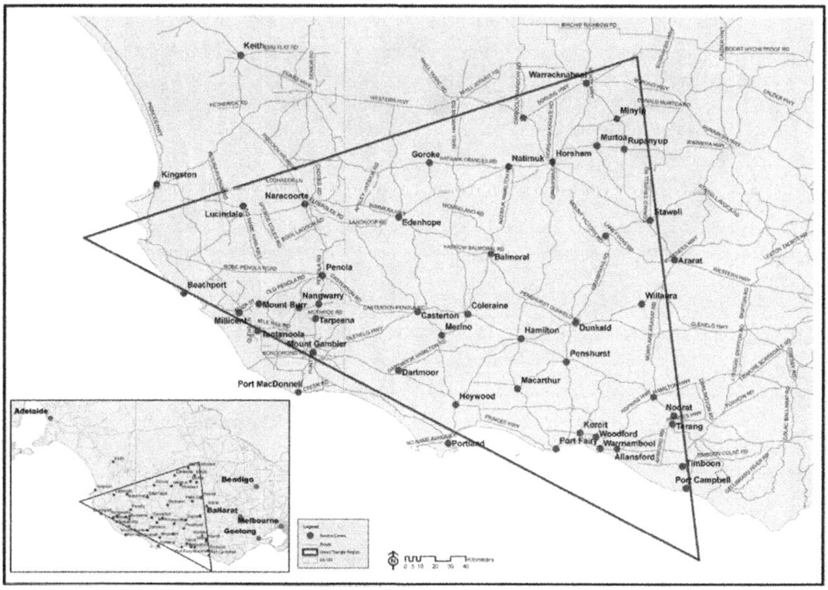

Figure 5.13 The "Green Triangle" region of South Eastern South Australia and western Victoria, Australia. *Reproduced with permission from Taylor, M. A. P., & Susilawati (2012). Remoteness and accessibility in the vulnerability analysis of regional road networks.* Transportation Research Part A: Policy and Practice, 46*(5), 761–771.*

model. In addition, and as shown in the inset in Figure 5.13, there are three "B" class cities nearby (Geelong, Ballarat, and Bendigo), all in Victoria. As indicated previously, there are no "B" class centers in South Australia.

The Green Triangle region was chosen as the case study area due to its location midway between Adelaide and Melbourne, and its economic importance in terms of industries including agriculture, paper manufacture, forestry, and tourism. Its regional road network is administered by two state transportation agencies, so coordination of network planning is of concern. The vulnerability assessment of the network is an important input into this process. This assessment was undertaken using the remoteness index defined in Equation (5.16), with equal weighting applied to all locations in the network.

Figure 5.14 shows the contour map for the *ARIA* for the full regional road network. The contours are drawn at intervals of 0.5 *ARIA* points, and the region falls in the range $1.4 < ARIA < 7.0$. Thus all locations fall into the "accessible" and "moderately accessible" categories. In the map more accessible locations are shown in green and less accessible locations in red. The most

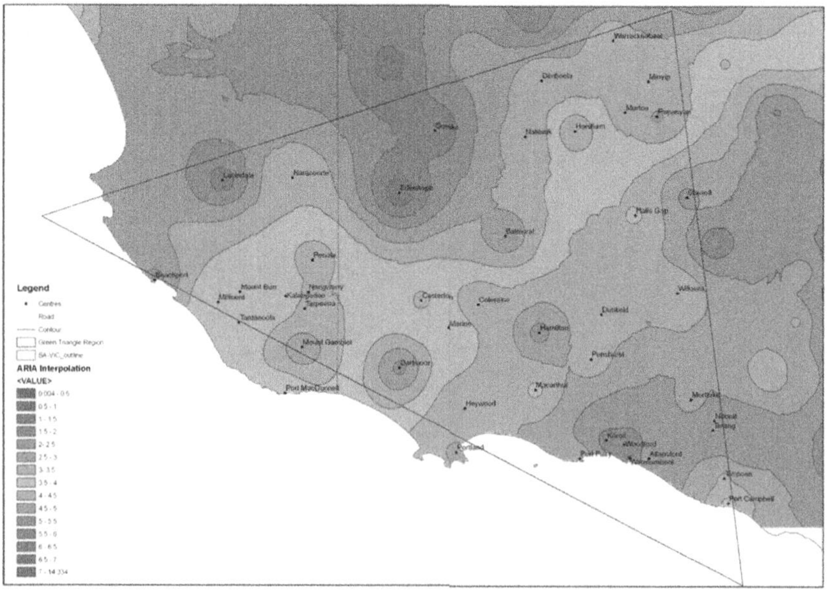

Figure 5.14 ARIA contour map for the full network of the "Green Triangle" region. *Reproduced with permission from Taylor, M. A. P., & Susilawati (2012). Remoteness and accessibility in the vulnerability analysis of regional road networks.* Transportation Research Part A: Policy and Practice, *46(5), 761–771.*

accessible population center is Warrnambool (population 26,700, *ARIA* = 1.457) and the most remote is Edenhope (population 770, *ARIA* = 6.254). Table 5.6 lists the computed *ARIA* values for all the settlements. The overall *ARIA* remoteness volume for the region with the full network was computed to be 1814. The remoteness volume was computed using a numerical approximation to Equation (5.12) available as the surface volume tool in the spatial analysis module of the ArcGIS software package.

The vulnerability assessment was undertaken on the basis of degrading the road network by failing specific links in the road network, and computing the changes in the *ARIA*. The four most critical links were found to be:

- Glenelg Highway near Dunkeld,
- Glenelg Highway near Hamilton,
- Glenelg Highway near Casterton, and
- Tarpeena—Penola Road.

The Glenelg Highway links are in Victoria, while the Tarpeena—Penola Road is in South Australia. Figure 5.15 locates these links in the region. Figure 5.16 provides the impacts of failure of each of these links on a number of settlements in the region.

Figure 5.16 shows the major impact of the failure of the Glenelg Highway near Dunkeld, which emerged as the most critical link in the network. The township of Dunkeld itself experienced an increase of 57.3% in its *ARIA* (3.32—5.22) under this scenario, a significant increase in the level of remoteness. The overall *ARIA* remoteness volume for the region increased to 1864 (a change in total volume of 2.8% for the region). Figure 5.17 shows the *ARIA* contours for the region in this scenario. By comparing this map with that in Figure 5.14, the large extent of increased remoteness in the region can be seen. For instance, the already remote region near Edenhope suffers further increase in its *ARIA* of about 8.7%.

The overall impact of network degradation by failure of the four most critical links is summarized in Table 5.7, which shows the increase in *ARIA* remoteness volumes under each separate link failure. While some centers experience significant changes in the value of their *ARIA*, no centers change their remoteness classification. On the other hand, the effects of the closures are seen in many of the population centers. For instance closure of the Glenelg Highway near Dunkeld affects 17 population centers, and the town of Dunkeld experiences a 57% increase in its *ARIA* (3.32—5.23).

Table 5.6 *ARIA* for Settlements in the Green Triangle Region for the Full, Intact Road Network

Center Name	*ARIA*	Service Center Class	Remoteness Classification	Center Name	*ARIA*	Service Center Class	Remoteness Classification
Adelaide[a]	0	A	HA	Allansford	1.848	F	A
Melbourne[a]	0	A	HA	Balmoral	4.772	F	MA
				Beachport	5.099	F	MA
Ballarat[a]	0.294	B	A	Dartmoor	4.551	F	MA
Bendigo[a]	0.355	B	A	Dunkeld	3.322	F	MA
Geelong[a]	0.186	B	A	Edenhope	6.254	F	MA
				Goroke	5.826	F	MA
Mount Gambier	2.479	C	A	Halls Gap	3.523	F	MA
Warrnambool	1.457	C	A	Kalangadoo	3.990	F	MA
				Lucindale	5.663	F	MA
Hamilton	2.374	D	A	Macarthur	3.563	F	MA
Horsham	3.105	D	MA	Merino	3.978	F	MA
Portland	2.962	D	MA	Minyip	4.376	F	MA
Stawell	2.141	D	A	Mortlake	2.645	F	MA
				Mount Burr	3.851	F	MA
Casterton	3.452	E	MA	Murtoa	4.056	F	MA
Coleraine	3.089	E	MA	Nangwarry	3.442	F	MA
Dimboola	4.021	E	MA	Natimuk	4.316	F	MA
Heywood	3.089	E	MA	Noorat	2.326	F	A
Koroit	1.924	E	A	Penshurst	3.204	F	MA
Millicent	3.617	E	MA	Port Campbell	3.625	F	MA
Naracoorte	4.057	E	MA	Port MacDonnell	3.831	F	MA
Penola	3.265	E	MA	Rupanyup	4.548	F	MA
Port Fairy	2.252	E	MA	Tantanoola	3.658	F	MA
Terang	2.107	E	MA	Tarpeena	3.376	F	MA
Warracknabeal	4.026	E	MA	Timboon	3.048	F	MA
				Willaura	3.435	F	MA
				Woodford	1.878	F	A

Remoteness classification: *A*, accessible; *HA*, highly accessible; *MA*, moderately accessible; *R*, remote; *VR*, very remote.
[a]Also showing *ARIA* values for the major population centers external to the region.

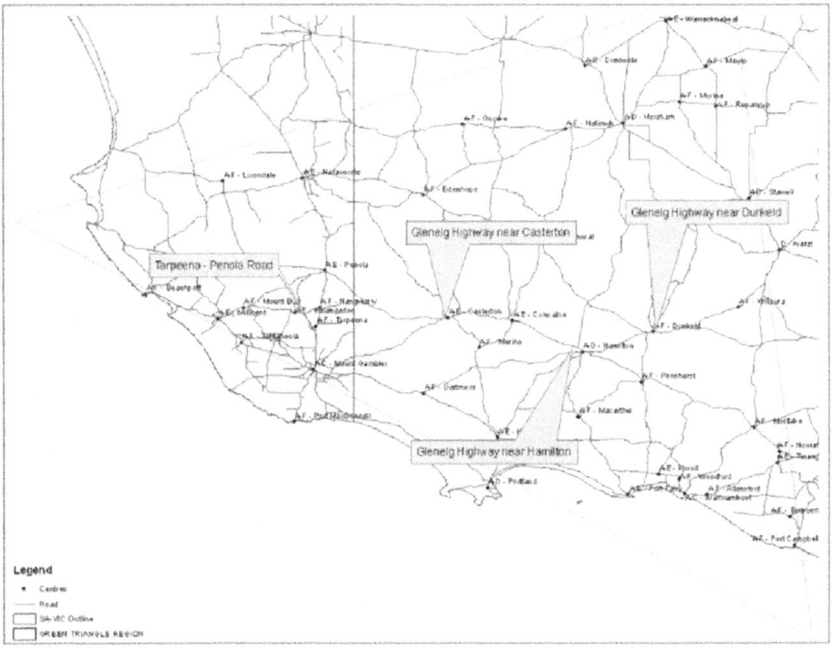

Figure 5.15 The four most critical links in the Green Triangle regional road network.

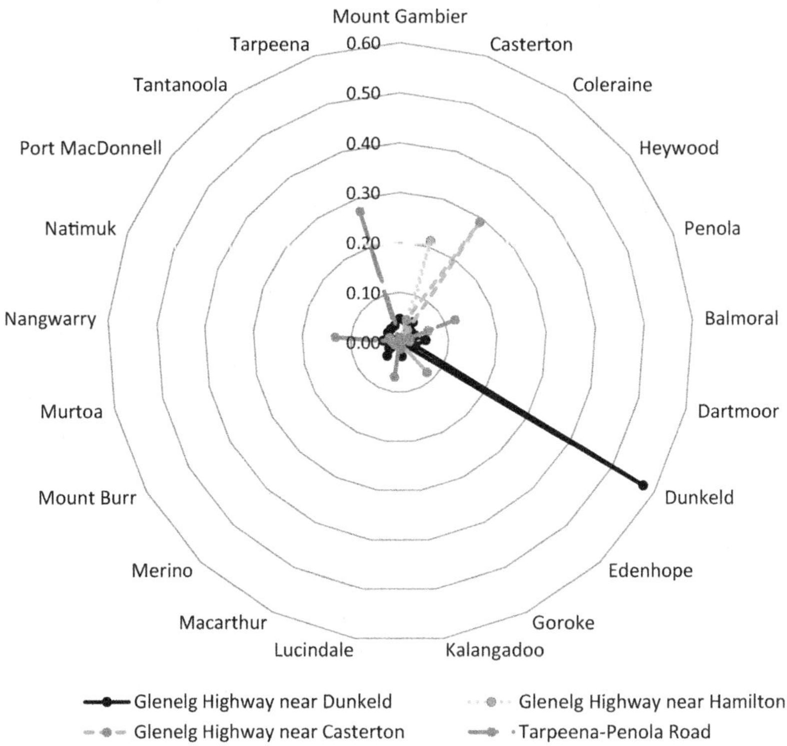

Figure 5.16 Percentage changes in *ARIA* for settlements in the Green Triangle region, given failure of each of the four critical links.

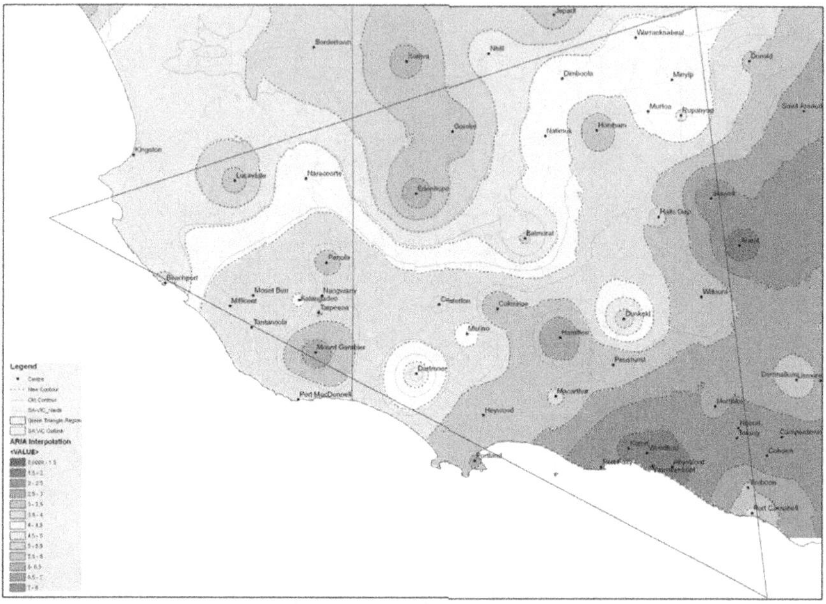

Figure 5.17 *ARIA* contour map for the degraded network (closure of Glenelg Highway near Dunkeld). *Reproduced with permission from Taylor, M. A. P., & Susilawati (2012). Remoteness and accessibility in the vulnerability analysis of regional road networks.* Transportation Research Part A: Policy and Practice, *46(5), 761–771.*

5.4 URBAN NETWORKS

Urban networks present a different challenge. The road and street networks are dense, with potentially many alternative paths for any origin–destination pair, and yet there may be significant bottlenecks to disrupt traffic flows. Traffic congestion is often a major factor in urban networks, and congestion can be exacerbated by incidents and other blockages occurring at different locations in the network. Section 3.5 discussed traffic congestion and its aspects, and the serviceability methods in Chapter 4 are often concerned with mitigating the impacts of congestion, especially the irregular (i.e., unexpected) congestion that results from temporary blockages in the network. The capacity of the urban area road network is likely to be tested to a much higher degree than that of a rural region. In addition, the multimodal nature of urban transportation systems may exert a strong influence: (1) where some transit modes (e.g., bus or street car) share road space with other traffic and (2) where those modes with separate rights-of-way (e.g.,

Table 5.7 *ARIA* for Settlements in the Green Triangle Region With Link Failures, for Those Population Centers Experiences Changes

Center Name	*ARIA*	Service Center Class	Remoteness Classification	New *ARIA* Values Under Link Failures			
				Glenelg Highway Near Dunkeld	Glenelg Highway Near Hamilton	Glenelg Highway Near Casterton	Tarpeena-Penola Road
Mount Gambier	2.479	C	A	2.595			2.504
Casterton	3.452	E	MA	3.601	4.187	3.613	
Coleraine	3.089	E	MA	3.238	3.178	3.989	
Heywood	3.089	E	MA	3.184			
Penola	3.265	E	MA	3.381	3.467	3.335	3.663
Balmoral	4.772	F	MA	5.027	4.869		4.772
Dartmoor	4.551	F	MA	4.700			
Dunkeld	3.322	F	MA	5.227			
Edenhope	6.254	F	MA		6.766	6.766	
Goroke	5.826	F	MA				5.849
Kalangadoo	3.99	F	MA	4.106	4.045	4.045	
Lucindale	5.663	F	MA				6.061
Macarthur	3.563	F	MA	3.570	3.563	3.563	3.563
Merino	3.978	F	MA	4.127	3.997	4.006	
Mount Burr	3.851	F	MA	3.947	3.892	3.892	3.851
Murtoa	4.056	F	MA	4.056	4.056	4.056	4.056
Nangwarry	3.442	F	MA	3.558	3.500	3.490	3.895
Natimuk	4.316	F	MA		4.412	4.412	
Port MacDonnell	3.831	F	MA	3.947			3.839
Tantanoola	3.658	F	MA	3.774	3.658	3.658	3.658
Tarpeena	3.376	F	MA	3.492	3.379	3.379	4.300

Remoteness classification: *A*, accessible; *HA*, highly accessible; *MA*, moderately accessible; *R*, remote; *VR*, very remote.

suburban heavy rail and light rail transit) still interact with the road system at at-grade intersections (e.g., level crossings), as discussed in Section 2.2.

Accessibility-based vulnerability analysis applied in urban networks therefore needs to take an alternative approach. This section discusses a method for assessing critical locations in urban networks, perhaps congestion "hot spots," which may be applied in anticipating potential vulnerabilities to incident-related congestion, and take proactive action to avoid excessive congestion rather than be obliged to react to it. Expected outcomes would then be reduced congestion, delays, and pollution; significantly improved performance from the existing urban road system; and reduced pressure to build more roads. The method involves modeling of travel demand, network topology, capacity and road geometry, the identification and assessment of impacts of traffic incidents at specific locations in a road network, and the use of accessibility analysis to assess network vulnerability in terms of the impacts of incident-based network degradation. This impact analysis is undertaken using an accessibility modeling framework that can account for time of day, transport mode and destination choices and level of traffic congestion among other factors. The resulting vulnerability analysis may be used to indicate the most critical locations in an urban road network, where network failure will have the greatest overall impacts. Given the complexity of urban networks, the proposed method does not involve a vulnerability scan to locate most critical locations; rather it is based on the selection of potential critical locations on the basis of professional judgment and the history of incidents in a given network.

Section 3.3 introduced the consumer surplus (*CS*) metric of accessibility, based on the use of a set of discrete choice models of traveler behavior (Equations (3.21)–(3.23) define this metric). One advantage of the use of *CS* is that it can be expressed in real and tangible units of quantity, which are either money ($) or time. Thus changes in accessibility can be interpreted in ways that have real meaning—as long as the underlying choice models and their parameters are reasonable. Chen, Yang, Kongsomsaksakul, and Lee (2007) offered the following description of a nested choice process for travel demand decisions which follows the sequence of choices leading to the derivation of *CS*. In this process the choice set is:

1. An individual at location i in time period t wishing to undertake some activity (e.g., study, work, shopping, and recreation) decides whether to travel to another location j at that time for the activity. The probability that the individual will travel at this time is $\Pr\{t|i\}$. If there are N_{it} individuals at the location, then the total number of trips from i in t is $H_{it} = N_i \Pr\{t|i\}$.

2. Given that the individual decides to travel, the conditional probability that an individual will choose destination j is $\Pr\{j|i,t\}$ and the number of trips from i to j in t is $H_{ijt} = H_{it}\Pr\{j|i,t\}$.
3. Then the individual selects a mode m for the trip. The conditional probability of choosing mode m is $\Pr\{m|i,j,t\}$ and the number of trips using m to travel from i to j in t is $H_{ijtm} = H_{ijt}\Pr\{m|i,j,t\}$.
4. The individual then selects a route r for the trip by mode m. The conditional probability for this is $\Pr\{r|m,i,j,t\}$ and the number of trips using route r in mode m for travel from i to j in t is $H_{ijtmr} = H_{ijtm}\Pr\{r|m,i,j,t\}$.

This nested choice structure is shown in Figure 5.18. Commonly a discrete choice model such as the multinomial logit model would be used for each choice decision, i.e., the probability that individual k will select alternative s from a set of choices is

$$\Pr\{s,k\} = \frac{\exp(Y_{sk})}{\sum_{s}\exp(Y_{sk})} \tag{5.17}$$

where Y_{sk} is the (deterministic part of the) utility of alternative s to the individual. This choice model lied behind the inclusive value (IV) formulation for the set of nested choices, introduced in Section 3.6 (see Equation 3.21) and illustrated in Figure 5.18.

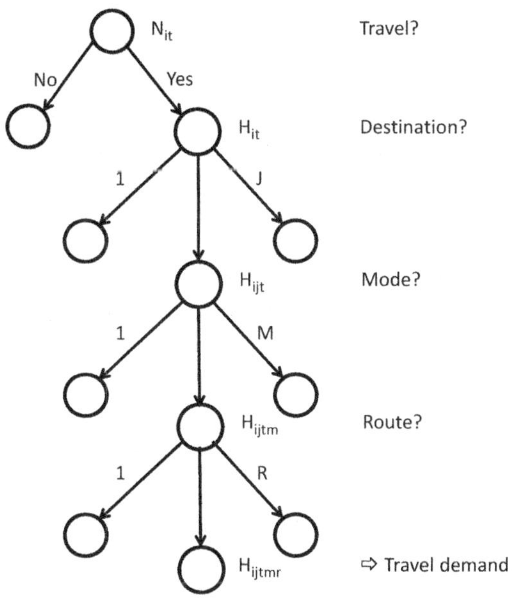

Figure 5.18 Nested choice set for travel decisions by an individual considering participation in an activity.

As discussed in Section 3.3 *CS* can be used as an accessibility metric derived on the basis of discrete choice models of travel behavior. In addition, the *IV* (sometimes termed as the "logsum value") has also been used as an accessibility metric (e.g., Primerano & Taylor, 2005; Chen et al., 2007). The two metrics are related, and it is useful for the following discussion to reiterate the formulation of these metrics. The *IV* is given by

$$IV_k = \log \sum_{S_n} \exp(Y_{sk}) \tag{5.18}$$

where IV_k is the deterministic component (observable attributes) of the maximum utility for individual k over all choices considered by the individual and Y_{sk} is the deterministic component of each secondary choice s in the set of choices S_k. This measure represents in a single value the overall benefit that an individual obtains from a set of alternatives. The *CS* is then given in terms of the *IV* and a coefficient (α) representing cost to estimate *CS* as follows:

$$E(CS) = \frac{1}{\alpha} \log\left(\sum_{n=1}^{N} \exp(IV_n) \right) + K \tag{5.19}$$

where α represents the negative of the coefficient of time or money cost (depending on the choice of unit) from the deterministic part of the utility function, and K is an unknown constant that represents the difference between the actual value of *CS* and the estimated value (Train, 2009). The estimated change in *CS* is then given as

$$\Delta E\left(CS^{AB}\right) = \frac{1}{\alpha}\left[\log\left(\sum_{n=1}^{N^A} \exp\left(IV_n^A\right) \right) - \log\left(\sum_{n=1}^{N^B} \exp\left(IV_n^B\right) \right) \right] \tag{5.20}$$

where the superscripts B and A represent "before" and "after" scenarios, respectively, and the two logsum terms represent the *IV*s derived from behavioral models under the two scenarios. Equation (5.20) thus gives an estimated change in *CS* with a measurement unit (e.g., hours or dollars) depending on the choice of α (Train, 2009). Thus the change in *CS* represents an accessibility metric with a well-known physical unit (money or time), and hence is amenable to useful interpretation.

Primerano and Taylor (2005) developed an accessibility framework using the hierarchy of travel choices in a set of discrete choice models. The framework was developed to combine the strengths of existing accessibility measures for use in transport and urban planning. The aim was to have a framework where policies related to transport and urban form could be tested and implemented to improve accessibility for all socioeconomic groups. The method used to develop the framework was activity-based rather than just location-based. This means that the accessibility framework determines the accessibility of an individual to an activity rather than the accessibility between locations. Considering accessibility in this way implies that accessibility is dependent on three components, namely the:

- traveler (individual or group),
- transport system (modes, roads, and service and traffic characteristics), and
- land use (characteristics of land uses at origins and destinations).

The flow chart in Figure 5.19 shows the framework. In this figure:

- choices are represented as rectangular boxes;
- the attributes of the traveler are shown as oval shapes;
- the alternatives in a choice set are shown as rounded-rectangular boxes; and
- constraints, which restrict the choices (e.g., the time—space prism which limits the spatial range of the individual in a given time period because of the possible speed of travel), are shown as diamond-shaped boxes.

In addition the framework includes a set of feedback lops, indicating that the traveler learns from previous experiences and so may adapt future travel

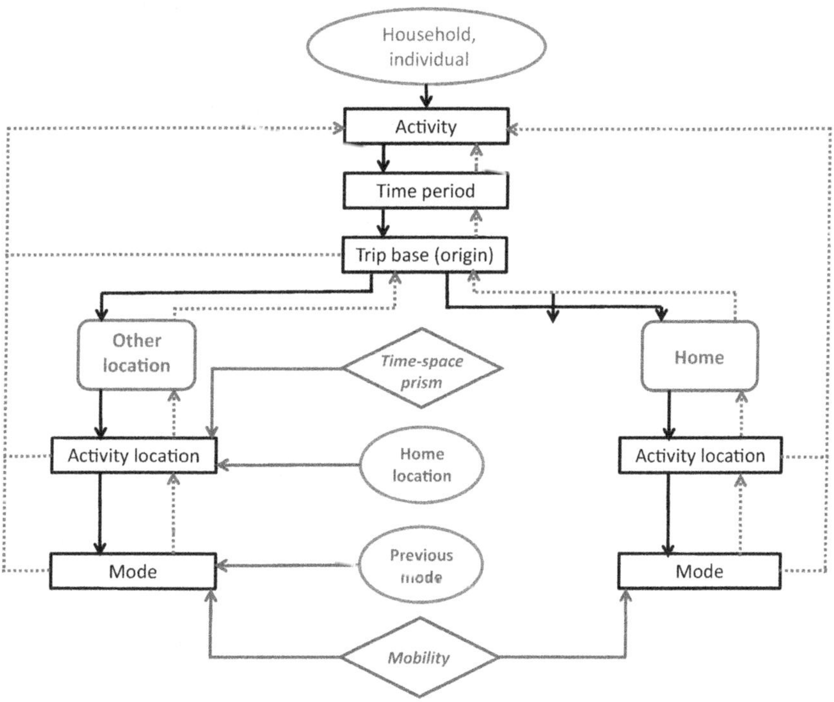

Figure 5.19 An accessibility framework for multimodal urban transport systems.

Figure 5.20 The Adelaide metropolitan area and its transportation system networks.

choices and behavior. Five types of travel choices are included in the framework: activity, time period, trip base (origin), activity location, and travel mode. Activity choice is the main choice—the individual decides to participate in an activity and then chooses when to travel, where to go to undertake the activity, and the mode of travel to reach that location. Trips starting at the individual's home may differ from those starting at some other location (e.g., work place or school).

A case study involving use of the accessibility framework was described by Taylor (2008b). This study involved the Adelaide metropolitan system and used the existing set of discrete choice models for that network as described in Primerano and Taylor (2005). Figure 5.20 shows a set of maps of the metropolitan area and its transportation system: (1) the spatial area divided into traffic activity zones (TAZ) for the travel demand model, (2) the bus route network, and (3) the main road and rail networks, including the O-Bahn guided busway. A module for the accessibility framework of Figure 5.19 was developed and attached to the metropolitan travel demand model. This module enabled computation of *IV* and *CS* values at the level of the "statistical local area" (SLA) across the region by time of day.[5]

[5] The metropolitan area contains 287 TAZ, which were divided between the 30 SLAs used in the analysis.

For the case study example the impacts of a major network failure were simulated, and new *IV* and *CS* values were calculated and compared to those for the full network. The network failure chosen was blockage of the two (directional) tunnels (the "Heysen Tunnels") on the South Eastern Freeway. The location of the Heysen Tunnels is shown in Figure 5.20. The freeway is the major link between the metropolitan area [especially the central business district (CBD) and surrounding suburbs] to the commuter towns in the Adelaide Hills, and is also the start of the major road link between Adelaide and Melbourne. In the vicinity of the tunnels the terrain is mountainous and there are only minor roads of much lesser quality available as alternative routes. The tunnel blockage incident was assumed to extend over a period of many hours, perhaps extending into days. The vulnerability of the network was explored using the *IV* and *CS* accessibility metrics for this situation.

Table 5.8 summarizes the overall impact on accessibility of the tunnel blockage incident in terms of changes in *IV*. It shows the *IV* for the full network and the degraded network by SLA and for the whole metropolitan area. The table is sorted in terms of *IV* in full network, with the most accessible SLA (Adelaide, the city center) at the top, and the northern and southern peripheral SLAs (Gawler, and Willunga and Noarlunga, respectively) at the bottom (i.e., the SLAs with the least accessibility in the metropolitan area). This accessibility measure covers accessibility to employment, education, shopping, and social and recreational activities, by all available transport modes.

Table 5.8 also shows the relative accessibility of each SLA in the full network and the degraded network, relative to the metropolitan-wide average. The incident has the most significant effects on the SLAs of Stirling (which represents the residential areas accessed by the freeway) and East Torrens (its neighbor). The accessibility of Stirling falls from just below the metropolitan average (relative *IV* in full network 0.996) to a value much below the average (relative *IV* in degraded network 0.956), implying a significant impact on that area. The effects on East Torrens are smaller, but are still an order of magnitude higher than those for any other SLA. The overall accessibility of the metropolitan area as measured by the *IV* is lowered by about 1%. Figure 5.21 charts the relative *IV* values in both full and degraded networks, and reinforces the results of the impacts on Stirling and East Torrens compared to the rest of the metropolitan area.

Table 5.8 Overall Vulnerability Impacts of the Tunnel Blockage Incident on Metropolitan Adelaide SLA, as Measured by Changes in *IV*

SLA Name	Full Network *IV*	Incident-Induced Change in *IV*	Degraded Network *IV*	Full Network Relative *IV*[a]	Degraded Network Relative *IV*[a]
Adelaide	6.335	−0.009	6.326	1.2016	1.2011
Glenelg	6.261	−0.005	6.256	1.1876	1.1878
Prospect	6.143	0.000	6.143	1.1652	1.1663
Unley	6.139	−0.009	6.13	1.1645	1.1639
St Peters	5.978	−0.007	5.971	1.1339	1.1337
Walkerville	5.778	−0.005	5.773	1.0959	1.0961
Burnside	5.765	−0.007	5.758	1.0935	1.0932
West Torrens	5.635	0.000	5.635	1.0689	1.0699
Mitcham	5.625	−0.006	5.619	1.0669	1.0668
East Torrens	5.618	***−0.053***	5.565	***1.0656***	***1.0566***
Thebarton	5.600	0.000	5.600	1.0622	1.0632
Port Adelaide	5.591	0.000	5.591	1.0605	1.0615
Payneham	5.554	−0.003	5.551	1.0535	1.0539
Munno Para	5.522	−0.002	5.520	1.0474	1.0480
Hindmarsh	5.469	0.000	5.469	1.0374	1.0384
Woodville	5.469	0.000	5.469	1.0374	1.0384
Kensington & Norwood	5.466	−0.001	5.465	1.0368	1.0376
Elizabeth	5.411	0.000	5.411	1.0264	1.0273
Henley & Grange	5.355	0.000	5.355	1.0157	1.0167
Tea tree Gully	5.324	−0.001	5.323	1.0099	1.0106
Enfield	5.263	−0.003	5.260	0.9983	0.9987
Stirling	5.252	***−0.215***	5.037	***0.9962***	***0.9563***
Campbelltown	5.232	−0.001	5.231	0.9924	0.9932
Happy Valley	5.148	−0.003	5.145	0.9765	0.9768
Marion	5.139	−0.001	5.138	0.9748	0.9755
Brighton	4.986	0.000	4.986	0.9458	0.9466
Salisbury	4.944	0.000	4.944	0.9378	0.9387
Noarlunga	4.821	−0.001	4.820	0.9145	0.9151
Willunga	4.572	−0.001	4.571	0.8672	0.8679
Gawler	4.365	0.000	4.365	0.8280	0.8287
Metropolitan average	5.272	−0.005	5.267	1.000	1.000

SLA name (*bold + italic*) indicates the two SLAs most affected by the tunnel blockage.
[a]Value of SLA *IV* relative to metropolitan average.

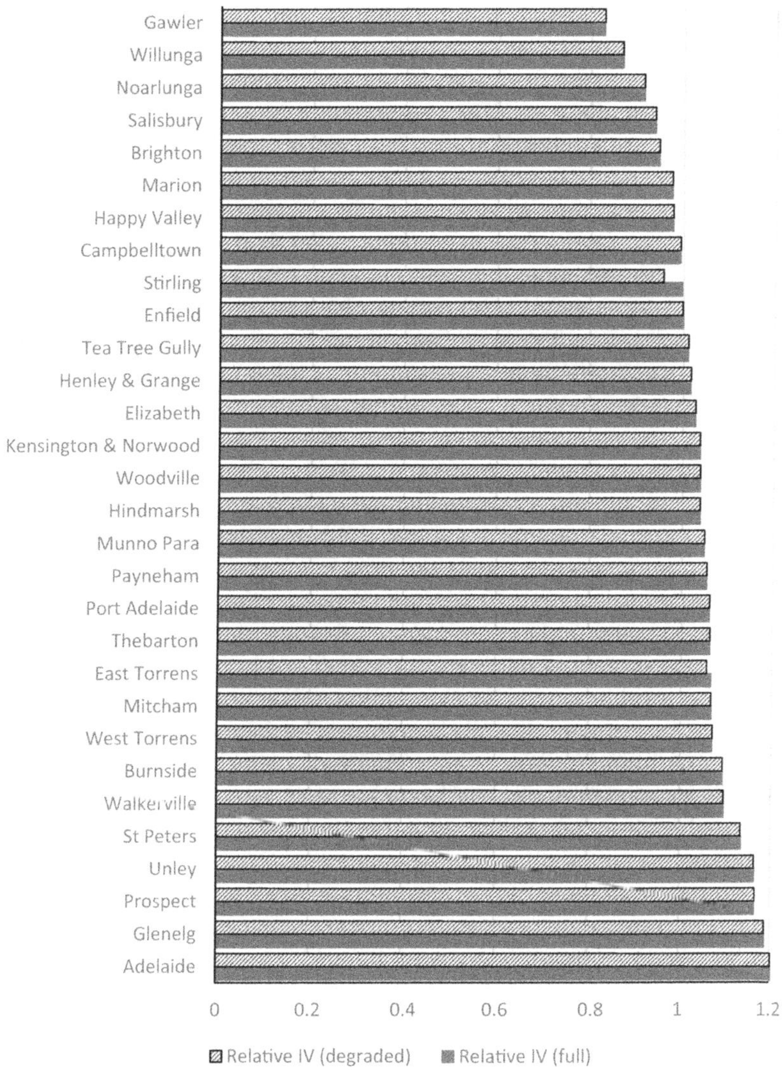

Figure 5.21 Relative *IV* accessibilities by SLA in metropolitan Adelaide with the tunnel blockage incident.

Interestingly, the accessibility values for many of the less accessible SLAs (those in the outer northern and outer southern suburbs) are not much affected by the incident, but there are noticeable effects on the accessibilities of the SLAs in the central areas (Adelaide city center and neighboring SLAs). These spatial effects can be seen in the thematic maps of Figure 5.22. Figure 5.22A shows the *IV* accessibilities of the SLAs in the full network,

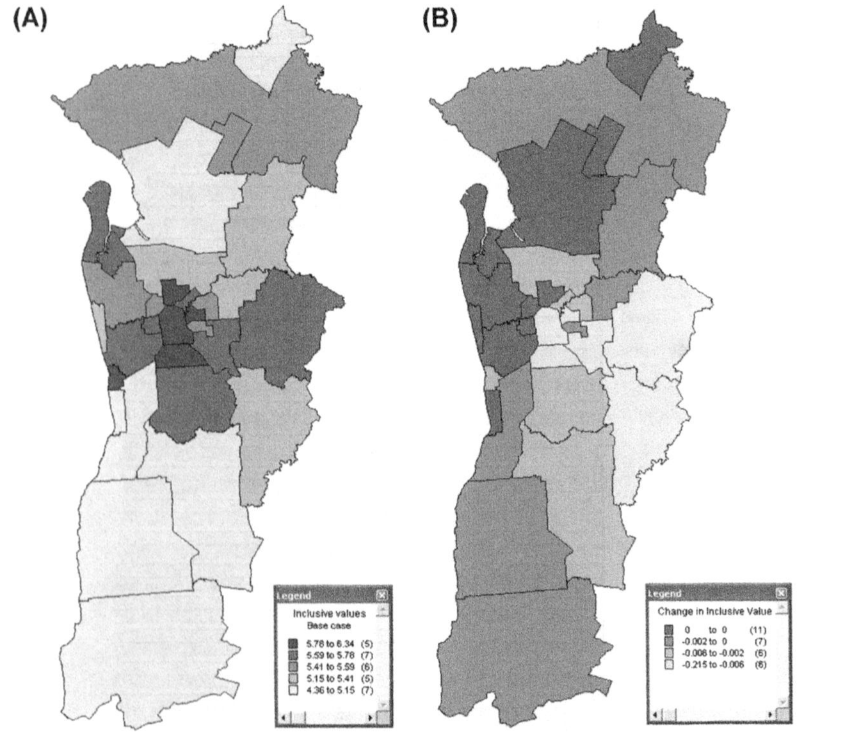

Full network *IV* values by SLA   Changes in *IV* values by SLA with tunnel blockage

Figure 5.22 Inclusive value accessibilities by SLA in metropolitan Adelaide: (A) *IV* values for the full network and (B) changes in *IV* under the tunnel blockage incident.

while Figure 5.22B shows the changes in the *IV* with the tunnel blockage incident. Figure 5.22A shows the overall pattern of decreasing accessibility of SLAs with distance from the city center. Figure 5.22B indicates the effects of the incident on Stirling and East Torrens, and also the otherwise "high accessibility" corridor into the city center from the south east. There is a noticeable (quantum) jump in the *IV* changes for these SLAs (Unley, Burnside, Walkerville, and St Peters in Table 5.8) compared to the rest of the metropolitan area. The overall effect of the incident is quite apparent in these maps, but given that the *IV* is an abstract measure, a full appreciation of the impact of the tunnel closure needs also to be based on a more tangible measure. The *CS* accessibility metric, here expressed in the units of money, can be used for this purpose.

The computed changes in *CS* based on Equation (5.20) provide a direct measure of the impact of the tunnel blockage incident. Table 5.9 summarizes

Table 5.9 Change in Social-Welfare Cost of Tunnel Blockage Incident for Adelaide SLA, Measured in Terms of Change in *CS*.

SLA Name	SLA Population	Change in Total *CS* ($ p.a.)	Change in per Capita *CS* ($/day/capita)
Stirling	13,025	−$8,028,957	**−$2.49**
Adelaide	12,785	−$514,820	*−$0.16*
East Torrens	27,410	−$1,098,446	*−$0.16*
Unley	36,663	−$1,398,972	*−$0.15*
Walkerville	6968	−$219,122	*−$0.13*
Burnside	42,110	−$1,151,929	*−$0.11*
Mitcham	61,878	−$980,180	−$0.06
Enfield	47,828	−$691,720	−$0.06
Munno Para	41,394	−$513,006	−$0.05
Campbelltown	18,993	−$199,028	−$0.04
Happy Valley	68,750	−$566,247	−$0.03
St Peters	21,507	−$175,008	−$0.03
Marion	44,900	−$317,900	−$0.03
Payneham	15,835	−$104,735	−$0.03
Tea tree Gully	98,449	−$432,058	−$0.02
Noarlunga	66,822	−$240,436	−$0.01
Glenelg	18,873	−$57,868	−$0.01
Salisbury	107,819	−$307,995	−$0.01
Woodville	21,507	−$49,209	−$0.01
Kensington & Norwood	9670	−$19,105	−$0.01
West Torrens	28,112	−$31,551	$0.00
Willunga	33,108	−$36,610	$0.00
Hindmarsh	50,296	−$49,209	$0.00
Brighton	14,350	−$9496	$0.00
Henley & Grange	31,284	−$11,849	$0.00
Prospect	19,185	−$4957	$0.00
Thebarton	23,731	−$4156	$0.00
Port Adelaide	54,831	−$4565	$0.00
Elizabeth	26,014	−$893	$0.00
Gawler	17,859	−$91	$0.00
Metropolitan average	1,081,956	$17,220,118	$0.06

SLA name (*italic*) indicates the five SLAs most affected by the tunnel blockage.

the results at the SLA level and for the entire metropolitan area. This table lists the total change in consumer welfare ($ p.a.) for each SLA as a consequence of the incident. Given the population of each SLA, this *CS* value can be converted into an amount in \$/day/capita for each working day of the year that the tunnel was blocked. Across the metropolitan area, the value is a decrease of 6 cents per person/day. Residents of Stirling experience a decrease in *CS* more than 40 times greater than this, at \$2.49 per person/day. This area undergoes a massive severance as a result of the incident. The SLAs of Adelaide, East Torrens, Unley, Walkerville, and Burnside all experience decreases in *CS* of 11 cents or more per person per day. All other SLAs experience changes in *CS* of 6 cents or less per person/day, indicating the spatial focus of the incident. Figure 5.23 provides a chart of the per capita changes in *CS* for each SLA, clearly showing the dramatic outcome for Stirling.

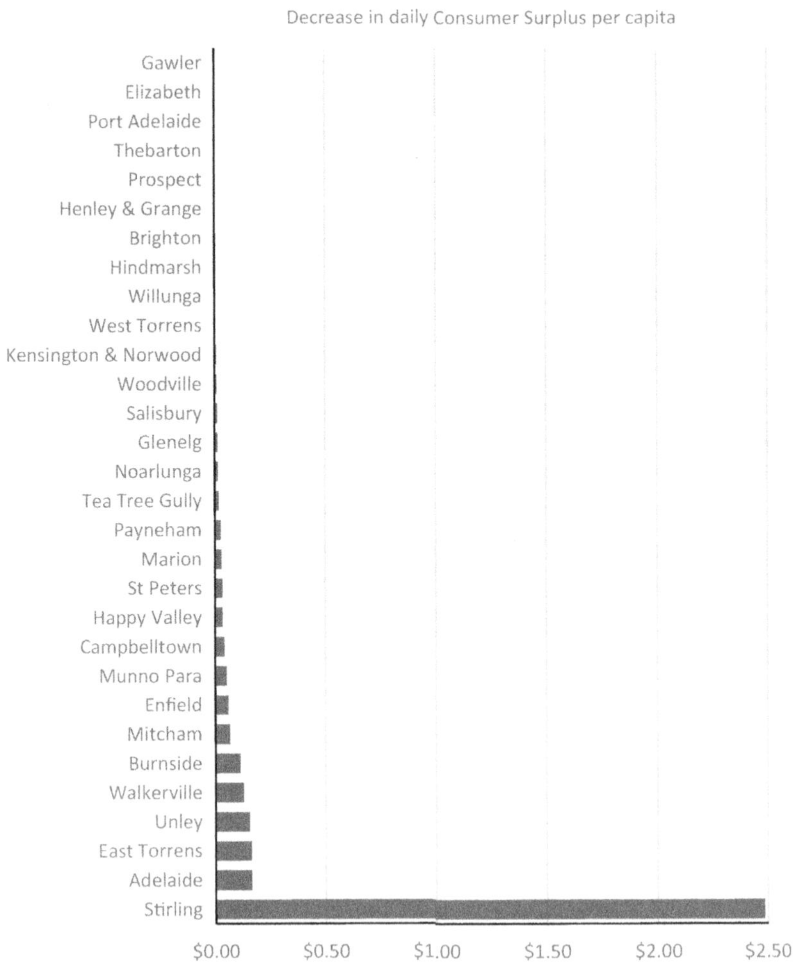

Figure 5.23 A social-welfare accessibility metric—change in *CS* (\$/day/person) with the tunnel blockage incident by SLA in metropolitan Adelaide.

The spatial impacts of the changes in per capita *CS* due to the incident may be seen in Figure 5.24. Again the significant effect on Stirling and the substantial effects on the SLAs between it and including the city center are apparent.

This analysis, together with the analysis of the impacts on the *IV* accessibility metric, provides a useful tool for assessing the transport and related (social and economic) impacts of a major incident on a metropolitan transport network.

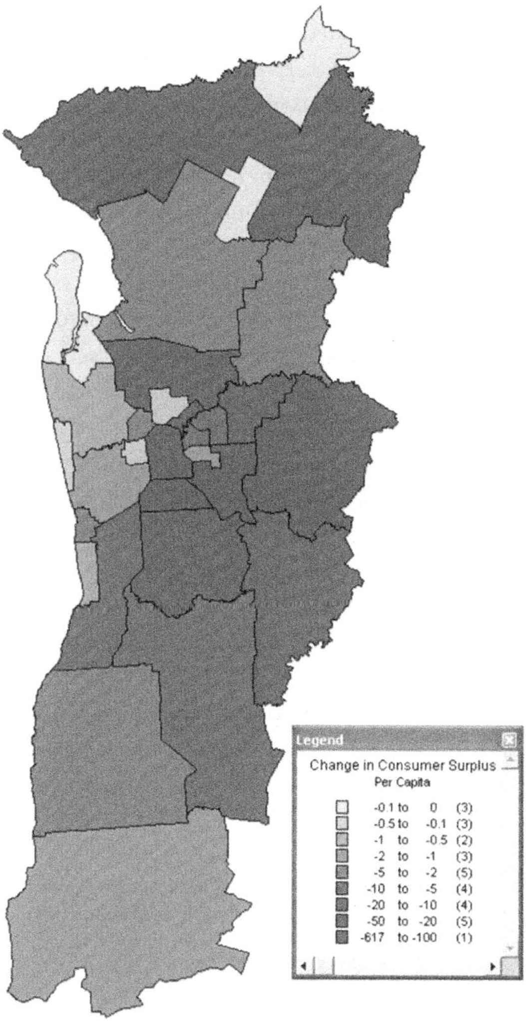

Figure 5.24 Changes in per capita *CS* from the tunnel blockage incident by SLA in metropolitan Adelaide.

5.5 SUMMARY

Accessibility-based vulnerability analysis provides a methodology which allows the effects of network degradation on the wider social and economic systems of the region served by the network. Starting from the discussion of accessibility and its metrics in Section 3.6, this chapter has introduced a set of accessibility measure each suitable for application at different spatial scales and levels of detail concerning the study region and its networks. Changes in accessibility metrics between an intact network and a degraded and/or congested network can be used to infer the likely economic and social impacts of network degradation.

At the broadest level a node-based metric such as the Hansen accessibility index may be used to study the interaction between large, separated population centers. In situations where there are few such population centers, alternative indices may be required. One such index, the *ARIA*, was used in two case studies, first for a state-wide road network covering an area with a large number of small population centers, and second, in a regional area of dispersed populations where the index was used on a locality basis. In the final case study two accessibility metrics based on discrete choice models of travel behavior were used. These metrics were applied to a multimodal urban transportation system and can account for changes in aspects of transportation service delivery. One of these metrics, *CS*, allowed a direct insight into the social-welfare aspect of degraded transport network performance because this metric could be expressly in terms of money loss across a population. The *CS* metric with its *IV* partner can also be used to study detailed spatial impacts of network degradation in a study area.

The Adelaide metropolitan case study further introduces the need to consider vulnerability analysis for public transit systems as a separate area from the consideration of road networks upon which much of the discussion in Chapters 4 and this chapter has dwelt. This leads into Chapter 6, where vulnerability analysis for public transportation is the focus.

REFERENCES

Bil, M., Vodak, R., Kubecek, J., Bilova, M., & Sedonik, J. (2015). Evaluating road network damage caused by natural disasters in the Czech Republic between 1997 and 2010. *Transportation Research Part A: Policy and Practice, 81*, 90–103.

Chen, X.-Z., Lu, Q.-C., Peng, Z.-R., & Ash, J. E. (2015). Analysis of transportation network vulnerability under flooding disasters. *Transportation Research Record, 2532*, 37–44.

Chen, A., Yang, C., Kongsomsaksakul, S., & Lee, M. (2007). Network-based accessibility measures for vulnerability analysis of degradable transportation networks. *Networks and Spatial Economics, 7*(3), 241–256.

DHAC. (2001). *Measuring remoteness: Accessibility/remoteness index of Australia (ARIA) (revised edition)*. Occasional paper, new series no 14. Department of health and aged care, DHAC 2001., measuring remoteness: accessibility/remoteness index of Australia (ARIA) (revised edition). Occasional paper, new series no 14. Canberra, Australia: Department of Health and Aged Care.

GISCA. (2009). *Centre for the social applications of geographic information systems*. Adelaide: University of Adelaide. Retrieved from http://www.gisca.adelaide.edu.au/products_services/ariav2_about.html.

Jenelius, E., Petersen, T., & Mattsson, L.-G. (2006). Importance and exposure in road network vulnerability analysis. *Transportation Research Part A: Policy and Practice, 40*(7), 537–560.

Primerano, F., & Taylor, M. A. P. (2005). An accessibility framework for evaluating transport policies. In D. M. Levinson, & K. J. Krizek (Eds.), *Access to destinations* (pp. 325–346). Oxford: Elsevier.

Rupi, F., Bernardi, S., Rossi, G., & Danesi, A. (2015). The evaluation of road network vulnerability in mountainous areas: A case study. *Networks and Spatial Economics, 15*(2), 397–411.

Sohn, J. (2006). Evaluating the significance of highway network links under the flood damage: An accessibility approach. *Transportation Research Part A: Policy and Practice, 40*(6), 491–506.

Taylor, M. A. P. (2008a). Vulnerability analysis of regional road networks. Session "Traffic Network Management". In *Proc 23rd ARRB Conference. August, Adelaide*. Melbourne: ARRB Group Ltd. CD-ROM ISBN: 1 8765 9254 0.

Taylor, M. A. P. (2008b). Critical transport infrastructure in urban areas: Impacts of traffic incidents assessed using accessibility-based network vulnerability analysis. *Growth and Change, 39*(4), 593–616.

Taylor, M. A. P., & Susilawati. (2012). Remoteness and accessibility in the vulnerability analysis of regional road networks. *Transportation Research Part A: Policy and Practice, 46*(5), 761–771.

Taylor, M. A. P., Sekhar, S. V. C., & D'Este, G. M. (2006). Application of accessibility based methods for vulnerability analysis of strategic road networks. *Networks and Spatial Economics, 6*(3), 267–291.

Train, K. (2009). *Discrete choice methods with simulation* (2nd ed.). Cambridge: Cambridge University Press.

CHAPTER SIX

Public Transport Networks

Serviceability and accessibility methods discussed in Chapters 4 and 5 focused mainly on road networks. The last decade has seen the advent of analysis methods expressly designed for application to public transport networks, primarily the rail networks. Much of the interest has been on urban metro systems. There are significant differences between rail and road networks, and between the natures of the vehicular flows on them. In particular, while road traffic flows are considered as continuous flows, rail network flows are composed of large, discrete flow units, namely trains, and these flows are sometimes seen as granular in nature. Rail flow units (vehicles, or "train sets") are large, and well separated from each other by stringent operating rules that do not exist for road traffic. For fixed rail movements, overtaking is not possible unless special passing loops are installed, or at multiplatform stations, and therefore passing maneuvers are limited to these locations. Disruption of services halting one train will thus curtail the operations of all other trains on the same line. Road networks often provide useful detours, at least for short-term operations. Thus (fixed rail) public transport networks tend to be more sensitive to disruptions than road networks. Metro and other rail networks are usually sparse (i.e., have few connecting links between nodes) which can add to the difficulties generated by disruptions.

Section 2.2.2 provided a basic description of the features and characteristics—right-of-way, technology, and service type—of public transport networks, while Appendix B provides an introduction to the capacity of railway systems.

Much of the research on vulnerability analysis for rail networks has used network topology. As argued by Mattsson and Jenelius (2015), this is largely because the serviceability- and demand-based methods require advanced modeling tools that while common for road networks are not generally available in usable form for public transport systems. Nevertheless, as shown in Sections 6.3 and 6.4, serviceability- and demand-based methods are

Vulnerability Analysis for Transportation Networks
ISBN: 978-0-12-811010-2
http://dx.doi.org/10.1016/B978-0-12-811010-2.00006-X

available in some circumstances, where they have proven very useful[1]. The application of topological analysis to public transport networks is also useful in providing insights into the ways these networks operate.

Risk management for public transport is also a major concern in the modern world. With large numbers of people using urban public transport systems in constrained spaces (stations and trains), open access (stations), safety, and security issues are the most important issues for system managers and urban authorities. Minor crime involving transit passengers is an ongoing concern, while planned attacks on urban metro systems are a major threat in an era of terrorism. Bentler et al. (2014) presented a framework for risk and crisis management for implementation as part of the normal operating procedures for urban transit systems. Vulnerability analysis is an important component of the risk- and crisis-management system. Given the ongoing cyclical operations of urban transit systems and their requirements to move large numbers of people, resilience—basically the time required for a system to recover and resume normal operations after a shock or disruption—is also an important consideration. Resilience of networks was introduced in general terms in Section 2.5. Mattsson and Jenelius (2015) and D'Lima and Medda (2015) discussed resilience as it would apply to public transport systems. Mattsson and Jenelius suggested that the consequences of a system failure will depend on its duration and the numbers of travelers affected, the ability of travelers to find alternatives in time and space, and the level of information supplied to assist them in doing so. D'Lima and Medda stressed the need to consider dynamic resilience, "the speed at which a system returns to equilibrium after a disturbance away from equilibrium" (D'Lima & Medda, 2015, p. 38). This involves consideration of the resilience triangle, as discussed in Section 2.5. Zhang, Song, Zhang, and Liu (2014) considered the interdependency of urban mass transit systems, especially the interdependency between the rail transit network and the power-supply and communications systems for a modern transportation system. They introduced a framework for analysis of vulnerability of interdependent infrastructure systems and applied this to the Shanghai metro, suggesting that the highest betweenness node-based attack to the power grid and the largest degree node-based attack to the communications network would result in the most severe losses of function

[1] At present, the main issue with the method is its requirement for a detailed, transit-oriented travel demand model to support it. Such models only exist in a few places.

for the metro network. Interdependency of infrastructure systems was discussed in Section 2.1. It is an issue of increasing importance in a changing world of growing complexity.

6.1 FEATURES OF TRANSIT NETWORKS

Rail transit networks possess a number of features that are unique or at least important in the consideration of network performance and the potential vulnerability of a network and its components. While Section 2.2.2 discussed technical features of transit networks, network configuration, structure, and topology are of interest in the development of methods for vulnerability analysis of these networks. In particular, transit networks tend to be sparse, with a low ratio of number of links to number of nodes, and are often arranged on a line or route basis, with few connections (transfer points) between the lines. These features can be explained diagrammatically and by considering some network properties. Figure 6.1 shows a small urban metro network as an example. "Metro M" is a fictitious network although it bears some resemblance to the Montreal metro, and is intended to illustrate the typical properties of a metro network configuration. Figure 6.1A shows the network with all stations represented as nodes, while Figure 6.1B shows the network with only those nodes (A—I) which are either line terminals or transfer stations (where passengers can switch from one line to another). These networks clearly show the sparseness of the network in terms of numbers of links compared to the number of nodes (e.g., as

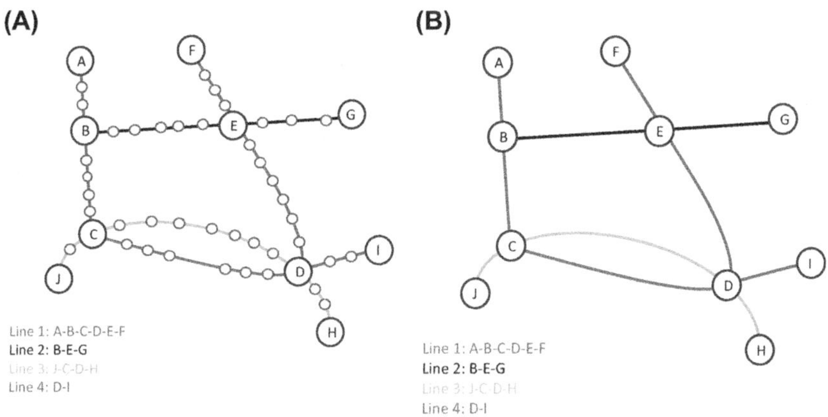

Figure 6.1 An example of a small metro network (Metro M) with *four lines*: (A) showing all stations as nodes, (B) showing only those station nodes where passengers can transfer between lines and line-terminal nodes.

indicated by the degree of a node, as discussed below[2]). Figure 6.1B represents the basic network that would be used in topological analysis, for it contains complete information about redundancy and availability of alternatives. Figure 6.1A is more useful for studies of passenger flows, for all the stations represent the points where passengers can enter or leave the system and thus indicate the origin–destination flow patterns.

In terms of network (graph) theory a transit network in its simplest form can be described as an undirected[3] graph $G = \{V, A\}$ composed of a set of nodes (vertices) V and set of links (edges) A. Two basic network indicators, as suggested by Derrible and Kennedy (2010a), are the β indicator, which refers to network complexity and the degree of connectivity (γ).

The β indicator is straightforward, which is merely the ratio of the number of links (S) to the number of nodes (N):

$$\beta = \frac{S}{N} \tag{6.1}$$

A small value of β indicates that the network is relative simple in structure.

The γ-indicator of connectivity is a topological measure of how much a network is connected compared to how much it could be connected, and is broadly defined as the ratio of the actual number of links to the potential maximum number of links for the network. In a general n-dimensional space and for an undirected network, this maximum number of links is $\frac{1}{2}N(N-1)$, which is the possible number of connections between all nodes, halved to avoid double counting in an undirected graph. However, in a planar network, to which transit networks generally belong, this number of connections is infeasible: two links crossing each other would automatically generate another node. Derrible and Kennedy (2010a) indicated that for a planar network the maximum possible number of links is $3(N-2)$, for $N \geq 3$. Thus the definition of γ in this case is

$$\gamma = \frac{S}{3N-6} \tag{6.2}$$

[2] See also Section 2.3 and Appendix A.

[3] An undirected graph means that flow is possible in both directions for a link a between nodes i and j, which is generally the case for metro systems—one exception is the directional loop of Line 10 in the Paris Metro, between stations "Boulogne-Jean Jaurès" and "Javel-André Citroën." Directional networks, where some links only accommodate unidirectional flows, are often found in road transport networks, e.g., in cities with one-way street systems.

The first and the basic property of a network node is its degree (k_i), defined as the number of links connecting the node to the rest of the network. Equation (2.4) defined the degree of the node, i.e., $k_i = \sum_{j \neq i} \delta_{ij}$ where

$$\delta_{ij} = \begin{cases} 1 & \text{if link } a_{ij} \text{ exists} \\ 0 & \text{otherwise} \end{cases}$$

The average degree of the network is $C^D = \frac{1}{N} \sum_i k_i$. Node degree is of interest while considering network structure which provides more detail to support the β indicator. A scale-free network (Barabasi & Albert, 1999) is one in which the probability density function $p(k)$ of the number of connecting links ($k = 1, 2, 3, \ldots$) of a node follows a power law, i.e., $p(k) \propto k^{-\lambda}$ with scaling factor λ. There is a body of research (e.g., Derrible & Kennedy 2010a, 2010b; Sienkiewicz & Holyst 2005; Von Ferber, Holovatch, Holovatch, & Palchykov, 2009; Zhang, Zhao, Liu, & Xu, 2013) suggesting that many, but not all, metro networks can be described as scale-free. In addition, the "small-world" property is also of interest for the analysis of transit networks. Small-world networks have two principal properties: (1) they exhibit high clustering, and (2) they have short average minimum path lengths. Clustering considers the number of connections between the nodes in a neighborhood, where the neighborhood of node i is all of the nodes directly connected to i (i.e., by physical links). There are k_i such nodes. Using the concept presented by the γ-indicator (Equation 6.2), for a planar neighborhood network (with $k_i \geq 3$), there would be a maximum $3(k_i - 2)$ possible connections, so that the clustering coefficient C_i for node i is

$$C_i = \frac{k_i}{3(k_i - 2)} \quad \text{if } k_i \geq 3 \tag{6.3}$$

and thus the overall clustering coefficient for the network (CC), which is the average node clustering coefficient, is

$$CC = \frac{1}{N} \sum_i C_i \tag{6.4}$$

In terms of shortest paths in the networks, three relevant indices were introduced in Chapter 3. These indices were the global efficiency of the network ($\eta(G)$, given by Equation 3.5), the local efficiency ($\eta_{\text{loc}}(G_i)$ for node i, where G_i is the subgraph of G comprising the node, its neighbors, and the links between them as defined in Equation 3.6), and the betweenness centrality (C_i^B) of node i as defined in Equation (3.7). Among these indices, betweenness centrality has been frequently used in the analysis of transit networks. This index is computed by considering the total numbers of shortest paths n_{hd} over all origin–destination pairs h-d in the network and the numbers of those shortest paths that pass through node i ($n_{hd}(i)$). Then, given N_{hd} is the number of origin–destination pairs,

$$C_i^B = \frac{1}{(N_{hd}-1)(N_{hd}-2)} \sum_{h,d \neq i} \frac{n_{hd}(i)}{n_{hd}} \tag{6.5}$$

If the length of the minimum cost path from h to d is L_{hd} then the average minimum cost path length in the network is

$$\overline{L} = \frac{1}{N_{hd}} \sum_{hd} L_{hd} \tag{6.6}$$

This parameter is often termed the "characteristic path length" of the network.

It is also possible to have a betweenness index for links, as used in Cats and Jenelius (2014).

On the basis of their analysis of 33 metro networks across the world, Derrible and Kennedy (2010b) concluded that these largely satisfied the small-world properties of high clustering and short minimum path lengths, and clustering became more apparent as the networks grew in size.

Von Ferber et al. (2009) introduced a valuable multifaceted view of transit systems, by representing the system with alternative network configurations in different spaces, which they designated as *L-Space*, *B-Space*, *P-Space*, and *C-Space*. Defining the network configuration in each of these spaces enables the analyst to use some of the network indices described above to answer different questions about the network and its connectivity. Briefly, the four spaces may be defined as follows:

- In *L-Space* the network representation of the transit system is as a schematic map in which each station is a node and a link exists between any two nodes if these are consecutive stations on one or more transit lines.
- In *B-Space* the representative network is constructed with all lines and stations as nodes. Each line node is connected by a link to each station node on the line, and there are no direct links between nodes of the same kind. A transfer node is then connected to two or more line nodes.

- In *P-Space* the network nodes are the stations, and there are links between any two station nodes if they are serviced by one or more common lines.
- In *C-Space* the network nodes are the lines, and there is a link between two nodes if they share a station.

Constructing the different networks for each of these four spaces for a given transit system provides a multidimensional perspective on how the system will operate. As an example, Figure 6.2 shows the networks for each space for the transit system seen in Figure 6.1. Table 6.1 lists the descriptions for the different space networks and their respective properties. The degree of a node and the characteristic path length in each network are of interest. These properties indicate the level of movement required to travel between stations and the need for transfers in doing so.

Zhang et al. (2013) provided a comparative analysis of 30 metro systems from few cities across the world and suggested that the most vulnerable nodes were those with the highest betweenness centralities.

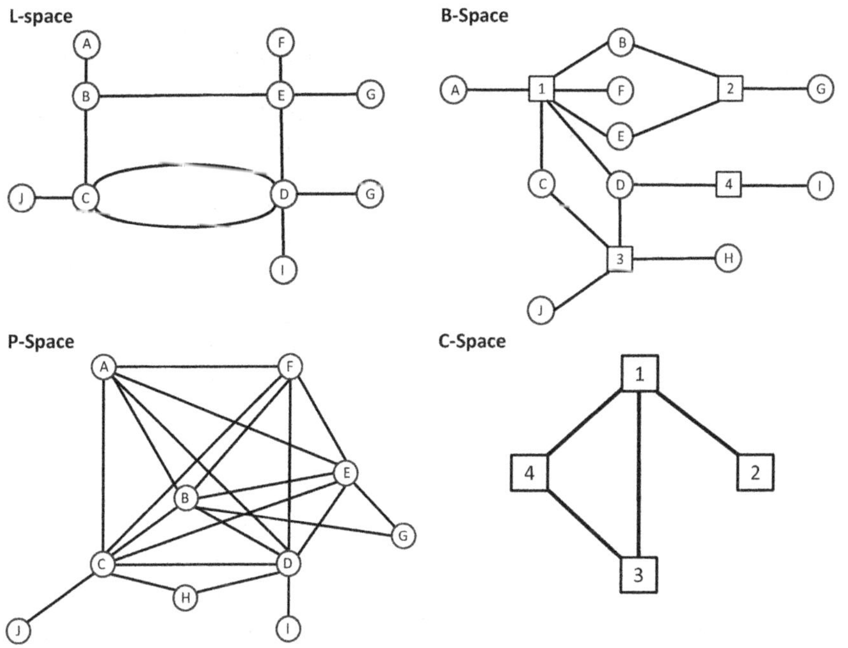

Figure 6.2 *L-Space, B-Space, P-Space,* and *C-Space* network representations of the Metro M transit system shown in Figure 6.1. (Lines 1, 2, 3, and 4, Stations A, B, C,..., I).

Table 6.1 Characteristics of *L-Space, B-Space, P-Space*, and *C-Space* Representations of Transit Networks

Space	Description	Properties
L-Space	A schematic physical/geographic layout of the network. Each station is a node. Any two nodes are connected by a link if these are two consecutive stations on one or more transit lines.	Characteristic path length $(\overline{L})$[1] equals the average minimum number of stops on a line between any two stations. The degree of a node (station) equals the number of stations reached by one stop from that node.
B-Space	All lines and all stations are nodes. Each line node is linked to all station nodes that fall along the line. There are no direct links between nodes of the same kind.	The degree of a station node equals the number of lines servicing it. The degree of a line node equals the number of stations along the line.
P-Space	Nodes represent the stations. There is a link between any two stations if they are serviced by one or more common lines.	$\overline{L}$ equals The average minimum number of transfers needed to travel between any two stations. The degree of a node (station) equals the number of stations reached without transferring to a different line.
C-Space	Nodes represent the lines. There is a link between two nodes if the lines share a station.	$\overline{L}$ equals The average minimum number of transfers needed to pass between any two lines. The degree of a node (line) equals the number of other lines available for direct transfer from it.

[1]The characteristic path length is the average length of the minimum paths between all (origin–destination) node pairs in the network, as defined by Equation (2.3). For the case of the L-Space network, each link is of unit length (i.e., represents one stop along the line, implying that the network is unvalued and is undirected).

Deng, Li, and Lu (2015) went beyond network layout to develop a framework for the vulnerability analysis of metro systems by considering the physical and functional components of the system. The physical infrastructure system was represented by a directed network, in which the nodes represented the components of the real infrastructure system (e.g., trains, tracks, power-supply system, signaling system, communications, and fare-collection system) and the links represented the relationships between the components. Vulnerability assessment was done assuming that if a component fully or partially lost its function then the node representing the component was deleted from the functional representation network, using the network modeling the topological indices defined by Equations (6.1)–(6.5). Using the Nanjing metro as a case study application, the authors demonstrated that the train component was perhaps the most vulnerable to functional failure. While the study focused on the signaling system as the source of failure, the analysis could be repeated with failures of other components such as the automatic fare-collection system.

Derrible and Kennedy (2010a) took a broader view of the transit system and its role in the urban system to which it belonged. They did so by considering three broad network characteristics that could be related to activities in the urban system:

- The *state* of the network, which referred to the current development phase of the system and the degree of connectivity in it. To do so they employed the β and γ indicators discussed earlier (see Equations 6.1 and 6.2). More highly developed systems had higher levels of connectivity.
- The *form* of the network, which indicated how the transit system was integrated into the built environment. Metro networks play different roles depending on how they were planned, with a basic distinction between providing regional services that bring people from residential areas to employment centers or on providing local services for people living in one locality. To do so they took three broad parameters of a transit system: the number of lines (n_L), the number of stations (n_S), and the total system route length (SL). Average line length (SL/n_L) provided a first measure, with regional systems typically having longer line lengths. At the same time, the number of stations was also important as a network with low average line length and many stations will offer more local coverage. Average interstation spacing (SL/n_S) adds further detail. A network with large interstation spacing is probably regionally focused. Shorter spacings generally mean lower speeds and therefore longer travel times—including both running time and dwell time at stations. A trade-off between regional accessibility and local coverage then often featured in transit system planning.
- The *structure* of the network is concerned with the need for transfers between lines to complete journeys, or alternatively as the level of directness available for travelers, and the structural connectivity of the network (as opposed to the degree of connectivity consider in *state*). Derrible and

Kennedy (2010a) defined a directness indicator as $n_L/Xmax$, where $Xmax$ is the maximum number of transfers required to make any nominated journey in the network. A well-designed network should be capable of simultaneously providing good performance in both connectivity and directness.

Going beyond topology and the physical state and configuration of a transit system, network is necessary if the operational serviceability of the system is to be studied. Passenger flows and the choice of alternative routes are of importance. A key part of this consideration is the development of a generalized travel-time model for the metro network. Cai, Zhu, Yang, Fan, and Xu (2016) described the development and use of such a model, more or less akin to the generalized travel-cost model as discussed in Chapter 4 and illustrated in Equation (4.1), with the condition that the transit travel-time model, while considering all the different components of travel time, is only concerned with those components and not other aspects of a traveler's journey.

The primary focus of this section has been on urban rail transit networks, represented by metro systems. Similar work can be taken for long-distance (intercity and regional) railway systems. For example Wang, Liu, Li, and Jiang (2010) considered vulnerability in a national railway system and identified four broad factors affecting vulnerability:

1. External attacks, as acts of deliberate sabotage, warfare or terrorism, which are likely to be targeted attacks
2. Extreme weather events and natural disasters, which are likely to be random in nature, though the susceptibility to specific events may be understood—while weather events can also be subject to the influences of climate change
3. Network failure, involving the failure of particular components of the railway system, both in terms of physical infrastructure and operating systems; in the main, the probability distributions for these failures are likely to be known, and
4. Unstable travel demands, when seasonal variations and special events can combine to disrupt or even overwhelm the existing services in some circumstances.

Peterson and Church (2008) considered network failure, and identified bridge and tunnel failures as primary sources of disruption—and hence vulnerability—in a large national railway system (as in the United States). They developed a system-optimization model to deal with these failure situations which considers the opportunities to reroute freight trains.

6.2 TOPOLOGICAL METHODS

There is a body of research tackling the vulnerability of transit systems from the perspective of changes in network performance, as measured by topological performance indices such as betweenness and network efficiency. The general approach is to test a network's performance on the basis of the failure of one or more nodes. Zhang et al. (2013) presented an analysis of the topological vulnerability of the metro systems from 30 cities on 5 continents, examining:

- the distribution of node degree in each network
- betweenness centrality of nodes, for each network
- the distribution of shortest path lengths between origin—destination pairs in each network
- the unit degree betweenness distribution in each network, which is the ratio of the node betweenness to the node degree and thus is an indicator of the loads placed on the links
- the distribution of average node betweenness across the 30 networks, and
- network failure modes.

They also identified two sets of potential network failures: random failures and malicious attacks. Random failures include:

- random failure of links and
- random failure of nodes,

while malicious attacks include:

- highest betweenness link-based attacks,
- largest degree node-based attacks,
- highest unit degree betweenness node based attacks, and
- highest betweenness node-based attacks.

These six failure modes were used in simulations of network failure for each of the 30 metro systems. System performance was assessed using the critical threshold f_c, $0 \leq f_c \leq 1$, the fraction of removed nodes (or links) leading to network breakdown (i.e., when there is no longer any connected subnetwork in the system). For fraction $f < f_c$ some network operation is still possible, but for $f \geq f_c$ the network is shut down[4]. The researchers concluded that highest betweenness node-based attack was the most effective method to disable a metro network.

[4] Using the definitions provided by Wang et al. (2015) and described later in this section, c_S corresponds to a fraction of ½ of the nodes (f_{50}).

Berche, Von Ferber, Holovatch, and Holovatch (2009) performed a similar study on 14 metro systems. They adopted the criterion of the characteristic concentration (c_S) of removed nodes, being the concentration at which the largest operational subnetwork in the full network has half the number of nodes of the original, full network. If the size (number of nodes) of a network/subnetwork is $N(c_S)$ where c_S is the number of nodes removed, then

$$N(c_S) = \frac{1}{2}N(0) \tag{6.7}$$

On the basis of this criterion Berche et al. found that some networks were especially vulnerable to attack while others were strongly resistant. Behaviors under attack ranged from smooth decay of performance to abrupt change.

Ouyang, Zhao, Liu Hong, and Pan (2014) considered failure in railway networks in terms of the average proportion of stations accessible from each station. If N_S is the number of stations available normally then passengers from any one origin station can reach $(N_S - 1)$ destination stations. If n_σ^i is the number of stations that can be reached from the ith station immediately after a service disruption σ, then Ouyang et al. defined the average accessibility A_σ of the network as

$$A_\sigma = \frac{1}{N_S(N_S - 1)} \sum_i n_\sigma^i \tag{6.8}$$

The topological vulnerability of the railway network was thus given by

$$V_{T\sigma} = 1 - A_\sigma = 1 - \frac{1}{N_S(N_S - 1)} \sum_i n_\sigma^i \tag{6.9}$$

given that the accessibility index for the intact network is unity.

Deng et al. (2015) used the network efficiency indicator (see Equation 3.4) as their measure of network performance. For a given network $G = (V, A)$ with N nodes under scenario σ, where $\sigma = 0$ is the intact network and $L_{ij}(\sigma)$ is the shortest path length from node i to node j, the network efficiency is

$$\eta(G, \sigma) = \frac{1}{N(N - 1)} \sum_{ij, j \neq i} \frac{1}{L_{ij}(\sigma)} \tag{6.10}$$

The vulnerability metric for the network is then

$$V(G, \sigma) = 1 - \frac{\eta(G, \sigma)}{\eta(G, 0)} \tag{6.11}$$

This is a familiar result but there is more at play. First, as indicated above, Deng et al. (2015) did not restrict their analysis to the physical form of the network alone. Rather, they formed alternative network representations of the metro system for different functional components in it. The study dealt in detail with the signaling system, but they actually identified 31 different functional modules. Second, they proposed a method for the assessment of the criticality of different failure modes, so that the criticality $C_m(k)$ of the kth failure mode and the degree of risk associated with that failure mode, could be estimated using

$$C_m(k) = \alpha_j \beta_j \lambda_p t \tag{6.12}$$

where $\alpha_k =$ the ratio of the frequency of occurrence of the kth failure mode to that of all possible failure modes; $\beta_k =$ the failure effect probability, i.e., the conditional probability that the system endures some criticality due to the kth failure mode (a value likely to be estimated on the basis of expert knowledge); and $\lambda_p =$ the failure rate of the component, being the probability that it will fail during its working design lifetime t.

Application of this approach to the Nanjing metro indicated that the train component was the most vulnerable functional component to failure of the signaling system.

In their study of vulnerability of the Shanghai metro system Sun, Zhao, and Lu (2015) also used network efficiency as their measure of vulnerability. They considered the physical layout of the metro system, but focused on the vulnerability of the stations in it. They also made allowance for passenger flows, therefore enabling an analysis to consider those stations catering to the largest numbers of passengers as well as all other stations as of equal importance. Station efficiency $\eta_S(i)$ for station i was defined as

$$\eta_S(i) = \eta(G, 0) - \eta(G, i) \tag{6.13}$$

where $\eta(G, 0)$ is the efficiency of the full network (with all stations operational) and $\eta(G, i)$ is the network efficiency when station i is removed.

For the Shanghai system, they concluded that:

1. The efficiency of the intact network was quite poor to begin with.
2. Random attacks caused minimal losses in network efficiency—a loss of 10% of the network nodes decreased network efficiency by some 38%.
3. Malicious attacks could cause much larger losses in efficiency. For instance, removing the top 10% of nodes based on largest node degree or highest node betweenness reduced network efficiency by 90%.

4. In terms of station efficiency, removal of either of the top two efficient stations would decrease the overall network efficiency by 11%.

Sun and Guan (2016) used betweenness centrality as their measure of network performance. They introduced a modified version of this centrality, called "passenger betweenness centrality," to include the impact on passenger flows and travel demands in the system. Their model is described in more detail later in this chapter, in Section 6.4.

Wang, Koc, Derrible, Ahmad, and Kooij (2015) employed the robustness indicator r^T (Derrible & Kennedy, 2010b) along with the "effective network conductance" (C_G) as overall indicators of network vulnerability, and correlated these indicators with the "critical thresholds" f_c and f_{90}. Critical thresholds indicate the fraction of nodes that have to be removed from a network so that the size of the largest connected subnetwork equals a nominated fraction of the original size of the network. The threshold f_{90} is the first point at which the size of the largest connected subnetwork is less than 90% of the original network size. Threshold f_c is the first point at which the network completely disintegrates, i.e., the size of the largest connected subnetwork is one (node)[5]. The Derrible–Kennedy robustness index in its first form is

$$r_T = \frac{\rho - N_L^m}{N_S} \tag{6.14}$$

in which N_S is the total number of stations (not restricted to transfer and terminal stations); N_L^m is the number of multiple links between two nodes (i.e., overlapping lines) in the network; and ρ is the cyclomatic number representing the total number of alternative paths in the network. Given L as the number of links, N as the number of nodes and P as the number of subnetworks,

$$\rho = L - N + P \tag{6.15}$$

In their normal state all transit networks are connected, i.e., $P = 1$. N_S as the denominator of Equation (6.14) represents the likelihood of failure; it implies that the larger the system, the more stations have to be maintained and therefore the more likely that a station failure will occur.

[5] Using the notation of Wang et al. (2015) the characteristic concentration (c_S) used by Berche et al. (2009) would be described as f_{50}, the first point at which the network's largest subnetwork contained 50% of the total number of nodes.

Wang et al. (2015) employed a simplified version of the robustness index in their study. This study used only the number of transfer and terminal nodes (N) and ignored the existence of multiple lines connecting any two stations—even when two stations were directly connected by two or more lines, it was assumed that these only represent one link. Equation (6.14) was thus rewritten as

$$r_T = \frac{L - N + 1}{N} \tag{6.16}$$

Note that the robustness index is a theoretical metric for the metro system. A second theoretical metric is C_G, the network conductance, which is determined by an analogy with an electrical circuit network in which R_{ij} is the effective resistance between nodes i and j. The effective network resistance R_G is found by considering R_{ij} over all node pairs and is given by

$$R_G = N \sum_{k=1}^{N-1} \frac{1}{\mu_k} \tag{6.17}$$

where μ_k is the kth nonzero eigenvalue of the Laplacian matrix $\mathbf{Q}$, which is an $N \times N$ matrix defined as $\mathbf{Q} = \mathbf{Z} - \boldsymbol{\Delta}$ with $\boldsymbol{\Delta}$ being the incidence matrix of the network (see Section 3.4 and Appendix A) and $\mathbf{Z}$ is an $N \times N$ diagonal matrix with elements $z_{ii} = d_i$ where d_i is the degree of node i. Then

$$C_G = \frac{N - 1}{R_G} \tag{6.18}$$

Critical thresholds were determined by simulation, involving (1) random removal of nodes and (2) degree-based removal of nodes. On the basis of this analysis, Wang et al. (2015) concluded that:

- r_T and C_G reflect different aspects of the robustness of metro networks, with r_T focusing on the number of alternative paths (thus favoring large networks) and C_G focusing on the lengths of minimum paths (favoring small networks),
- the robustness metric r_T was correlated with critical threshold f_c, and
- the conductance metric C_G was correlated with critical threshold f_{90}.

Although these results were not definitive and suggested that further investigation was needed to explore network robustness in a holistic fashion.

While the topological vulnerability analysis is useful for examining the structural properties and identifying potential weaknesses and critical locations in networks, as pointed out by Ouyang et al. (2014) and Sun et al. (2015) among others, there is a need to consider passenger flows and travel demand in full vulnerability analysis of transit networks. The remainder of this chapter thus discusses methods involving flows and travel demand.

6.3 SERVICEABILITY METHODS

Following the system for appraisal of road network vulnerability, it is possible to identify serviceability-type models and demand/accessibility-type models for analysis of public transport networks. This section considers methods and models that can fit under the serviceability category, and which consider (passenger and freight) flows on the network and generalized travel costs, i.e., that consider functional vulnerability by considering the susceptibility to incidents that result in reductions in system functionality, through network disruption and full or partial service suspension, increased delays and congestion, or reduced access for passengers due to station or platform closures. The methods described in this section are, as for the topological methods, largely intended for use in railway systems, but they can also be used in multimodal urban public transport systems. Such systems may include railway services including the modes metro, suburban and long-distance rail (these two sometimes operating on the same tracks), light rail transit and streetcars, bus rapid transit, and general bus systems. Streetcars and general buses operate on the road network and are therefore subject to road-based traffic congestion. What this means is that public transport systems may have much greater complexity than road networks even if their network structures seem simpler. Multimodal service operations and passenger movements may include transfers between lines and services, the use of transport hubs, and walking links associated with transfers. In general the connectivity of public transport networks is lower than that of (urban) road networks and transit networks are less dense, with fewer alternative paths between any two nodes. Further, the vehicular flows on public transport networks can be described as "lumpy" or granular, the number of vehicle flow units being restricted, and with service levels varying in discrete packets due to diurnal, weekly, and seasonal timetables. This may imply that public transport networks could be more vulnerable than road networks because a few critical links or nodes may dictate the operating state of the network at any time.

Ouyang et al. (2014) provided a simple approach to the inclusion of passenger flows into station-based vulnerability analysis by suggesting a flow-based equivalent of their station accessibility model (see Equations 6.8 and 6.9). Instead of the fraction of reachable stations after a disruption, this metric was for the fraction of available operating trains. If N_T is the number of trains running during a normal day and X_σ^i, $i = 1, 2, \ldots N_T$, is the status of the ith train after service disruption σ, where $X_\sigma^i = 1$ if that train can still operate or zero if it cannot, then the train flow performance metric is

$$F_\sigma = \frac{1}{N_T} \sum_i X_\sigma^i$$

and the train-based vulnerability index for the event is

$$V_\sigma^F = 1 - F_\sigma \qquad (6.19)$$

which is the proportion of trains that are unavailable. Ouyang et al. (2014) then indicated that if the trains are segregated by type then the train-based vulnerability could be calculated for each train type.

Sun et al. (2015) suggested a station vulnerability index based on consideration of passenger flows as an extension of their station vulnerability index defined by Equation (6.13).

A more ambitious approach was suggested by Cats and Jenelius (2014), which they subsequently refined and extended in a series of further papers (e.g., Cats & Jenelius, 2016; Cats, Yap & Van Oort, 2016; Jenelius & Cats, 2015). This approach takes a dynamic and stochastic view of the operation of urban public transport systems and needs to be underpinned by a detailed model of system and service supply that accounts for the granular nature of public transport services. While such models are not widely known or available, they are used in some cities. A few authors have made use of these models, including the "BusMezzo" model for Stockholm (Cats & Jenelius, 2014) and the "OmniTRANS Zenith" model for the Randstad Zuidvleugel region in The Netherlands (covering the area from The Hague to Rotterdam, see Cats et al., 2016). These models incorporate dynamic supply so that the travel costs associated with alternative paths to destinations are time-dependent, and thus the path choices of passengers can vary over time. This dynamic influence is essential because it enables the inclusion of the accumulated effects of a service disruption. A disruption of a network element means that the public transport vehicles can neither enter nor exit that element, which can mean a spill-back effect for upstream services and a removal of downstream services possibly persisting for some time after the disruption is removed. The impact of a service disruption may depend on two factors: (1) the local crowding levels at stations in the vicinity of the disruption, and (2) traveler reactions to the change in service supply. Passengers do not all have perfect knowledge of the system they are attempting to use, and so path choice needs to be assessed on a probabilistic basis in which the selection of alternative paths will depend on passenger characteristics and preferences. The provision of real-time information on system operations is one way system managers may assist in this process.

To provide the necessary information for the dynamic vulnerability analysis, the public transport systems model needs to represent the interactions between traffic dynamics, public transport operations, and traveler decisions in a multimodal transportation system. Uncertainties in operations may result from traffic conditions, vehicle capacity, dwell times, vehicle schedules, and fluctuations in demand, and therefore these features need to be included in the model. In addition, service disruptions at different locations in the network will need to be simulated. Dynamic path choices by travelers arise from successive decisions based on anticipated or assumed conditions downstream, and factors such as timetables, transfers, and walking distances are required for the estimation of passenger loads under different conditions.

Cats and Jenelius (2014) defined the public transport network as a *directed* graph $G(S, A)$ in which the node set S represents stops and stations (hereafter referred to as stops, for simplicity) and the link set A represents the direct connections between stops. There are N_S stops and N_A links in the network. Each link $a \in A$ can be used by one or more public transport lines, with line l defined by the sequence of stops $l = (s_{l,1}, s_{l,2}, \ldots, s_{l,n})$ where $o_l = s_{l,1}$ is the origin terminal of the line and $d_l = s_{l,n}$ is the destination terminal. The set of all origin–destination terminals is denoted as $S_T \subseteq S$, the set of lines between origin terminal $o \in S_T$ and destination terminal $d \in S_T$ is identified as L_{od} and the set of all lines is L (there are N_L lines). Link a is in line l ($a \in l$), if there is a link $a = (s_{l,i}, s_{l,i+1})$ for some i. Each link has a riding time, which is the time taken between the departure from the upstream stop and the arrival at the downstream stop. $RT_{sl}(t)$ is the riding time from stop s to the next stop on line l at time of day t, and is a stochastic variable. Likewise, each stop has a dwell time $DT_{sl}(t)$ (for stop s on line l at time t), which is also stochastic. Each line l operates with a set of vehicle trips according to a schedule, which may be based on a timetable or perhaps on the basis of a minimum allowable headway (as in a metro system). The departure time of vehicle trip k on line l from the origin terminal is a function of the scheduled departure time and the arrival time of the previous trip, which can again be regarded as a stochastic variable. $K_l(t, \Delta t)$ is the set of vehicle trips traversing some part of line l during a time interval $(t, t + \Delta t)$. This is also a stochastic variable. The variables introduced in this paragraph represent the supply side of the public transport system and define its operating state at any point in time. They represent the system from the perspective of the system managers.

The perspective of the passengers is found by considering the travel demand to use the network. Demand is connected to the network through a subset of origin–destination nodes, $S_{hd} \subseteq S$. There are $N_{hd}(t, \Delta t)$ people traveling from origin h to destination d in the time interval $(t, t+\Delta t)$, with a total of $N(t, t+\Delta t)$ travelers over all origin–destination pairs. In the Cats–Jenelius model, passenger departure rates are assumed to be inelastic, i.e., not affected by changes in travel times or other system factors. However, the number of travelers in a time interval can be stochastic due to day-to-day variations. The route taken by a traveler is defined by a sequence of stops from the origin to the destination, i.e., $j = (s_{j,1}, s_{j,2}, \ldots, s_{j,m})$ where $h_j = s_{j,1}$ is the origin stop and $d_j = s_{j,m}$ is the destination stop. The set of all available routes between origin h and destination d is J_{hd}. The specific route chosen by a given traveler at a specific time of day on a given day depends on the properties of the different transit lines and the operating conditions on that day, according to the traveler's preferences. In a dynamic, stochastic environment the probability that individual n uses route j is $p_n(j)$. A suitable route choice model is needed to estimate this probability.

Cats and Jenelius (2014) sought a suitable vulnerability metric for an urban transit system. They began by considering betweenness centrality at the link level. For link a, this was taken as the fraction of shortest paths (with path length measured in terms of the number of stops encountered along the path) between all origin–destination pairs that included the link, including the inclusion of multiple shortest paths between origin–destination pairs. If the fraction of shortest paths from s_1 to s_2 that use a is $f_{s_1,s_2}(a)$ then the conventional link betweenness centrality of link a is

$$C^B(a) = \frac{1}{N_S(N_S - 1)} \sum_{s_1 \in S} \sum_{s_2 \in S/s_1} f_{s_1,s_2}(a) \tag{6.20}$$

For a dynamic, stochastic network with varying travel demands, this index may not be adequate for use in identifying critical links, for it assumes that:

1. all node pairs are equally important for the centrality of the link, and
2. the only relevant paths between a pair of links are the shortest paths, which thus ignores probabilistic path choice.

Consequently, Cats and Jenelius (2014) developed two alternative formulations of the betweenness index, one for system operators and another for passengers, based on the following system characteristics:

- dynamic environment, in which demand and supply may vary over time,
- probabilistic route choices, where not all travelers choose the same route between two nodes, and
- stochastic system, with inherent variability in demand and supply between hours of the day and days of the week.

For the system operator, a network link is central if a large number of lines and vehicle trips use it. Thus it is appropriate to weight each pair of stops by the number of lines and to weight each line by the number of vehicle trips between the stops. This latter condition introduces the dynamic element and requires consideration of the betweenness centrality over a time period (t, $t+\Delta t$). Further, the stochastic riding, dwell and departure times for the vehicles imply that the number of vehicles $|K_{la}(t,\Delta t)|$ on line l entering link a in the time interval is also stochastic, as is the total number of vehicles on the line, $|K_l(t,\Delta t)|$. Thus the *expected* numbers of vehicles are required. The operator's betweenness centrality $C_O^B(a|t,\Delta t)$ can then be shown to be (Cats & Jenelius, 2014)

$$C_O^B(a|t,\Delta t) = \frac{\sum_{l\in L} E\left[|K_{la}(t,\Delta t)|\right]}{\sum_{l\in L} E\left[|K_l(t,\Delta t)|\right]} \tag{6.21}$$

This metric is actually the expected number of vehicle trips entering link a during the time interval divided by the expected total number of vehicle trips in the system in that time period.

From a passengers' perspective, a link is central if large numbers of passengers use it. Thus it is useful to weight each pair of stops, i.e., the link, by the number of passengers traveling between those stops. To avoid double counting for the same traveler passing several stops along the route, only the origin and destination of each traveler should be used in setting the weights. Given that demand levels and line schedules can vary over time, the passenger betweenness centrality metric is again dynamic, and the numbers of travelers in the system in a time interval is stochastic (therefore expected values are again required). If $N_{hd}(t, \Delta t)$ is the total number of travelers between h and d in a time interval and $N_{hda}(t, \Delta t)$ is the number using link a then the passenger betweenness centrality of the link is

$$C_P^B(a|t,\Delta t) = \frac{\sum_{h\in S_{OD}} \sum_{d\in S_{OD}} E[N_{hda}(t,\Delta t)]}{\sum_{h\in S_{OD}} \sum_{d\in S_{OD}} E[N_{hd}(t,\Delta t)]} \tag{6.22}$$

Equation (6.22) thus defines the passenger betweenness centrality of a link as the ratio of the expected number of passengers entering the link in a time interval to the expected total number of passengers in the system in the same time period.

Considerations of vulnerability in the dynamic system require measures of the impact of a disruption, again from the perspectives of the operator and the passenger. For an operator, the total operating cost of the system $OC(\sigma|t, \Delta t)$ under a scenario σ in time interval $(t, t+\Delta t)$ is of concern, and can be assumed to be the sum of the operating cost of each vehicle trip during the interval (with $OC_k(\sigma)$ being the operating cost of individual vehicle trip k under scenario σ). These costs are stochastic and thus need to be represented by expected values, so that the expected total operating cost under scenario σ is

$$OC(\sigma|t, \Delta t) = E\left[\sum_{l\in L} \sum_{k\in K_l(t,\Delta t)} OC_k(\sigma)\right] \tag{6.23}$$

The impact of a disruption scenario σ for the operator is then

$$\Delta OC(\sigma) = OC(\sigma) - OC(\sigma_0) \tag{6.24}$$

where σ_0 represents a baseline (normal conditions) scenario occurring for the same incident and recovery time duration—noting that the time interval to be considered includes the time over which the disruption took place plus the time required for the system to return to its normal operating state.

For passengers, the impacts can be expressed in terms of welfare, which is taken to be the total utility of the passengers expressed in units of money. Four factors would be included in this utility: in-vehicle time, waiting time, walking time, and number of transfers made. If $W_n(\sigma)$ is the welfare of passenger n in scenario σ then the total welfare during time interval $(t, t+\Delta t)$ under the scenario is

$$W(\sigma|t, \Delta t) = E\left[\sum_{h\in S_{hd}} \sum_{d\in S_{hd}} \sum_{n\in N_{hd}(t,\Delta t)} W_n(\sigma)\right] \tag{6.25}$$

therefore the change in welfare over the total time of the disruption and recovery is

$$\Delta W(\sigma) = W(\sigma) - W(\sigma_0) \tag{6.26}$$

Cats and Jenelius (2014) applied this model of vulnerability assessment to the morning peak for the Stockholm inner city public transport system, which comprises seven metro lines, four trunk bus routes, and a light rail transit line. The effect of the provision of real-time travel information was also included in the analysis. The researchers found that link centrality, as measured by the conventional metric, did not necessarily imply link importance as measured by the total impact on welfare. Link importance also depended on the level of information provided to passengers and indeed the value of information provision varied for different disruption scenarios. Further, the availability of real-time information could, sometimes, worsen the impact of a disruption, implying that specific tailoring was needed on the nature and extent of information provision to meet specific circumstances and for particular locations.

The researchers saw the main benefit of their approach as being the provision of an analytical tool that system operators could use to determine management plans to handle different disruption scenarios. In addition, urban planners could use the tool in determining investment decisions in new infrastructure and technological improvements, including the design of transfer facilities. Their major conclusion was the necessity of adopting the dynamic, stochastic analysis framework described in their study on vulnerability analysis of complex urban public transport systems.

In more recent works, Cats and Jenelius (2016) broadened the scope of their model to account for partial capacity reductions in addition to the service shutdowns and link closures implied as the disruptions in their earlier work. This was done using the concept of the vulnerability curve, which enables an analyst to consider a set of disruptions of different scales and assess both individual impacts and the accumulated impacts of a set of minor disruptions. Figure 6.3 illustrates the concept of the vulnerability curve of deterioration in system performance. It shows the possible relationships between a relative capacity reduction[6] ($0 \leq \Delta x \leq 1$) in a system and the level of reduced performance (deterioration $\Delta w(\Delta x, \sigma)$) of the system under a scenario σ. Curve (a) in the figure is a straight line, implying that there is a uniform deterioration in performance with the decrease in system capacity. Curve (b) represents the case where small reductions in capacity have small impacts on performance, but as the level of capacity reduction grows, the

[6] A relative congestion reduction of $\Delta x = 1$ means that the system component has completely failed. A value $\Delta x = 0.5$ means that it is only operating at 50% of its full capacity.

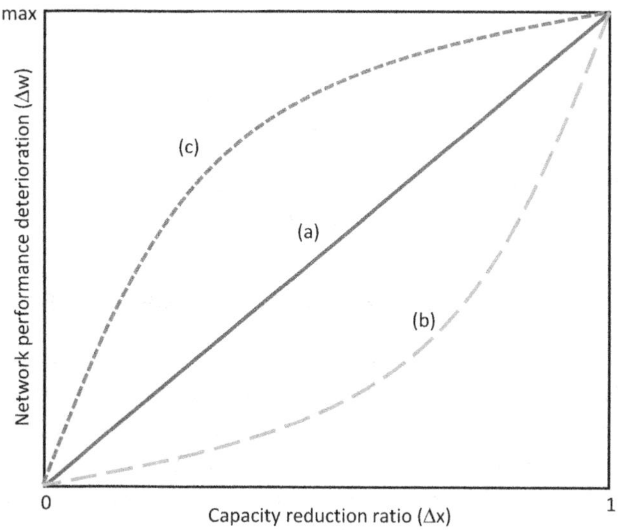

Figure 6.3 Illustrative alternative forms of the vulnerability curve, relating relative capacity reduction (Δx) to the deterioration in system performance (Δw): curve (a) is for uniform deterioration in performance with the decrease in system capacity; curve (b) indicates small reductions in capacity having small impacts on performance; curve (c) indicates an initial small reduction in capacity having an immediate large impact on performance.

system deteriorates more rapidly. Curve (c) represents the case where an initial small reduction in capacity has an immediate large impact on performance, with a less-pronounced impact of increasing capacity reduction.

The vulnerability curve can then be used in assessment of network vulnerability, by considering the accumulated impacts of capacity reductions using the integral of the curve with respect to capacity reduction:

$$D(\sigma) = \int_0^1 \Delta w(x, \sigma) dx \tag{6.27}$$

so that the normalized vulnerability of the system under partial failure when compared to complete failure is

$$V(\sigma) = 1 - \frac{D(\sigma)}{\Delta w(1, \sigma)} \tag{6.28}$$

In addition, while $V(\sigma)$ provides a measure of overall vulnerability of the system, the sensitivity of the system performance to small changes in the capacity of a system (network) element σ can be expressed as a marginal vulnerability, i.e.,

$$v_\sigma(x) = \frac{\partial}{\partial x}(\Delta w(x, \sigma)) \tag{6.29}$$

Marginal vulnerability can then be used to assess the likely effects of alternative capacity reductions of different network components.

6.4 DEMAND AND ACCESSIBILITY METHODS

Chapter 5 dealt with the use of accessibility metrics in the vulnerability analysis of road networks, where those metrics could be used to indicate impacts of network disruption not just on network performance but also on broader socioeconomic systems dependent on the transportation system. The literature review of vulnerability analysis did not find similar studies for public transport networks, although some avenues for future research on the topic are available.

The previous section of this chapter discussed the valuable, if not essential, role of passenger-flow data in studies of the operational vulnerability of urban public transport, building on and going beyond the structural vulnerability analysis using topological methods. While accessibility studies for public transport vulnerability are not yet apparent, there are several studies that have made use of travel demand data (origin–destination trip movements and line and link passenger flows) in that assessment. While these studies may not have the full dynamic capabilities of the Cats–Jenelius approach described in Section 6.3, they offer methods that can be applied in the common circumstances where a detailed, dynamic model of the public transport system does not exist.

As a starting point, Sun and Guan (2016) used modified betweenness, path length and efficiency indices in their study of the Shanghai metro. These indices used the origin–destination matrix of passenger flows, where H_{hd} is the number of passenger trips from origin station h to destination station d, and require knowledge of:

- the number of shortest paths from h to d, n_{hd};
- the number of shortest paths from h to d passing through a candidate node i, n^i_{hd};
- the length (distance) of the shortest path between h and d, L_{hd}, noting that for each required transfer between lines a fixed penalty distance was included in the path length calculation; and

- the number of passengers from h to d passing through node i, F^i_{hd}.

In addition, they defined B^l to be the set of stations on transit line l and m_l to be the number of stations on that line.

The first of the Sun–Guan indices is the "passenger betweenness centrality" (PC^B). For station i, this index is defined as

$$PC_i^B = \frac{\sum_{hd,d\neq h} F^i_{hd}}{\sum_{hd,d\neq h} H_{hd}} \tag{6.30}$$

This index is the ratio of the number of passengers passing through station i to the total number of passengers using the system, including those passengers who start or finish their trips at the station. The average passenger betweenness centrality for line l is then

$$\overline{P}\,\overline{C}_l^B = \frac{1}{m_l}\sum_{i\in B^l} PC_i^B$$

A line with higher $\overline{P}\,\overline{C}^B$ indicates that this line and its stations are used more frequently than others, suggesting that it is an important component of the network.

Sun and Guan then considered the average (minimum) path length, weighted by passenger numbers (APL_F):

$$APL_F = \frac{1}{\sum_{hd,d\neq h} H_{hd}} \sum_{hd} L_{hd}H_{hd} \tag{6.31}$$

Given that all passengers might not be able to complete their journeys under any network disruption, they assumed that the path length for those passengers should be assumed to be

$$L^* = \max_{hd}\{L_{hd}\} \tag{6.32}$$

i.e., the maximum shortest path length in the full, intact network. Then they proposed a weighted global efficiency ($\eta_f(G)$), as

$$\eta_F(G) = \frac{1}{\sum_{hd,d\neq h} H_{hd}} \sum_{hd,d\neq h} \frac{H_{hd}}{L_{hd}} \tag{6.33}$$

Determination of a station-based origin–destination matrix is now straightforward for a metro system with automatic fare collection using swipe cards to gain both access to and egress from stations, so that the matrix

$\{H_{hd}\}$ can be assumed to be readily available, and can be monitored over time. Sun and Guan gave no information on how to obtain F^i_{hd}, and presumably this data would need to be determined using an assignment model as indicated by Cats and Jenelius (2014). Similar assignment modeling was described by Rodríguez-Nunez and Garcia-Palomares (2014) and Cai et al. (2016). In the former case an "all shortest paths" assignment was used, and in the latter a probabilistic ("stochastic user equilibrium") assignment based on Dial's logit-based assignment model (Dial, 1971)[7], noting that all shortest paths assignment can be taken as a special case of logit-based assignment and can be performed using a sufficiently large value of Dial's diversion factor (Taylor, 1979). Rodríguez-Nunez and Garcia-Palomares (2014) based their vulnerability exposure metric on overall average travel times (weighted by passenger flows) in the network under different disruption scenarios, and identified critical links by those whose failure led to the largest changes in average travel time. Cai et al. (2016) used a version of network efficiency with minimum generalized travel time as the cost variable, and reassigned travel demand to the network for each disruption scenario, to simulate the different levels of congestion expected in each scenario.

Rodríguez-Nunez and Garcia-Palomares (2014) selected a limited number of scenarios for network disruption: (1) removing the most critical link, (2) removing the most critical sequence of five links, and (3) removal of five random links, using the Madrid network as their case study. Their impact measure was the change in system average travel time resulting from each scenario, which is basically a change in passenger-hours of travel, akin to vehicle-hours of travel, see Table 4.1, but calculated by considering all travelers. Vulnerability was assessed at the station level. A redistribution of trips was undertaken (i.e., new destinations were found for the trip movements) in each of the failure scenarios. The researchers concluded that different impacts were experienced under the failure scenarios, indicating that link location in the network and the numbers of trips usually using the link were also important. They also flagged the need to consider population characteristics in future analyses, on the basis that failures in lower socioeconomic areas of the city could have more profound effects if the residents were more dependent on the transit system. This is perhaps one indication of the potential utility of an accessibility-based method for transit network vulnerability

[7] See Section 2.4.1 and Equation (2.5) in particular for more details.

analysis. In addition, Rodríguez-Nunez and Garcia-Palomares also concluded that there was a need to consider time of day effects on vulnerability, following the approach of Cats and Jenelius (2014).

Cai et al. (2016) used a modified network efficiency index in which a generalized travel time (a sum of riding time, waiting times, and weighted transfer times) was used instead of the minimum path distance between origin–destination pairs. As waiting times were functions of travel demand, and hence included the effects of waiting passenger demands potentially exceeding train capacity, this model was sensitive to congestion levels in the network and thus to time of day impacts. A weight was put on transfer times because it was known that travelers attempted to minimize their needs for transfers.[8] Their analysis focused on disruptions to services at transfer stations in the Beijing metro, and by considering a wide range of failure scenarios they were able to construct vulnerability curves (of the form of curve (b) in Figure 6.3) for that system.

D'Lima and Medda (2015) used passenger-flow data in a different way. They were more concerned with dynamic resilience of a metro system, using the London Underground as their case study. Dynamic resilience concerns the time required for a system to recover, i.e., regain its normal (time-dependent) operating state after the shock of a service disruption, thus employing the resilience triangle discussed in Section 2.5. On the basis of a time series analysis of passenger flows, they were able to use the temporal pattern of passenger flows on a line and in the system at large to establish when recovery was complete.

As indicated in the start of this section, no published study on transit network vulnerability using an accessibility indicator was available. This is an area for future investigation, and some suitable accessibility indicators are available. One is the Primerano–Taylor accessibility framework described in Section 5.4, which is designed for use in a multimodal urban transportation system. More recently Farber and Fu (2017) have proposed an urban accessibility index based on the number of jobs accessible using public transport within a nominated travel time isochrone from an origin, with a 1 hour isochrones used in their case study application to Salt Lake City. The authors clearly infer that this accessibility metric could be used for urban area vulnerability analysis, but this has not yet been undertaken.

[8] Cai et al. (2016) estimated a weighting factor of 1.86 for transfer times in the Beijing metro, which is not so different to the "rule of thumb" value of 2.

The transit travel-time model proposed by Farber and Fu is dynamic and appears to provide a good representation of the actual travel times experienced by passengers. The door is thus open to a wider study of transit network vulnerability.

6.5 SUMMARY

This chapter described the methods now being employed for vulnerability analysis of public transport networks. The main focus of this work is on railway networks, particularly on urban metro systems. Metro systems are often iconic representations of the city to which they belong—the New York Subway, the Paris Metro, the London Underground, the Singapore MRT, to name a few—and the construction of a metro system is an indication of the economic and political power of a city.

Typological-based methods are widely applied, using the standard metrics of node degree, characteristic path length, centrality, and network efficiency, but the most advanced studies have gone further in defining new versions of these metrics that include variables such as passenger flows, origin–destination travel patterns, and generalized travel times. Perhaps the most advanced method is the serviceability method based on link centrality developed by Cats and Jenelius (2014) and their colleagues. This method is applicable to multimodal transit systems and is dynamic, able to handle time of day and day of week variations, the stochastic nature of transit line operations, and travel demand. Changes in passenger welfare as an impact of service disruption provide a vulnerability criterion for assessment of importance, exposure, and criticality using this method.

There is no reported application of an accessibility-based transit network vulnerability analysis, but the development of new accessibility indices expressly for urban transit systems can be seen as a precursor to such studies in the near future.

REFERENCES

Barabasi, A., & Albert, R. (1999). Emergence of scaling in random networks. *Science, 286*, 509–512.

Bentler, C., Baumgarten, C., Brauner, F., Kornmayer, T., Lotter, A., Mudimu, O. A., et al. (2014). An integrated risk and crisis management approach for terrorist attacks on public transport networks. In , *Proceedings of the 5th international disaster and risk conference: Integrative risk management – the role of science, technology and practice, IDRC Davos5th international disaster and risk conference: Integrative risk management – the role of science, technology and practice, IDRC Davos 2014. Davos, Switzerland; 24–28 August 2014; Code 110967* (pp. 89–92).

Berche, B., Von Ferber, C., Holovatch, T., & Holovatch, Y. (2009). Resilience of public transport networks against attacks. *European Physical Journal B, 71*(1), 125–137.

Cai, H., Zhu, J., Yang, C., Fan, W., & Xu, T. (2016). Vulnerability analysis of metro network incorporating flow impact and capacity constraint after a disaster. *Journal of Urban Planning and Development*. http://dx.doi.org/10.1061/(ASCE)UP.1943-5444.0000368.

Cats, O., & Jenelius, E. (2014). Dynamic vulnerability analysis of public transport networks: Mitigation effects of real-time information. *Networks and Spatial Economics, 14*(3), 435–463.

Cats, O., & Jenelius, E. (2016). Beyond a complete failure: The impact of partial capacity degradation on public transport network vulnerability. *Transportmetrica B: Transport Dynamics*. Retrieved from http://dx.doi.org/10.1080/21680566.2016.1267596.

Cats, O., Yap, M., & Van Oort, N. (2016). Exposing the role of exposure: Public transport network risk analysis. *Transportation Research Part A: Policy and Practice, 88*, 1–14.

Deng, Y., Li, Q., & Lu, Y. (2015). A research on subway physical vulnerability based on network theory and FMECA. *Safety Science, 80*, 127–134.

Derrible, S., & Kennedy, C. (2010a). Characterizing metro networks: State, form and structure. *Transportation, 37*, 275–297.

Derrible, S., & Kennedy, C. (2010b). The complexity and robustness of metro networks. *Physica A, 389*, 3678–3691.

Dial, R. B. (1971). A probabilistic multipath traffic assignment model which obviates path enumeration. *Transportation Research, 5*(2), 83–111.

D'Lima, M., & Medda, F. (2015). A new measure of resilience: An application to the London underground. *Transportation Research Part A: Policy and Practice, 81*, 35–46.

Farber, S., & Fu, L. (2017). Dynamic public transit accessibility using travel time cubes: Comparing the effects of infrastructure (dis)investments over time. *Computers, Environment and Urban Systems, 62*, 30–40.

Jenelius, E., & Cats, O. (2015). The value of new public transport links for network robustness and redundancy. *Transportmetrica A: Transport Science, 11*(9), 819–835.

Mattsson, L.-G., & Jenelius, E. (2015). Vulnerability and resilience of transport systems – a discussion of recent research. *Transportation Research Part A: Policy and Practice, 81*, 16–34.

Ouyang, M., Zhao, L., Liu Hong, L., & Pan, Z. (2014). Comparisons of complex network based models and real train flow model to analyze Chinese railway vulnerability. *Reliability Engineering and System Safety, 123*, 38–46.

Peterson, S. K., & Church, R. L. (2008). A framework for modeling rail transport vulnerability. *Growth and Change, 39*(4), 617–641.

Rodríguez-Nunez, E., & Garcia-Palomares, J. C. (2014). Measuring the vulnerability of public transport networks. *Journal of Transport Geography, 35*, 50–63.

Sienkiewicz, J., & Hołyst, J. A. (2005). Statistical analysis of 22 public transport networks in Poland. *Physical Review E, 72*, 046127.

Sun, D., & Guan, S. (2016). Measuring vulnerability of urban metro network from line operation perspective. *Transportation Research Part A: Policy and Practice, 94*, 348–359.

Sun, D., Zhao, Y., & Lu, Q.-C. (2015). Vulnerability analysis of urban rail transit networks: A case study of Shanghai, China. *Sustainability (Switzerland)*, 7(6), 6919–6936.

Taylor, M. A. P. (1979). Evaluating the performance of a simulation model. *Transportation Research, 13A*(3), 159–173.

Von Ferber, C., Holovatch, T., Holovatch, Y., & Palchykov, V. (2009). Public transport networks: Empirical analysis and modelling. *The European Physical Journal B, 68*, 261–275.

Wang, X., Koc, Y., Derrible, S., Ahmad, S. K. N., & Kooij, R. E. (August 1–2, 2015). Quantifying the robustness of metro networks. *Proceedings 6th International Symposium on transport network Reliability*. Nara, Japan: Kyoto University.

Wang, W., Liu, J., Li, H., & Jiang, X. (2010). The vulnerability assessment method of railway network. In , *Proceedings of the ASME Joint Rail Conference 2010, JRC2010: Vol. 1. ASME 2010 Joint Rail Conference, JRC2010. Urbana, IL, United States; 27–29 April; Code 81896* (pp. 461–465).

Zhang, J., Song, B., Zhang, Z., & Liu, H. (2014). An approach for modelling vulnerability of the network of networks. *Physica A, 412*, 127–136.

Zhang, J., Zhao, M., Liu, H., & Xu, X. (2013). Networked characteristics of the urban rail network. *Physica A, 392*, 1538–1546.

CHAPTER SEVEN

Integrated Framework for Vulnerability Analysis and Application

To this point, this book has identified and explained four alternative methods, risk-based inventory assessment, topological method, serviceability method, and accessibility method, used for vulnerability analysis in transportation networks. Each method has its own requirements and areas of application, yet they all share a number of common features. This chapter provides an integrated framework which can be used to bring the methods together and, indeed, if implemented, to allow different methods to be used together. This would allow a multifaceted approach to vulnerability analysis, enabling the analyst to fully comprehend the potential vulnerabilities in a given network.

7.1 COMMONALITIES AND DIFFERENCES

The common feature of the four methods is that they all use a core description of the network. The basic difference is that they each have different data demands and computational support requirements.

The core network description is that from graph theory; the representation of the network as a graph $G = (N, A)$, where N is a set of nodes and A is a set of links. In general transportation networks are planar networks which are directed and valued, i.e., there may be separate links for flows in opposite directions between a connected pair of nodes (and sometimes there may be only one such link, for flow in only one direction), and each link may have a different impedance (e.g., be of different length, or have different travel time and travel cost). While link distances can be regarded as static, travel time and cost can be dynamic, varying over time, e.g., in response to the demand to use the link and the different levels of congestion that can exist over any time of the day and day of the week. Another important feature, common to the four methods, is that flows in the transportation network occur between specified node pairs. A subset of the nodes in N act as origins and

Vulnerability Analysis for Transportation Networks
ISBN: 978-0-12-811010-2
http://dx.doi.org/10.1016/B978-0-12-811010-2.00007-1

destinations, and the travel demand using the network all moves between the sets of origins and destinations (sinks and sources).

Graph theory provides a set of metrics to describe the connectivity of a network, and the topological method uses these metrics to identify critical nodes and links in terms of their centrality and relative importance, and their potential use for movement through the network. This implies a minimum data requirement, which is summarized by the network incident matrix and a set of link impedance values (e.g., distance or assumed travel time) and is the key feature of this method. Topological analysis can be performed for any network given this basic description, with the identification of a set of origin–destination nodes sufficient to also allow the study of betweenness. Critical nodes and links can be identified on this basis. However, there may be a need to consider travel-demand levels and actual flows in the network in this process. Topological methods are widely used in the study of public transport network vulnerability.

The inventory methods require the assembly of detailed databases of network assets and components, including the locations on the network of features and facilities, such as bridges and tunnels along with the design details and current condition of the assets, of which road pavement (or rail track) is the major asset. Such databases are regularly available through the asset management systems used by modern transportation agencies. The agency is also likely to maintain databases on the traffic usage of the network. Data on climate and environment are also needed, and these data are generally available through other sources. The transportation agency will also seek projections of the future states of the network and its assets in the development of its maintenance, repair, rehabilitation, and replacement programs. Inventory-based vulnerability assessment seeks to identify locations and facilities at risk from specific phenomena, such as floods or landslides, and then to plan for remedial measures to overcome potential problems. The vulnerability-assessment framework developed by Federal Highways Administration (FHWA, 2012) and applied at state and regional levels across the United States is a prime example of the inventory approach, but other methods such as those developed in New Zealand (Scott & Dunn, 2015) and Japan (Pokharel & Ieda, 2016) also exist.

For both the serviceability and accessibility methods another (background) capability is required, a travel-demand model or a traffic performance model. These models enable study of congestion levels in a network in a given state of operation (e.g., intact or degraded, such as by full or partial loss of a link) and the (potential) identification of alternative routes from origin to destination in the event of degradation. These models may be used to estimate travel times (and costs) under different scenarios, which is necessary information for many instances of vulnerability analysis. Suitable models for road networks are well established and commonly used. Models also exist for public transport networks, but while the theory and model formulation are established there are relatively few implementations of these models for real-world urban public transport systems. Cats and Jenelius (2014) and Cats, Yap, and Van Oort (2016) identified and used two such models, as described in Chapter 6.

Both serviceability and accessibility methods also make use of databases on the population and land-use characteristics (land-use type, employment, services, and facilities) of the study region. For serviceability assessment, these data are necessary inputs to the travel-demand model, but may not feature directly in an analysis because this is concerned with the performance of the transportation system per se.[1] In accessibility analysis the population and land-use data are also used explicitly in the computation of the accessibility indices used as performance metrics.

The broad approach to vulnerability analysis requires the definition of a set of scenarios of network condition, including as a base case the full, intact network in a normal operating state, and then a set of different levels or types of network degradation, such as the failure of different links. Choice of the degraded network scenarios is largely a matter of expert judgment, given that it is rarely possible to (say) consider the failure of each and every link in a real-world regional network due to computational limitations. Probability of use (and hence topological betweenness) or actual current traffic load can be used as one approach to scenario selection, as can study of the propensity for natural disaster events such as flooding. However, there is not a single overall approach and expert judgment is perhaps a prerequisite. The choice needs to be wide enough to ensure that critical network components should not be overlooked, yet focused enough to retain computational feasibility. Bil, Vodak, Kubecek, Bilova, and Sedonik (2015) noted that careful definition of the study region network was required to ensure that the proper set of routes were included in the analysis.

[1] The exception to this is where population values for origin—destination nodes may be used as weighting factors in the study of exposure and importance, as for instance in Jenelius, Petersen, and Mattsson (2006) and Bil et al. (2015).

7.2 OVERALL SYSTEM FOR VULNERABILITY ANALYSIS

In designing an overall system for vulnerability analysis, a number of dimensions are to be considered. The first is the planning horizon of interest, i.e., the time period for which the analysis is to be made. Second is a consideration of circumstance. For normal operating conditions a long-term view is appropriate, extending over several years if not decades and concerned with future developments of network infrastructure and the regional population and economic systems that the network supports. However, there are also emergency situations that may have to be dealt with, perhaps in the aftermath of a natural or man-made disaster befalling the network. These situations may require exceptional actions, such as the installation of temporary features (e.g., a bailey bridge as replacement for a failed permanent structure). There is also a need for analysis to assist in the formulation of emergency plans to deal with specific disasters, such as the incidence of wild fires, hurricanes, tsunamis, and earthquakes. Creeping potential disasters such as the long-term impacts of climate change (and perhaps then sea-level rise or increased frequency and intensity of flooding) should also be considered. On this score the US FHWA (2012) framework for inventory-based vulnerability assessment for climate change adaptation can be taken as a prime example of a system for vulnerability analysis.

The FHWA framework was described in Chapter 2 and shown in Figure 2.6. At this stage it is worth revisiting that figure, which is reproduced here as Figure 7.1. The figure places vulnerability analysis in an overall planning and management system with five main components in a closed system:

1. definition of scope and the determination of planning and management objectives,
2. assessment of the vulnerability of transportation-system assets in the face of changes in climate, considering likelihood and risk,
3. inclusion of the assessment results in decision—making,
4. monitoring and revision of asset condition and environmental threats, and
5. revision of objectives, including the setting of new objectives.

As discussed subsequently, the FHWA vulnerability-assessment framework can be used to set an overall integrated framework for vulnerability studies for a wide set of alternative degradation scenarios. This includes a wider range of inventory-based assessments, such as those discussed by Scott and Dunn (2015) as well as the inclusion of the different methods for network vulnerability analysis. The following section describes the proposed framework.

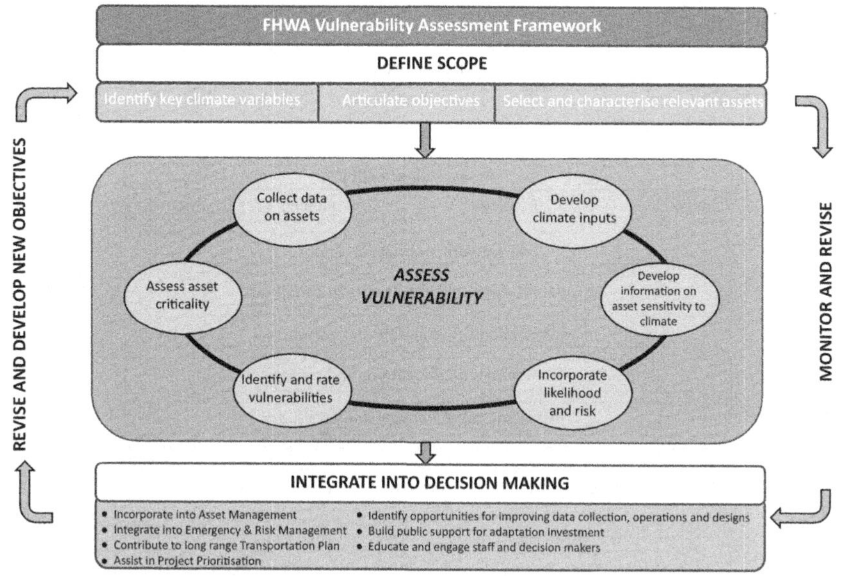

Figure 7.1 The FHWA assessment framework for climate change vulnerability of road assets. *Adapted from FHWA (2012).* The Federal Highway Administration's climate change and extreme weather vulnerability assessment framework. *Washington, DC: Federal Highway Administration, Retrieved from http://www.fhwa.dot.gov/environment/climate_change/adaptation/.*

7.3 AN INTEGRATED FRAMEWORK FOR ANALYSIS

The proposed integrated framework is presented in Figure 7.2. Similar to the FHWA framework, this framework places a multifaceted vulnerability-analysis module within a closed systems planning model.

The key components of the integrated framework are:

1. *definition of scope and* determination of planning and management *objectives*, as in the FHWA framework but with the identification of key factors expanded to include, or allow for, a wider range of influences and with a focus on relevant components of the network;
2. *vulnerability assessment including* the options for *inventory, topology, serviceability and accessibility* approaches to be adopted, separately or jointly, and including the five steps of
   - **a.** assessment of normal operating conditions in the full, intact network,
   - **b.** development of scenarios covering network degradations and abnormal conditions,

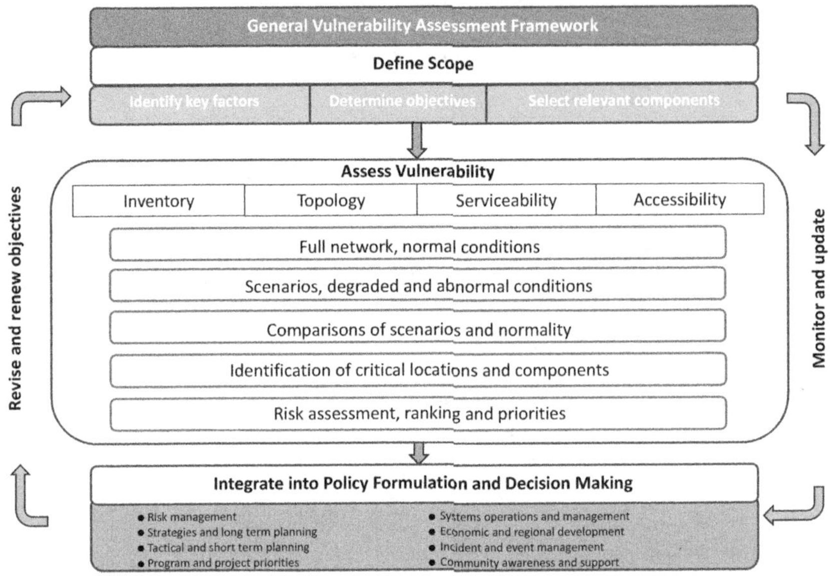

Figure 7.2 A proposed general framework for vulnerability analysis and its incorporation in transportation-systems planning.

   c. comparisons of the scenarios with normal operating conditions, and the computation of vulnerability metrics,
   d. identification of critical locations and components, and
   e. risk assessment of identified features, with ranking and priority determination;
3. *integration* of the vulnerability analysis results *into policy formulation and decision-making* for the network, including initiatives in
   a. risk management,
   b. strategy determination and long-term plans,
   c. tactical and short term planning,
   d. program and project priority determination,
   e. systems operation and management,
   f. wider considerations of economic and regional development,
   g. incident and event management, and
   h. community awareness, opinion and support;
4. *monitoring and update* of network assets, operations, and usage; and
5. *revision and renewal of* planning *objectives* in line with system developments over time.

The consideration of risk and probability (or, perhaps more loosely, likelihood) has to be a key feature in the implementation of the integrated framework. This remains an area requiring significant further research for vulnerability studies, as indicated by Mattsson and Jenelius (2015) and discussed in Chapter 8. Risk, as the product of probability and consequence, provides the measured impact of an event such as one causing network degradation. Chapter 3 argued for the inclusion of risk management as part of the vulnerability-analysis methodology, and presented general risk vulnerability approach (a flowchart in Figure 3.1). Figure 7.3 is a reproduction of the risk-management model from that earlier figure.

The risk-assessment model in Figure 7.3 was designed to be part of the inventory-based vulnerability-assessment method. It focuses, therefore, on network assets and relies on existing data sources including the network-asset management database and supporting databases on economic activity, population and demographics, facility locations, weather and climate, and physical environment. It is also applicable to a more general application by considering the top left-hand box of the flowchart which covers assets and their importance. The importance of individual components of a network is a key output from the other methods for vulnerability assessment, so the system of Figure 7.3 can be applied to assess the level of risk (low, medium, high) associated with each identified component. As a starting point, historical records on some degradation scenarios (e.g., flooding) can be accessed to determine both potential consequence and likelihood of a given event. For other events, generic assessment of likelihood and

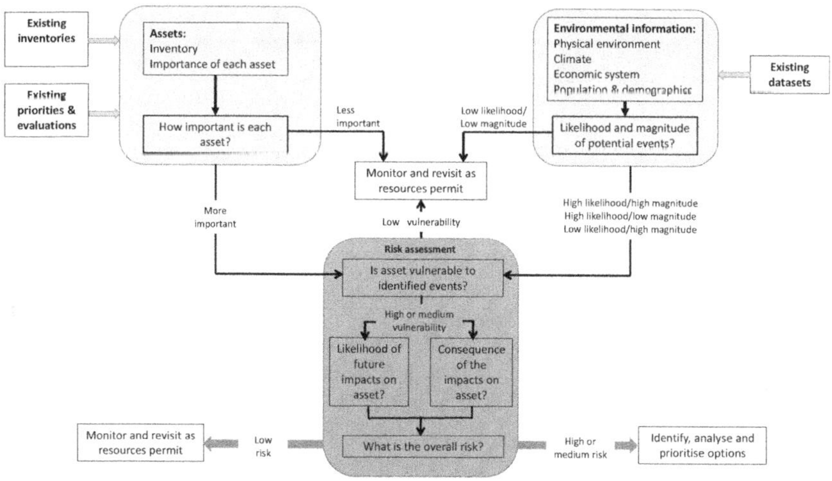

Figure 7.3 General framework of a vulnerability risk-assessment model specifically intended for inventory-based analysis, but applicable to the other assessment approaches as well.

consequence may be required, perhaps utilizing data from other regions where the particular events have been experienced, a process not unknown in other fields such as road-safety engineering.

It is useful to consider a specific implementation of the general framework to each of the four approaches to network vulnerability analysis.

7.3.1 A Framework for Inventory-Based Analysis

Figure 7.4 provides a version of the general framework designed for use in inventory-based analysis. The analysis is based on the assembly of data concerning topography and physical environment along with network configuration and assets, traffic loads, and network operating conditions (including travel conditions and road-safety performance). Degradation scenarios are then developed to study the impacts of different events on the network, followed by an impact assessment that indicates network components at risk in the scenarios. Vulnerability metrics (e.g., increased costs of travel) can then be determined, based on assumptions about changes in travel behavior under different scenarios. This may be informed by the use of transport and traffic models of the network, but this is not essential in this process and expert judgment and community opinion can be used instead. The metrics are then used to determine critical locations, facilities, and components, which

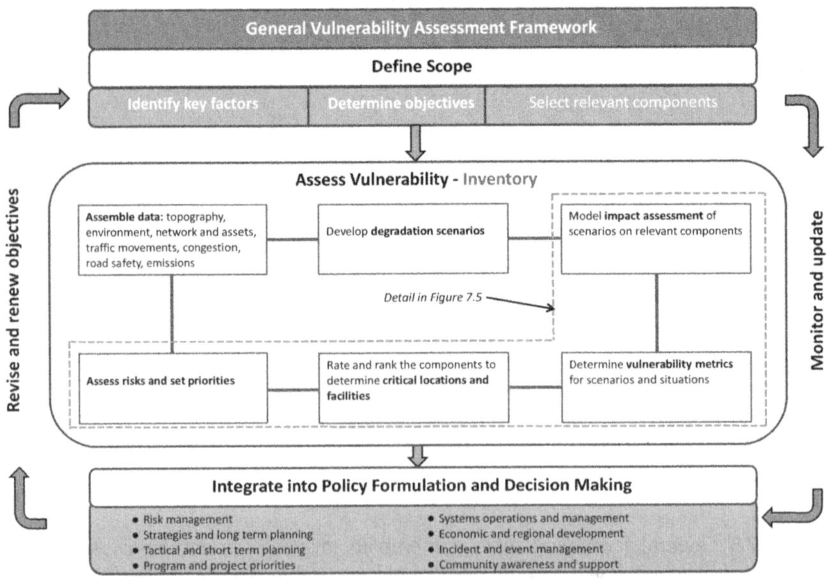

Figure 7.4 The general framework set up for inventory-based vulnerability assessment.

can be ranked and priorities for treatment set. These results are then fed into a decision-making process for action.

More detail is requires for the interpretation of the assessment procedures in the model of Figure 7.4. This detail concerns the four phases of impact assessment, vulnerability metrics, critical location determination, and risk assessment in the diagram, and enclosed within the dashed polygon in Figure 7.4. One approach for providing the detail is given in the Scott–Dunn analysis method used in New Zealand. Figure 7.5 represents this approach.

Here the network is divided into a number of routes, which comprise connected sets of network links and represent major or vital travel paths through the network. Detours around potential blockages along each route are then determined, for use in the assessment (e.g., additional travel times). The links along a route are then split into segments, on the basis of surrounding land use, road geometry and pavement type, detour points and traffic volumes, with road-safety performance (e.g., crash type and frequency) also being a key consideration. These properties and factors are then used to determine link performance attributes and exposure along with segment vulnerability metrics (see Section 3.3). An overall vulnerability score for the route is then computed, and used to compare and rank the routes.

7.3.2 A Framework for Topologically Based Analysis

The topological methods require a minimum amount of core data, concerning network structure and basic node and link characteristics, such as the

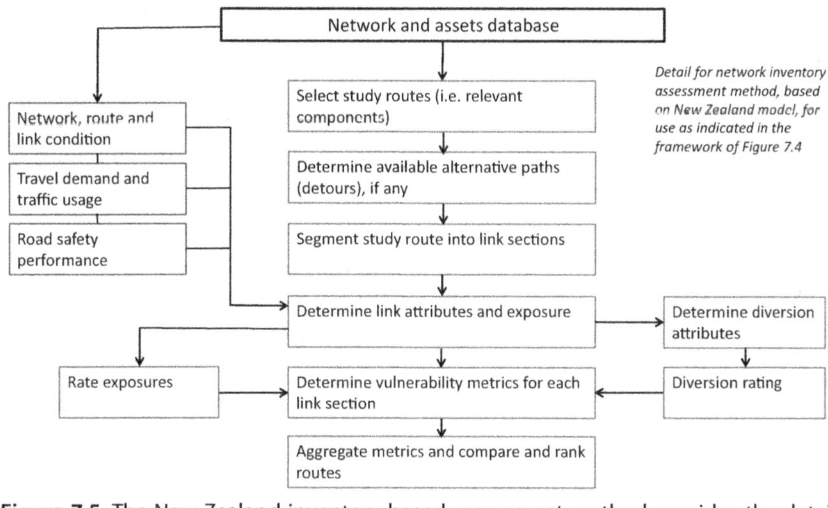

Figure 7.5 The New Zealand inventory-based assessment method provides the detail for the framework of Fig. 7.4.

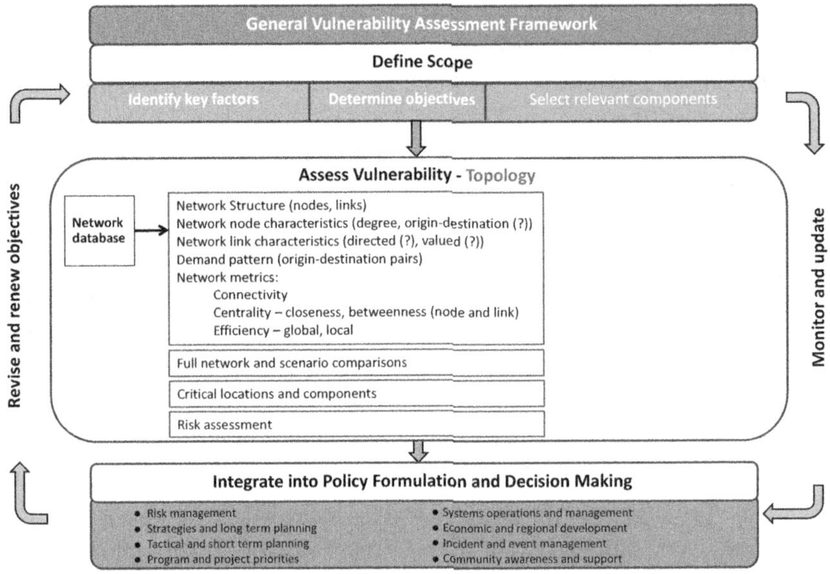

Figure 7.6 The general framework as applied to topologically based vulnerability assessment.

degree of connectivity and the presence of directed and/or valued links. Once a network is defined, e.g., by its incidence matrix and perhaps link lengths, there is sufficient information for a topological analysis. Knowledge of origin–destination nodes in the network can enhance the analysis but this is not essential.

Figure 7.6 presents the assessment framework using topological analysis. The core elements of the network database (as above) are required, and these enable computation of network metrics such a connectivity, closeness, and betweenness centrality (for both nodes and links, as necessary), and global and local network efficiencies. These indices, computed for the full network and for assumed degradation scenarios of it, can then be used to identify critical locations and components, which can be subject to risk assessment.

7.3.3 A Framework for Serviceability-based Analysis

Serviceability analysis requires more detailed network data of the forms generally used in travel-demand and traffic-systems-performance models and so, while demanding, are readily available in transportation planning. In addition to the core items of the network database used in topological assessment, serviceability analysis requires information on node and link attributes such as road type and road geometry, numbers of rail tracks,

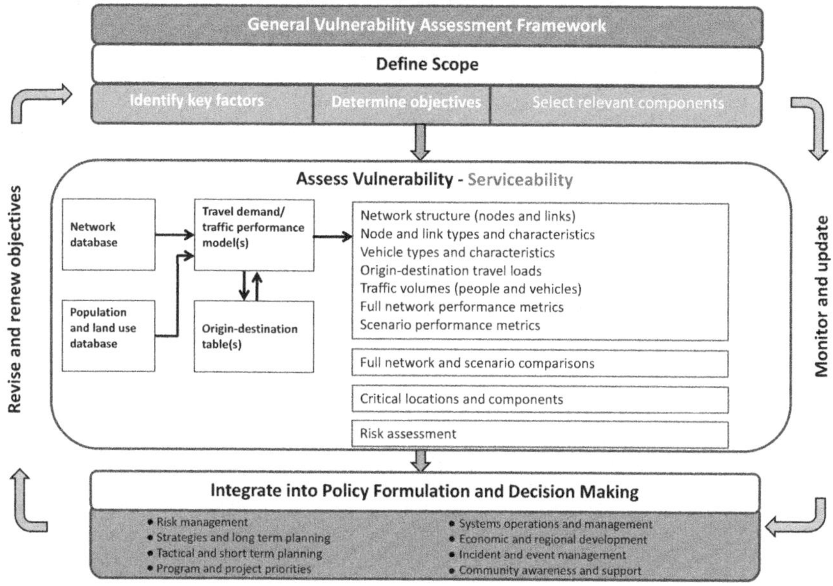

Figure 7.7 The general framework as applied to serviceability-based vulnerability assessment.

interchange, intersection and station characteristics, vehicle types and characteristics, as well as demand information (origin–destination flows and traffic loads), travel times, and travel costs throughout the network. These latter items are the outputs of the travel-demand model, which also uses population and land-use data in determining the origin–destination flows from which the traffic loads arise. As indicated in Chapter 6, travel-demand models for private road transport are in widespread use but similar models for public transport systems are rarer. Figure 7.7 presents the assessment framework based on serviceability.

In this analysis process the travel-demand or traffic-systems-performance model is applied to the full network and to each of the selected degradation scenarios. The outputs of the travel/traffic model for each scenario case are then compared to those for the full network, using the vulnerability metrics described in Chapter 4, and critical locations and components then identified and subject to risk assessment.

7.3.4 A Framework for Accessibility-Based Analysis

Figure 7.8 shows the assessment framework intended for accessibility analysis. It uses basically the same data about the network as for serviceability

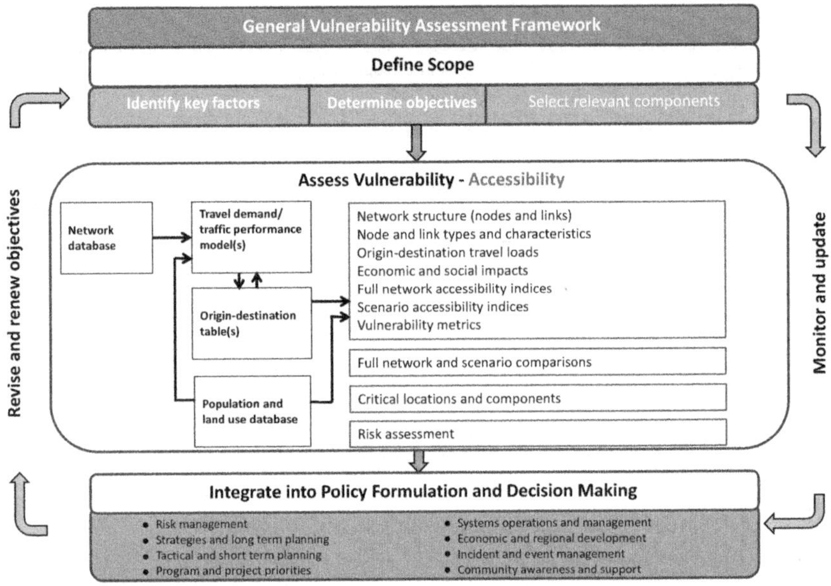

Figure 7.8 The general framework as applied to accessibility-based vulnerability assessment.

studies, but the population and land-use database now plays a direct part in the analysis because this is used in the determination of the accessibility indices.

In addition, the travel-demand model does not need to be connected directly to the accessibility assessment process. The output of that model, especially the origin–destination table(s) and travel times and costs under the selected scenarios, is the main requirement. More detailed outputs such as link volumes and travel costs are not needed explicitly. The vulnerability metrics are taken from the computed changes in accessibility indices under the various scenarios, and the type of accessibility index to be employed depends on the nature and location (e.g., urban vs. rural) of the network, as discussed in Chapter 5.

7.4 PLANNING AND SYSTEM MANAGEMENT

The integrated framework present in this chapter is intended to offer transportation planners a clear way to introduce and apply vulnerability analysis in their work, and in transport policy formulation and decision-making, on a systematic basis.

The implementation of the proposed assessment framework integrating the four vulnerability-analysis processes for real-world applications has still to be accomplished, and remains the subject of the ongoing research. Facilitation of the integrated method requires a universal spatially oriented database platform, which can be provided by a geographical information system (GIS). Modern GIS platforms integrate disparate databases sharing common spatial attributes (i.e., that pertain to a specified region and include spatial location variables, such as longitude and latitude). They also often link to other modeling platforms, such as travel-demand models or environmental-impact models. Figure 7.9 provides a generic view of the use of a GIS platform to host vulnerability assessments, including the selection of degradation scenarios representing alternative natural and man-made disasters. For the natural events at least, there are often impact models (e.g., flood models as in Sohn, 2006) that can indicate the likely extent and duration of flooding episodes in different parts of a region and thus affecting different parts of the transportation network. The GIS software can then indicate the likely level of network degradation occurring under a specified flood event, from which the vulnerability analysis can be conducted.

In this GIS-based implementation the analyst is able to choose the required method(s) for vulnerability analysis and can then obtain alternative sets of critical locations and components relating to the different assessment

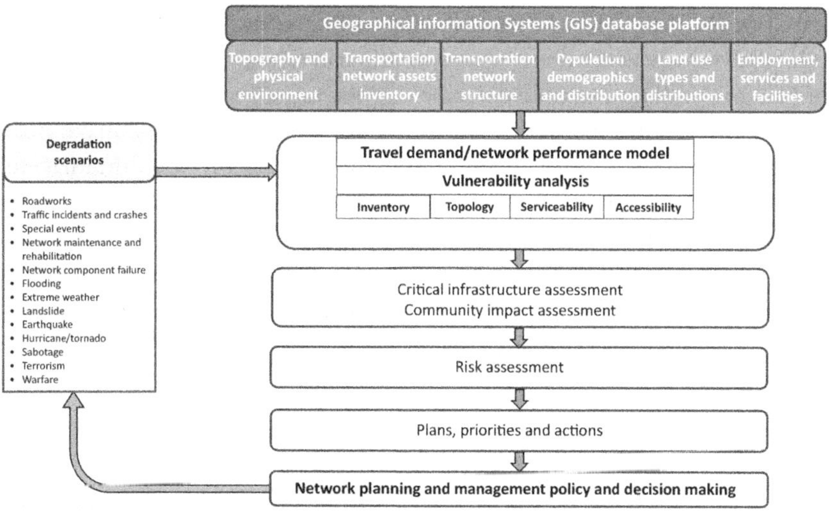

Figure 7.9 A proposed GIS database platform for multifaceted vulnerability assessment.

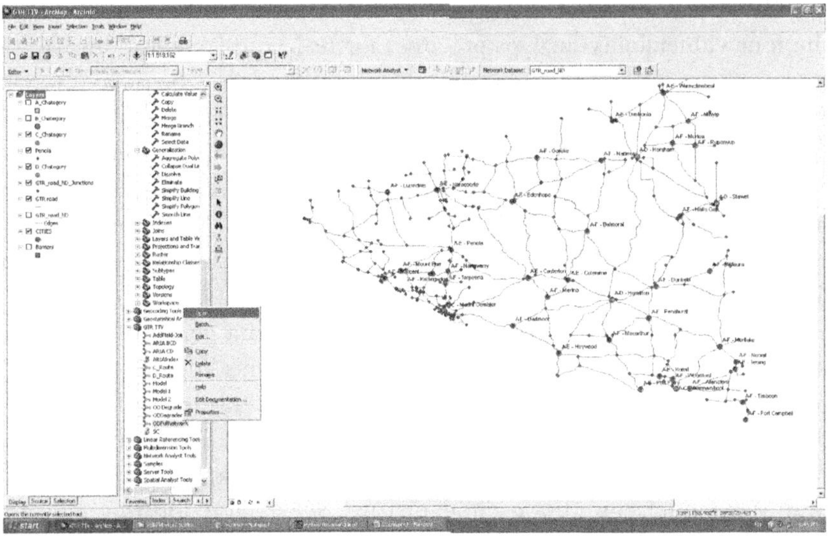

Figure 7.10 Screenshot of the GIS platform used for accessibility-based vulnerability analysis in the "Green Triangle" region of southeast Australia. *Reproduced by permission from Susilawati, S. (2017). Private communication.*

methods. These sets can then be compared to establish final ratings and rankings, and so far better inform the decision-making and policy and planning processes. Figure 7.10 provides an indicative screenshot of the pilot implementation in a GIS of the integrated framework. This view shows the road network for the "Green Triangle" region of southeast Australia, used as a case study of the accessibility-based method in Section 5.3. The capabilities of GIS in handling multiple databases for the same region, in incorporating analytical tools and in connecting to external model packages, make it the preferred platform for a full implementation of the multifaceted vulnerability-assessment framework described in this chapter.

This is not, however, the end of the story. There is considerable scope and indeed need for further research and development in the field, as discussed in Chapter 8, the final chapter of this book.

REFERENCES

Bil, M., Vodak, R., Kubecek, J., Bilova, M., & Sedonik, J. (2015). Evaluating road network damage caused by natural disasters in the Czech Republic between 1997 and 2010. *Transportation Research Part A: Policy and Practice, 81*, 90–103.

Cats, O., & Jenelius, E. (2014). Dynamic vulnerability analysis of public transport networks: Mitigation effects of real-time information. *Networks and Spatial Economics, 14*(3), 435–463.

Cats, O., Yap, M., & Van Oort, N. (2016). Exposing the role of exposure: Public transport network risk analysis. *Transportation Research Part A: Policy and Practice, 88*, 1–14.

FHWA. (2012). *The Federal Highway Administration's climate change and extreme weather vulnerability assessment framework*. Washington, DC: Federal Highway Administration. Retrieved from http://www.fhwa.dot.gov/environment/climate_change/adaptation/.

Jenelius, E., Petersen, T., & Mattsson, L.-G. (2006). Importance and exposure in road network vulnerability analysis. *Transportation Research Part A: Policy and Practice, 40*(7), 537–560.

Mattsson, L.-G., & Jenelius, E. (2015). Vulnerability and resilience of transport systems – a discussion of recent research. *Transportation Research Part A: Policy and Practice, 81*, 16–34.

Pokharel, R., & Ieda, H. (2016). Reliability and vulnerability of road network: An accessibility and network closure vulnerability approach. *Asian Transport Studies, 4*(1), 37–56.

Scott, V., & Dunn, R. (2015). A prototype method to rate the link vulnerability of strategic rural roads. *Road and Transport Research, 24*(2), 3–12.

Sohn, J. (2006). Evaluating the significance of highway network links under the flood damage: An accessibility approach. *Transportation Research Part A: Policy and Practice, 40*(6), 491–506.

Susilawati, S. (2017). *Private communication*.

CHAPTER EIGHT

Summary Overview and Conclusions

Network vulnerability analysis emerged as a new and active area of research in transportation planning and modeling at the turn of the 21st century. Since the early works, reported in Bell and Iida (2003), the area has grown immensely and spread across the globe to a wide research community. One account of the development of research interest in network vulnerability since then can be found in Mattsson and Jenelius (2015). This reveals the wide extent of the research field and provides a useful summary of it. This book serves as a full discussion of network vulnerability and has described the development of a number of alternative approaches. It also proposes the development of an integrated framework for vulnerability assessment and for the incorporation of this framework in the systems planning process applied to transportation networks.

8.1 EXISTING METHODS

The current methodology for vulnerability analysis can be described in terms of four main approaches:

- inventory-based risk assessment, which considers transportation network components and assets which can be affected by degradations, such as those from climate change or natural hazards;
- topologically based assessment, which analyses a network in terms of its basic structure and connectivity and identifies critical locations in the network on the basis of their centrality and contributions to network connectivity;
- serviceability-based assessment, which considers the transportation network and its component (node and link) attributes in detail and examines the operational performance of the network in different states of degradation and perhaps under different travel-demand loads. It identifies critical locations and components in terms of the impact on network operations of given degradation; and
- accessibility-based assessment, which again considers the transportation network in detail but focuses on the broader impacts of network

Vulnerability Analysis for Transportation Networks
ISBN: 978-0-12-811010-2
http://dx.doi.org/10.1016/B978-0-12-811010-2.00008-3

degradation in terms of the impacts on the social and economic systems in the region served by the network, and thus treats travel demand as a derived demand resulting from socioeconomic activities, and the ability of individuals and communities to participate in that activity.

Each of these methods has its appropriate domains for application, and these were described and illustrated in Chapters 3–6.

Chapter 7 noted the similarities and differences in approach, data needs and modeling procedures of the four approaches, and offered an integrated framework that can incorporate the approaches. The framework also offers the means to place vulnerability analysis in the planning process. This chapter outlines the next steps in research, development, and implementation for the framework, and summarizes future research needs as apparent to the author.

8.2 THE WAY FORWARD

"Moving forward," to use the modern parlance, involves the transfer of research knowledge and analytical skills and methods from academic research to transportation planning practice. Given the uptake of considerations of vulnerability by agencies such as the FHWA (e.g., FHWA, 2012), the Japanese Ministry of Land, Infrastructure and Transport (Pokharel & Ieda, 2016) and the Organization for Economic Cooperation and Development (ITF, 2016), this task can begin from a firm footing. There is still, however, much work to be done in many countries. Development and implementation of the integrated framework for vulnerability analysis proposed in Chapter 7 should offer a substantial vehicle to assist in this process.

There is a growing need for an understanding of vulnerability in transportation networks internationally, due to pressures of world population growth; the maturity of transportation infrastructure systems in the developed world with diminishing opportunities to provide new, additional infrastructure; the converse needs for rapid development of new infrastructure in the developing world; and the shortening time frames expected by operators, users, and customers of transportation services. Much of our existing infrastructure operates "on the edge," with small perturbations potentially leading to major failures in system supply. Vulnerability analysis can assist through the identification of critical locations and facilities, and by testing alternatives proposed to overcome identified vulnerabilities. System resilience is increasingly gaining importance in transportation planning decisions.

GIS software packages would appear to offer the best location for the implementation of vulnerability-analysis tools, given their ability to integrate different data sets pertaining to a nominated study region. Software "add-ons" to travel-demand modeling packages might offer an alternative avenue for implementation, but this approach may suffer from the need for such software modules to be specifically written for particular proprietary software.

Road transportation networks are generally well covered by available travel demand and traffic systems performance models and the transportation asset databases held by transportation agencies, so that implementation of all of the four methods for vulnerability analysis.

The greater use of vulnerability analysis for study of public transport systems is to be encouraged, and is relatively easy to accomplish in terms of the topological approach. The wider implementation of transit-oriented travel demand and transportation-system performance-analysis tools is needed before serviceability methods can be more widely used for these networks, although there is considerable value in seeking this development, for better understanding of transit system operations as a wider goal than vulnerability analysis alone. This issue is discussed further in the next section on future research and development.

8.3 AREAS FOR RESEARCH AND DEVELOPMENT

No research study can ever avoid conclusions pointing to the needs for further research on the topic in question. This is illustrated *par excellence* by the quotation attributed to Isaac Newton: "I do not know what I may appear to the world; but to myself I seem to have been only like a boy playing on the seashore, and diverting myself in now and then finding a smoother pebble or a prettier shell than ordinary, whilst the great ocean of truth lay all undiscovered before me" (Brewster, 1855). Our quest for further knowledge (and perhaps even understanding) is only reinforced by gaining new knowledge. This is the case for vulnerability analysis for transportation networks.

A number of areas present themselves for further research interest:

- The inclusion of elastic demand considerations in the travel-demand modeling for degraded network scenarios. Present approaches are largely confined to inelastic demand models and only allow for alternative route choice. This means that the origin—destination matrices used in the analysis are static, so that travelers have no choices with regard

to alternative modes, destinations, or when to travel (or decide not to travel). The inelastic demand case is acceptable for short-term disruptions, perhaps of hours' duration or a day or two at least, but for longer disruption periods this may not be the case
- The concept of system resilience and the "resilience triangle" as described in Section 2.5 is one requiring substantially more research (D'Lima & Medda, 2015; Mattsson & Jenelius, 2015; Reggiani, 2013). The ability of a transportation system to recover from a shock over a time interval is key to its ongoing operations and the socioeconomic activities that it facilitates.
- Dynamic vulnerability studies relate to study of resilience, and are particular relevant to public transport network vulnerability, given the changes in service provision and schedules that such systems employ over the course of a day or a week.
- As a related topic, the further development and wider implementation of public transport travel-demand models, to make these as sophisticated and as widely available as those for road networks, is a requirement for the enhanced implementation and use of transit-oriented vulnerability-analysis tools that tackle the operations of real world transit systems.
- In a broader concept, the study of vulnerability curves that allow for the study of the impacts of incremental network degradations as introduced by Cats and Jenelius (2016) is likely to be an important area for new development of vulnerability analysis for all transportation systems.
- The accessibility approach requires the development of new accessibility indices specifically related to the network under study, and particular for public transport networks. While Chapter 5 suggested a range of accessibility indices and identified some that were suitable for transit systems, there are no current reported studies of their use for public transport networks.

What is clear, however, is that vulnerability analysis is a well-founded area for transportation research that stands to make great improvements in transportation planning practice. The author hopes that this book will provide a basis and facilitation for that development.

REFERENCES

Bell, M. G. H., & Iida, Y. (Eds.). (2003). *The network reliability of transport*. London: Emerald Publishing.

Brewster, D. (1855). *Memoirs of the life, writings, and discoveries of Sir Isaac Newton*. Edinburgh: Thomas Constable and Co.

Cats, O., & Jenelius, E. (2016). Beyond a complete failure: The impact of partial capacity degradation on public transport network vulnerability. *Transportmetrica B: Transport Dynamics*. http://dx.doi.org/10.1080/21680566.2016.1267596.

D'Lima, M., & Medda, F. (2015). A new measure of resilience: An application to the London underground. *Transportation Research Part A: Policy and Practice, 81*, 35–46.

FHWA. (2012). *The Federal Highway Administration's climate change and extreme weather vulnerability assessment framework*. Washington, DC: Federal Highway Administration. Retrived from http://www.fhwa.dot.gov/environment/climate_change/adaptation/.

ITF. (2016). *Adapting transport to climate change and extreme weather: Implications for infrastructure owners and network managers. International transport forum, ITF research reports*. Paris: OECD Publishing. http://dx.doi.org/10.1787/9789282108079-en.

Mattsson, L.-G., & Jenelius, E. (2015). Vulnerability and resilience of transport systems – a discussion of recent research. *Transportation Research Part A: Policy and Practice, 81*, 16–34.

Pokharel, R., & Ieda, H. (2016). Reliability and vulnerability of road network: An accessibility and network closure vulnerability approach. *Asian Transport Studies, 4*(1), 37–56.

Reggiani, A. (2013). Network resilience for transport security: Some methodological considerations. *Transport Policy, 28*, 63–68.

APPENDIX A

Network Topology for Transportation Networks

A network or connected *graph* is a set of nodes and links (vertices and edges), which allows the flows of information or objects through an n-dimensional space. The network G may then be described in the form $G = (N, A)$, where N is the set of nodes and A is the set of links. If two nodes i and j are connected, then a_{ij} is the link between them. The set of links for network G is described by the incidence matrix Δ, where the elements of Δ are δ_{ij}, such that

$$\delta_{ij} = \begin{cases} 1 & \text{If link } a_{ij} \text{ exists in the network} \\ 0 & \text{otherwise} \end{cases} \tag{A.1}$$

In its simplest form, the network is undirected and unvalued:

1. undirected—links in an undirected network permit the flow in either direction, from i to j and from j to i, equivalently, and
2. unvalued—there is no differentiation in the cost of travel on any link in an unvalued network (all links may be regarded as having unit travel cost).

Land transportation networks can be assumed to be valued (or "weighted") (all links have travel costs associated with them, and each link may have a different cost) and are sometimes directional (the link a_{ij} may not have a two-way pair, a_{ji})—the definition of the incidence matrix (Equation A.1) can accommodate one-directional flows. The first link travel cost in a transportation network is the link length (distance) x_{ij}, but often transportation planners and analysts use a general travel cost $c(a_{ij})$ (alternatively c_{ij}) to represent the cost of travel on a link. Travel time is an obvious type of travel cost, but a generalized cost of travel may also be used, for instance to combine money costs (tolls or fares paid) and travel time. Directional transportation links occur for instance in the one-way street systems used to manage traffic flows in many cities. The incidence matrix of an undirected network will be symmetric, but that for a directed network will not.

Links in transportation networks will also possess a large number of properties and characteristics besides their length. These would include the number of lanes (for a road link) or tracks (for a rail link), the type of road (physically and functionally), presence of traffic control devices and information signs or beacons, and management restrictions (e.g., parking restrictions and speed limits on urban roads). These characteristics and properties all serve to affect the travel time and travel cost on a link, which will also be influenced by the demand to use the link and the congestion levels experienced on it.

In n-dimensional space, links may overlap (i.e., not intersect), but in a planar network crossing links will form a node at their point of intersection, and hence the direction of flow can be changed at those nodes. While airline networks might be considered as having large parts that are n-dimensional, land transportation networks are in the main planar, unless special grade separation (overpasses or underpasses) have been provided at specific locations so that links can cross over or under each other without physically intersecting.[1]

A.1 PATHS THROUGH NETWORKS

A path Ψ_{hd} from origin node h to destination node d exists if there is a connected set of links $(a_{hr}, \ldots, a_{ij}, \ldots, a_{sd})$ from h to d. The cost of travel on this path is L_{hd}, given by

$$L(\Psi_{hd}) = \sum_{a_{ij} \in \Psi_{hd}} c(a_{ij}) \tag{A.2}$$

where $c(a_{ij})$ is the travel cost on link a_{ij}. The minimum path cost L_{hd} is given by

$$L_{hd} = \min_{\Psi_{hd}} \{L(\Psi_{hd})\} \tag{A.3}$$

This value and a minimum path through the network corresponding to it may be computed using an appropriate algorithm, such as the Dijkstra algorithm described later. In a connected network there will be at least one minimum path between h and d. Equally, in a degraded network where one or more nodes or links have failed, there may be no available path between these nodes and in that case $L_{hd} = \infty$.

The interconnectedness of the network can be described in the first instance by two metrics: (1) the characteristic path length $(\overline{L})$, which is

[1] In a road network there would still have to be connecting links at this interchange if traffic is to be permitted to transfer from one road to the crossroad.

the average length of the minimum paths between all node pairs (h, d) in the network (Latora & Marchiori, 2001), i.e.,

$$\overline{L} = \frac{1}{|N|(|N|-1)} \sum_{hd:h \neq d} L_{hd} \tag{A.4}$$

and (2) the average degree (C^D) of the network, which is average number of direct connections from a node to all other nodes in the network, i.e.,

$$C^D = \frac{1}{|N|} k_i = \frac{1}{|N|} \sum_{j,j \neq i} \delta_{ij} \tag{A.5}$$

where $|N|$ is the number of nodes, k_i is the degree of node i, the number of links connecting i to the rest of the network, which is given by the size of the set of links emanating from node i, i.e., summing across the row of the incidence matrix for i.

$$k_i = \sum_{j,j \neq i} \delta_{ij} \tag{A.6}$$

There can be a multitude of paths through a network between a random pair of nodes, and a classification of possible paths is as follows:

- *Cyclical* paths involve one or more loops along the path, so that the same link may be used more than once. These paths are not generally relevant in transportation analysis, except perhaps for the case of a driver circulating a city block in search of a parking space
- An *efficient* path is one on which each node used or link traversed takes the traveler closer to the destination. If $p(i)$ is the potential (or minimum path cost) from node i to the destination and j is the next node along the path to the destination, then on an efficient path $p(j) < p(i)$.
- A *minimum cost* path is a path with the least travel cost incurred in moving from the origin to the destination. It will be a special case of an efficient path, and it is possible for there to be more than one minimum cost path between any two node pairs.

Much of transportation network analysis is concerned with identifying minimum cost paths and alternatives to them. This is done, for instance, in probabilistic path assignment (e.g., Dial, 1971; Taylor, 1979) and in search for the n best paths through a network. A useful review of methods and algorithms for determining the n best paths is available in Chen, Li, and Lam (2016).

A.1.1 The Dijkstra Algorithm

A widely used algorithm for determining minimum paths in a network is given by Dijkstra (1959). The algorithm is efficient in both computing time and computer memory and storage, and has a number of attractive properties. It can be used to find the minimum path tree from a given origin node, or to find the minimum path between any pair of nodes, or to find the minimum paths from the origin to an arbitrary set of nodes. The minimum path tree from an origin is the combined set of minimum paths from that node to all other nodes in the network. The algorithm works by fanning out from the origin node, considering each node directly connected to it (i.e., a link exists between nodes i and j), and then repeating that procedure for each node that has already been reached.

At any stage of operation of the algorithm, the nodes in the network can be split into three separate sets: Set **S**, which contains all those nodes for which the minimum path has been successfully computed; Set **T**, which contains nodes which are candidates for inclusion in Set **S** (i.e., a path has been found to each node in Set **T**, but this may not yet be the actual minimum path); and Set **X**, containing all other nodes in the network. Sets **S** and **T** are each described as a "triplet" $[J, L(J), c(J)]$, where J is a network node, $L(J)$ is "the last node back" from J, i.e., the node connected to J by a link that is on the path from the origin H to J, and $c(J)$ is the cost of travel to J on that path. The minimum path from H to any node i is determined by "backtracking," using the last node back i.e., the path from H to i is given (in reverse topological order) by the sequence of links $\{i, L(i), L(L(i)), \ldots, H\}$.

At commencement, Sets **T** and **S** are empty, and Set **X** is all of the nodes in the network.

At completion (of the calculation of the minimum path tree), Set **S** contains all nodes that can be reached from the origin, Set **T** is empty, and Set **X** will only contain those nodes that cannot be reached from the origin, i.e., if there is a cut or discontinuity in the network. For a network with no discontinuities Set **X** will be empty at the finish.

The steps in the algorithm are:

Step 0. Put the origin node (h) in Set **T**. The travel cost (potential) of node H from itself is assumed to be zero. Thus

$$\text{Set } \mathbf{T} = [h,\ h,\ 0]$$

Step 1. Remove the triplet with the smallest cost from **T**, say $[i, L(i), p(i)]$ (where $p(i)$ is the potential (minimum cost separation) of node i from h, and insert it into Set **S**. Thus

$$\mathbf{T} \leftarrow \mathbf{T} - [i, L(i), p(i)]$$

$$\mathbf{S} \leftarrow \mathbf{S} + [i, L(i), p(i)]$$

Step 2. Consider each node j adjacent to i, except those nodes already in Set **S**. Calculate the cost for the shortest path to j passing through i (i.e., $p(i) + c(i, j)$), where $c(i, j)$ is the travel cost on link (i, j)). If a triplet for j does not already exist in Set **T**, insert the new triplet in **T**, i.e.,

$$\mathbf{T} \leftarrow \mathbf{T} + [j, i, p(i) + c(i, j)]$$

If there is a triplet for j already in Set **T**, replace it by the new triplet *only* if the new cost is less than the old cost.

Step 3. If Set **T** is empty, go to Step 4, otherwise go to Step 1.

Step 4. Stop. Set **S** now contains the minimum path tree from h to all other nodes.

Note that if the algorithm were to be used to find the minimum path from h to d, then Step 3 would be "If node d is now in Set **S**, stop." This is because the Set **S** that only contains those nodes for a minimum path is found.[2] Once a node is put in Set **S**, the minimum path to it has been set.

A.1.2 Path Counting Algorithm

The following algorithm, originally provided by Taylor (1981), can be used to compute the number of efficient paths $n_C(i, d)$ of travel cost C through the network from node i to destination node d. Path $\Psi(h,d) = \{h = i_1, i_2, \ldots, i_{m-1}, i_m = d\}$ as a connected node sequence through the network is an efficient path if each node i_r, $r = 2, \ldots, m$ is closer to the destination than its predecessor i_{r-1}, i.e., on an efficient path $p(i_r) < p(i_{r-1})$. The algorithm requires the following inputs:

- $|N|$, the number of nodes in the network,
- $c(a_{ij})$, the cost of travel on link a_{ij} from node i to node j,

[2] Note that the Dijkstra algorithm only finds one minimum path to any node. It will always find a path if one exists, but if there are multiple equivalent minimum paths only one of these will be found by the algorithm. Other methods are required to find a full set of the minimum paths in this situation. See for example Chen et al. (2016).

- $\Omega(i)$, the set of all nodes j reach directly from node i (i.e., for which there is a link a_{ij}),
- Path potentials $p(i)$ from d sorted into forward topological order (i.e., closest to furthest), with $s(k)$, $k = 1, 2, \ldots, |N|$ being the kth closest node to d, and
- Matrix Λ_{li}, $i \in N$, with $n_C(i) = \Lambda_{C-p(i),i}$ and $\Delta p = C - p(i) > 0$.

The algorithm is:

Step 0. Set $i = d$ and $k = 1$, and

$$\begin{array}{ll} \Lambda_{0d} = 1 & \\ \Lambda_{0d} = 0 & l = 1, 2, .., l\max \end{array}$$

Step 1. Consider the next closest node to i, i.e., $i = s(k \leftarrow k + 1)$. Examine all nodes $j \in \Omega(i)$. For each j, if $p(i) > p(j)$ then let $\Lambda_{li} \leftarrow \Lambda_{li} + \Lambda_{l-\Delta l,j}$ where $\Delta l = p(j) + c(a_{ij}) - p(i) \geq 0$ and $l = \Delta l, \Delta l + 1, \ldots, l_{\max}$. (Paths of cost $C = p(i) + l$ through i must come from paths of cost $C - c(a_{ij})$ through j).

Step 3. If $k < |N|$ go to Step 1, as not all nodes have been examined. If $k \geq |N|$, stop.

On termination Λ_{li} holds the number of paths of length $C = l + p(i)$, $l = 0, 1, 2, \ldots, l_{\max}$ between i and d.

A.2 NETWORK CONFIGURATIONS

Networks come in many forms, with differing degrees of complexity, shape, and form. Two basic network indicators, as suggested by Derrible and Kennedy (2010), are the β indicator, which refers to network complexity, and the degree of connectivity (γ).

The β indicator is straightforward. It is merely the ratio of the number of links $|A|$ to the number of nodes$|N|$:

$$\beta = \frac{|A|}{|N|} \tag{A.7}$$

A small value of β indicates that the network is relative simple in structure.

The γ-indicator of connectivity is a topological measure of how much a network is connected compared to how much it could be connected, and is broadly defined as the ratio of the actual number of links to the potential maximum number of links for the network. In a general n-dimensional space this maximum number of links is $|N|(|N|-1)/2$, which is the possible number of connections between all nodes, halved so as to avoid double counting in an undirected graph. In an n-dimensional network the γ-indicator is given by

$$\gamma = \frac{2|A|}{|N|(|N|-1)} \tag{A.8}$$

However, in a planar network, to which transportation networks generally belong, this number of connections is infeasible: two links crossing each other automatically generate another node. Derrible and Kennedy (2010) indicated that for a planar network the maximum possible number of links is $3(|N|-2)$, for $|N| \geq 3$. Thus the definition of γ for a planar network is

$$\gamma = \frac{|A|}{3(|N|-2)} \quad \text{for } |N| \geq 3 \tag{A.9}$$

The average degree (C^D) of the network was defined in Equation (A.5). Node degree is of interest when considering network structure and provides more detail to support the β indicator. Two general network structures of interest are random networks and scale-free networks. A random network is one in which the link connections between nodes can be assumed to occur at random (although node neighbors are most likely to be connected). A scale-free network (Barabasi & Albert, 1999) is one in which the probability density function $p(k)$ of the number of connecting links ($k = 1, 2, 3, \ldots$) of a node follows a power law, i.e., $p(k) \propto k^{-\lambda}$ with scaling factor λ. There is some evidence (e.g., Derrible & Kennedy, 2010) that many (but not all) metro networks can be described as scale-free. Barabasi and Albert indicated that scale-free networks can be more resilient to random attacks than random networks, but may suffer more under targeted attack of critical nodes.

In addition, the "small-world" property is also of interest for the analysis of transportation networks. A small-world network is one in which most nodes are not neighbors of each other, but the neighbors of any given node are likely to be neighbors of each other, and most nodes can be reached from every other node by a small number of links. More precisely, a small-world network is defined as one in which the typical separation (travel cost between any random pair of nodes) L is proportional to the logarithm of the number of nodes in the network, i.e., $L = \beta \log_e(|N|)$ where β is a constant. Small-world networks have two principal properties: (1) they exhibit high clustering and (2) have short average minimum path lengths. Clustering considers the number of connections between the nodes in a neighborhood, where the neighbourhood of node i is all of the nodes directly connected to i (i.e., by physical links). There are k_i such nodes. Using the concept presented by the γ-indicator (Equation A.9), for a planar neighborhood network (with $k_i \geq 3$) there would be a maximum $3(k_i - 2)$ possible connections, so that the clustering coefficient C_i for node i is

$$C_i = \frac{k_i}{3(k_i - 2)} \quad \text{if } k_i \geq 3 \tag{A.10}$$

and thus the overall clustering coefficient for the network (CC), which is the average node clustering coefficient, is

$$CC = \frac{1}{|N|} \sum_i C_i \tag{A.11}$$

A.3 CENTRALITY AND BETWEENNESS

Consideration of clustering in networks leads to the concept of centrality (Freeman, 1979; see also Porta, Crucitti, & Latora, 2006; Mattsson & Jenelius, 2015). This is used to help identify the most important nodes or links in a network. Two common indices used to assess centrality are "closeness centrality," which considers the proximity of a node to all other nodes, and "betweenness centrality," which considers the importance of a network component in terms of its use for movement through the network—were importance is usually taken to mean the component's role in minimum path movements across the network.

Closeness centrality is the reciprocal of the average shortest path distance from a node (L_i) to all other nodes, i.e.,

$$C_i^C = \frac{1}{L_i} = \frac{|N| - 1}{\sum_{j \neq i} L_{ij}} \tag{A.12}$$

While this index is useful for a connected network, where it indicates the spatial accessibility of a node, it is not useful for a cut network where some of the L_i may be infinite unless an assumption about the values of L_i can then be made. It is also dependent on network size, so that it cannot be readily used to compare different networks.

Betweenness centrality considers the importance of a node in terms of the proportion of shortest paths which pass through the node. If n_{hd} is the total number of shortest paths between h and d and $n_{hd}(i)$ is the number of those shortest paths that pass through node i then the betweenness centrality C_i^B of the node is given by

$$C_i^B = \frac{1}{(|N|-1)(|N|-2)} \sum_{h,d \in N; h,d \neq i} \frac{n_{hd}(i)}{n_{hd}} \tag{A.13}$$

A similar betweenness index for the link a_{ij} can also be defined, given $n_{hd}(a_{ij})$, the number of minimum paths from h to d using that link:

$$C_{a_{ij}}^B = \frac{1}{(|N|-1)(|N|-2)} \sum_{h,d \in N; h,d \neq i} \frac{n_{hd}(a_{ij})}{n_{hd}} \tag{A.14}$$

A.4 NETWORK EFFICIENCY

The efficiency of a network is a measure of how easily it permits flows or movement. Network efficiency metrics can be applied at both global and local scales. Global efficiency indicates the overall capability of the network to facilitate flows, while local efficiency indicates the network's resilience to small scale failures, i.e., the local efficiency of a node indicates the ability of its neighbors to facilitate flows when that node fails.

One measure of network efficiency was introduced earlier in this appendix. This is the characteristic path length $(\overline{L})$, see Equation (A.4), the average length of the minimum paths between all node pairs (h, d) in the network. The characteristic path length is a measure of efficiency of the network because the lower the value of $\overline{L}$, the higher the speed of movement between any node pair. This metric has a difficulty, however, in that it is not defined if there is a cut (discontinuity) in the network—i.e., if the network is split into separate components due to failure of a link or node—because then for some node pairs $L_{ij} \to \infty$. Thus an alternative measure, the global efficiency $\eta(G)$ is commonly used where G represents the network. The global efficiency is defined as

$$\eta(G) = \frac{1}{|N|(|N|-1)} \sum_{i,j \in N; i \neq j} \frac{1}{L_{ij}} \tag{A.15}$$

This metric remains defined in a cut network because $\frac{1}{L_{ij}} \rightarrow 0$ when $L_{ij} \rightarrow \infty$.

In an unvalued network in which all links can be taken as of unit length $\eta(G)$ is [0, 1], thus representing a normalized value. The global efficiency $\eta(G) = 1$ in an "ideal" network (in n-dimensional space), where a link connects each and every node pair. There will be $|N|(|N| - 1)/2$ such links in that ideal network.

In a valued network the global efficiency defined by Equation (A.15) is not normalized, for the links may have different lengths. A normalized global efficiency $E(G)$ can be defined by comparing the shortest path lengths through the network (sometimes referred to as geodesic distances) to the Euclidean straight line distances between the node pairs (Latora & Marchiori, 2001; see also Porta et al., 2006; Mattsson & Jenelius, 2015). If G_{id} is an ideal network with the same nodes as G in which each link a_{ij} has length equal to the Euclidean distance between i and j then

$$\eta\left(G^{id}\right) = \frac{1}{|N|(|N| - 1)} \sum_{i,j \in N; i \neq j} \frac{1}{L_{ij}^{Euclid}} \tag{A.16}$$

and the normalized global efficiency of the network can be then defined as

$$E(G) = \frac{\eta(G)}{\eta(G^{id})} \tag{A.17}$$

In addition to the global efficiency defined by Equation (3.6), a local efficiency $E_{loc}(G_i)$ can be defined (Mattsson & Jenelius, 2015), where G_i is the subgraph of G comprising node i, its neighboring nodes, and the links between them. The local efficiency is

$$E_{loc}(G_i) = \frac{1}{N} \sum_{i \in G} E(G_i) \tag{A.18}$$

Both global and local efficiencies are normalized in the range [0, 1], and thus these indices can be used to compare different networks or a given network in different states. Global efficiency is a measure of the directness of the connections between all node pairs while local efficiency indicates the average directness of the connections between the neighbors of a node.

A similar, alternative normalized measure of global efficiency, the "straightness centrality," defined by Vragovic, Louis, and Diaz-Guilera (2005), can also be considered. Straightness centrality is defined as

$$C_i^S = \frac{1}{|N|(|N|-1)} \sum_{j \in N; j \neq i} \frac{L_{ij}^{Euclid}}{L_{ij}} \tag{A.19}$$

This index is similar to normalized global efficiency but accounts for the straightness of each shortest path (i.e., path efficiency) separately. Straightness indicates the extent to which the connecting paths from i to all other nodes deviate from the (virtual) straight line path between them. The straightness centrality index was proposed on the basis that the shortest paths using a number of nodes (or links) can often be as efficient as direct links between node pairs, which of itself may contribute significantly to network efficiency. Straightness indicates the extent to which the connecting paths from i to all other nodes deviate from the (virtual) straight line path between them.

REFERENCES

Barabasi, A., & Albert, R. (1999). Emergence of scaling in random networks. *Science, 286*, 509–512.

Chen, B. Y., Li, Q., & Lam, W. H. K. (2016). Finding the *k* reliable shortest paths under travel time uncertainty. *Transportation Research B: Methodological, 94*, 189–203.

Derrible, S., & Kennedy, C. (2010). Characterizing metro networks: State, form and structure. *Transportation, 37*, 275–297.

Dial, R. B. (1971). A probabilistic multipath traffic assignment model which obviates path enumeration. *Transportation Research, 5*(2), 83–111.

Dijkstra, E. W. (1959). A note on two problems in connexion with graphs. *Numerische Mathematik, 1*, 269–271.

Freeman, L. C. (1979). Centrality in social networks: Conceptual clarification. *Social Networks, 1*, 215–239.

Latora, V., & Marchiori, M. (2001). Efficient behavior of small-world networks. *Physical Review Letters, 87*(19), 198701.

Mattsson, L.-G., & Jenelius, E. (2015). Vulnerability and resilience of transport systems – a discussion of recent research. *Transportation Research Part A: Policy and Practice, 81*, 16–34.

Porta, S., Crucitti, P., & Latora, V. (2006). The network analysis of urban streets: A primal approach. *Environment and Planning B: Planning and Design, 33*(5), 705–725.

Taylor, M. A. P. (1979). Evaluating the performance of a simulation model. *Transportation Research, 13A*(3), 159–173.

Taylor, M. A. P. (1981). Maximum likelihood estimation for a road traffic network model. *Applied Mathematical Modelling, 5*, 34–38.

Vragovic, I., Louis, E., & Diaz-Guilera, A. (2005). Efficiency of informational transfer in regular and complex networks. *Physical Review E, 71*, 036122.

APPENDIX B

Capacity of Railway Systems

As discussed in Chapters 2, 3 and 6, rail traffic flow is quite different from road traffic flow. The latter can be regarded as continuous, and the former as granular—consisting of large flow units (trains) with headways (time separations) dictated by stringent operating rules. In the main, these rules require that no two trains should occupy the same section (track, junction, or platform) at the same time. In general terms the capacity at any location in a railway system is then the maximum number of trains that can occupy that location over a time period τ, where τ is commonly taken to be an extended period of time such as an hour or, quite frequently, a day. If $\overline{h}$ is the required average headway between trains then the capacity (maximum number of trains) MT is given by

$$MT = \frac{\tau}{\overline{h}} \tag{B.1}$$

The average headway needs to be defined according to the particular component of the railway system under consideration:

- For rail lines, the average headway would be the average time gap between the front of a moving train and the front of the next moving train, as measured by an observer standing at the side of the track.
- For rail tracks at stations, the average headway is the time gap between two successive occupations of the track, irrespective of whether the trains stop or not.
- At junction nodes, the average headway is the time gap between two successive trains, departing from the same starting or finishing points in their paths.

Calculation of capacity using Equation (B.1) is further complicated by the facts that train arrivals are often stochastic, and that there may be irregular (not on-time) trains that have different impacts on each component of a railway system.

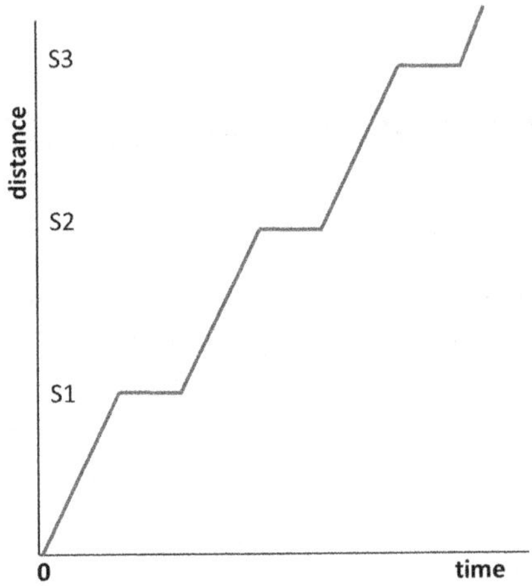

Figure B.1 Schematic train graph showing the movement of one train along a rail track.

The main idea behind railway capacity analysis is therefore to identify present and future bottlenecks in the railway system. Two aspects reflect all criteria that can be defined with respect to the capacity of railway infrastructure:

1. operational feasibility, which indicates whether a given traffic scenario can be performed on the infrastructure while satisfying a certain pre-defined quality of service criteria (in terms of punctuality, reliability, delay sensitivity, and stability) and
2. planning flexibility, which refers to the range of traffic scenarios that are feasible on the same infrastructure.

The evaluation of the capacity of railway systems is of key importance for planning the future infrastructure. Railway capacity can be defined as the maximum frequency of a certain pattern of train movements for which delays do not propagate unduly. The capacity of a railway system has to be determined using different methods for rail lines and for railway stations.

The starting point for railway capacity study is the "train graph," a trajectory diagram which shows the position of a train along a rail track over time. Figure B.1 is a schematic train graph showing the movement of one train along a rail track.

B.1 RAIL LINE CAPACITY

Rail line capacity has two basic dimensions:

- *Traffic capacity of a rail line*, which represents the maximum traffic volume expressed in trains or railcars on the respective line within a certain time frame (day or hour), depending on the existent fixed installations (infrastructure), the type and power of the locomotives, the types of cars and the way the traffic is organized.
- *Transport capacity of a rail line*, which represents the possible volume of freight traffic that can be hauled on a rail line during a year, expressed in million tons of freight. Transport capacity can be further classified as:
    - existing capacity,
    - potential capacity (designed), and
    - required capacity.

Existing capacity is determined taking into account the existing resources of the line (infrastructure, rolling stock, staff, etc.) and the method used to organize train traffic.

Potential capacity (designed) is calculated taking into account the designed resources of the line and the corresponding method of traffic organization.

Required capacity is calculated as a function of the planned transport volume and has to satisfy the traffic of the planned number of trains of a certain tonnage on the respective line, taking also into account the required reserve of capacity.

The reserve of traffic capacity is determined for each section of the rail track taking into account general technical and economic considerations, by calculating the difference between the existing traffic capacity of the line and the required traffic capacity. Generally, the reserve of capacity has to be:

1. for double track lines, 15%–20% of the maximum designed capacity and
2. for single track lines, 25%–35% of the maximum designed capacity.

The traffic capacity can be calculated globally for a rail line/section, and also locally for stations.

The principal elements of the technical installations which determine the traffic capacity are the:

- number of lines,
- length of the lines,
- profile of the line,

- type of locomotive,
- train tonnage,
- type of rail cars,
- signaling installations,
- number of sidings,
- maintenance lines,
- depot lines,
- fueling installations, etc.

The smallest value of the traffic capacity determined taking into account the stations, depots, and other installations, is the "resultant traffic capacity." The traffic capacity of each element of the technical installations Z is calculated as a function of the daily or hourly capacity consumed to serve a train, i.e.,

$$Z = \frac{1440 - T_{perm}}{t} \tag{B.2}$$

where T_{perm} is the time that the examined installation is occupied with permanent operations (not related to train traffic), in minutes per day, and t is the average time in minutes that the installation is occupied by a train.

Equation (B.2) represents the direct method of calculation for traffic capacity, and can be used when trying to calculate the capacity of a new line. Taking into account the coefficient of utilization of the capacity K_u, the traffic capacity can be written as

$$Z = \frac{\hat{Z}}{K_u} \tag{B.3}$$

where $\hat{Z}$ is the actual number of trains in the train graph and $K_u = \frac{tN'}{1440 - T_{perm}}$.

The traffic capacity can be calculated for both parallel and nonparallel graphs for all the elements of the technical installations. In a parallel rain graph (Figure B.2A), two successive trains travel at the same speed, keeping a set distance between them. Figure B.2B shows a nonparallel graph in which two trains travel at different speeds. If there is no location where the second train can pass the first, it must wait at a minimum distance behind the first train before it can move again.

B.1.1 Traffic Capacity—The Parallel Graph Case (Homogenous Traffic)

In the parallel graph case, the capacity is calculated only for the freight traffic or only for the passenger traffic. In the case of a parallel graph

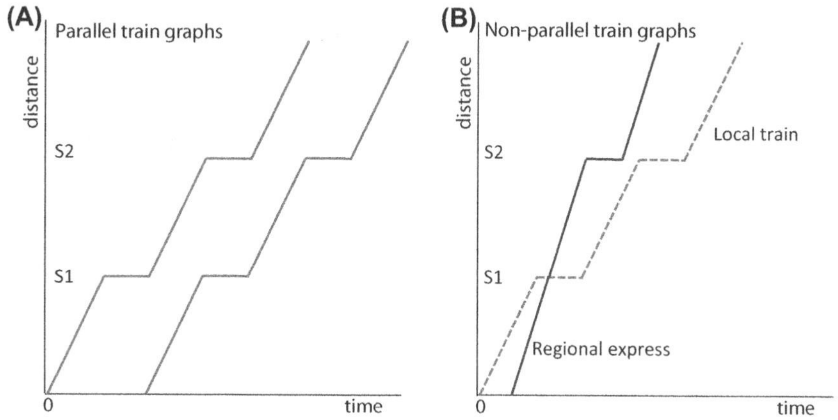

Figure B.2 Parallel and nonparallel train graphs: (A) parallel train graph, two successive trains traveling at the same speed and keeping a set distance between them; (B) nonparallel graph with two trains traveling at different speeds (e.g., local train and regional express train).

with no interruptions in the movement of the trains, $T_{perm} = 0$ and the traffic capacity Z is

$$Z = \frac{1440 N_T}{T_p} \tag{B.4}$$

where T_p is the period of the graph in minutes and N_T is the number of trains in that period. The traffic capacity of a single track line can then be determined, given that the period of the graph is calculated from:

$$T_p = t_1 + t_2 + \sum t_{st} + \sum t_{ss} \tag{B.5}$$

where t_1, and t_2 are the travel times without any stops, in both directions, Σt_{st} is the sum of station intervals and Σt_{ss} is the sum of times spent with the deceleration and acceleration of the train over all of its stops.

B.1.2 Traffic Capacity—The Nonparallel Graph Case (Heterogeneous Traffic)

In this case, which is the norm, different categories of trains have different speeds so their routes in the graph are not parallel. Although in the nonparallel traffic graph different categories of trains are represented, in general the traffic capacity is determined in terms of freight trains, taking also into account the time other trains take in the graph. The time that cannot be used for the traffic of the freight trains is called *reduction time of the freight trains due to the passenger trains*. This time reduction is made up of:

1. time a section of the track is occupied by transiting passenger trains, t_0 and
2. time that cannot be used for the traffic of the freight train because the interval between the passenger trains is not a multiple of the time required to fit in a freight train, the supplementary reduction time, t_{sr}.

Then the reduction time for a train (or pair of trains) will be $t_r = t_0 + t_{sr}$ and the traffic capacity for freight trains is:

$$N_f = \frac{1440 - t_r N_c}{T_p} \tag{B.6}$$

where N_f is the traffic capacity of freight trains (freight trains or pairs of freight trains) for the studied time period, N_c is the number of pairs of passenger trains, and all times are in minutes.

If $\frac{t_r}{T_p} = e_c$, the reduction coefficient of freight trains by passenger trains then

$$N_f = N - e_c N_c \tag{B.7}$$

where N is the maximum traffic capacity in the case of a parallel graph.

For the general case, the traffic capacity is calculated from:

$$N_f = N - \sum_{i=1}^{n} e_c^i N_c^i - \left(e_{trc}^f - 1\right) N_{trc}^f - \left(e_1^{mf} - 1\right) N_1^f \tag{B.8}$$

where $\sum_{i=1}^{n} e_c^i N_c^i$ = the sum of the reduction coefficients corresponding to different categories of passenger trains and their numbers, respectively, the number of freight train pairs eliminated from the graph by the passenger trains, e_{trc}^f, e_1^f = the reduction coefficients due to the traffic of other trains (e.g., local freight), N_{trc}^f, N_1^f = the number of other train pairs.

B.1.3 Transport Capacity of a Rail Line

The transport capacity C_t of a rail line in each direction is the total volume of freight that can be transported on the line over an extended period, e.g., a year. It is estimated using the equation

$$C_t = \frac{365 N_f Q_g \varphi}{10^6 K_n} + C_{trc} + C_{1m} \tag{B.9}$$

where C_t = in million tons per annum, N_f = the maximum number of long haul freight trains that can traverse the line in 24 h, Q_g = the gross tonnage of the freight trains, in tons, φ= the ratio of the net tonnage to the gross tonnage of the train, K_n = a monthly transport nonuniformity coefficient, C_{trc}, C_{1m} indicate the quantity of freight hauled by other freight trains (local freight, etc.), in million tons per annum.

The maximum number of long haul freight trains (N_f), i.e., the traffic capacity, expressed in freight trains (in the case of a double track line) can be estimated using:

$$N_f = N - \sum_{i=1}^{n} e_c^i N_c^i - (e_{trc} - 1)N_{trc} - (e_{1m} - 1)N_{1m} \tag{B.10}$$

where N = the traffic capacity in the case of a parallel graph, $\sum_{i=1}^{n} e_c^i N_c^i$ = the number of long haul freight trains eliminated from the graph by passenger trains (i is the number of categories for passenger trains), e_{tr}, e_{1m} = the reduction coefficient due to the traffic of other trains (local freight, etc.). N_{trc}, N_{1m} = number of other trains (local freight, etc.), φ is calculated using $\varphi = \frac{Q_n}{Q_g}$ where Q_n is the net tonnage per train.

The following equation can be used to analyze the transport capacity C_t (M ton p.a.) as a function of the structure of the freight hauled and the degree of utilization of the loading capacity of the rail freight cars:

$$C_t = \frac{365 N_f Q_g}{10^6 k_n 1 + \dfrac{k_t}{k_{ci}}} + C_{trc} + C_{1m} \tag{B.11}$$

in which k_{ci} is the coefficient of utilization of the car's loading capacity and k_t is the empty car coefficient, given by $k_{ci} = \frac{q_n}{q}$ and $k_t = \frac{q_t}{q}$ where q is the average loading capacity of the car in tons. Recommended values for φ in the Australian context are (1) for heavy freight (coal, minerals, metal, etc.), $\varphi = 0.75-0.9$, and (2) for light freight $\varphi = 0.6-0.65$. The average value in use on the Australian national railway network is $\varphi = 0.62-0.77$.

If the lengths of rail sidings limit a train's tonnage, then the transport capacity is calculated as follows:

$$C_t = \frac{365 N_f k_{ci} p_{ml} (L_u - n_1 l_1 - l_p)}{10^6 K_n l_v} \tag{B.12}$$

In this case the gross tonnage per train (Q_g, tons) is calculated from

$$Q_g = p_{ml}(L_u - n_1 l_1 - l_p) \tag{B.13}$$

where L_u = length of the siding (usually consider the smallest), in m, p_{ml} = the car load per meter, in tons/m, l_1 = the length of a locomotive in m, n_1 = number of locomotives in the train, l_p = length required for maneuvering/parking the train (15–30 m).

B.2 TRANSIT CAPACITY AND SERVICE CAPACITY OF A STATION

Station capacity is of particular importance for a railway system. The transit capacity and service capacity of a station involves two main aspects:

1. The existing capacity, corresponding to the different installations of a station (incoming/outgoing lines, waiting halls, lines for composing/decomposing trains, etc.) with the use of all reserves (available resources include equipment, buildings, installations, and human resources).
2. The required capacity, imposed by a certain volume of traffic, with the reserve designed to ensure the stability of the operations in the station under the conditions of nonuniform traffic and interruptions caused by repair and maintenance works of the station's buildings and installations (station infrastructure).

Existing transit capacity is the maximum number of trains of a certain type that can transit through the station within a determined time period (e.g., a day, 24 h), under a given station operation technology (e.g., technical checks, locomotive change, and train composition/decomposition) and a train graph which ensures the use of all existing resources.

Existing service capacity is the maximum number of freight trains of a certain tonnage that can be served (composed, decomposed) in the station during 24 h making use of the technology, to ensure the most rational use of the existing resources.

A direct calculation method can be used when determining the capacity of a station design, while indirect calculation may be needed when determining the capacity of an existing station. The direct calculation method uses

$$N = \frac{1440m - \sum T_{perm}}{t_{oc}} \tag{B.14}$$

where N = the transit/service capacity of a station expressed in trains per day, m = the number of elements of the same type of the examined compartment (e.g., number of incoming/outgoing lines), ΣT_{perm} = the time the examined compartment is occupied with permanent operations, in minutes per day, $t_{oc} = t_{oc}$, the train occupation time.

Occupation times account for the time intervals required for a train to enter a station, to dwell at a platform or siding (if required, e.g., to stop to embark or disembark passengers, to pick up or drop off freight, or perform the technical operations of crossing and overtaking), and to exit the station. The sum of these times is termed the "station interval." Station intervals can be identified as:

- nonsimultaneous arrival interval in the station of the trains coming from opposite directions, τ_{sn},
- crossing interval of the trains, τ_I,
- crossing interval of the trains when the trains do not stop in the station, τ_{ifo},
- following interval, τ_u,
- start and nonsimultaneous arrival, τ_{esn},
- start and nonsimultaneous arrival (the case of conflicting paths), τ_{sen}, and
- nonsimultaneous start and arrival of the train from opposite direction, τ_{ensc}.

Nonsimultaneous arrival interval τ_{sn} is the time elapsed from the arrival of a train in the station to the passing or arrival in this station of a train from the opposite direction. This interval occurs in the stations located on single track lines, when these lines cannot accommodate the arrival of simultaneous trains and crossing trains, as shown in Figure B.3 (see Figure B.2).

The crossing interval τ_I is the minimum time considered from the moment of the passing or arrival through/in the station of a train to the moment a train from the opposite direction is released on the same section of track; this last train has been stopped in the station in order to perform the crossing with the train that arrived before, as shown in Figure B.4.

The entrance and exit times of the trains can then be calculated using the following procedure. The entrance/exit time of a train is the time elapsed from the moment the entrance/exit command is given until the tracks are cleared. Entrance time (in minutes) is given by

$$t_i = t_p^1 + t_{di} \tag{B.15}$$

where t_p^1 is the time required to prepare the entrance track and to give the entrance command, and t_{di} is the time required by the train to travel the entrance into the station, over distance, D_i. The exit time (minutes) is given by

$$t_e = t_p^2 + t_{de} \tag{B.17}$$

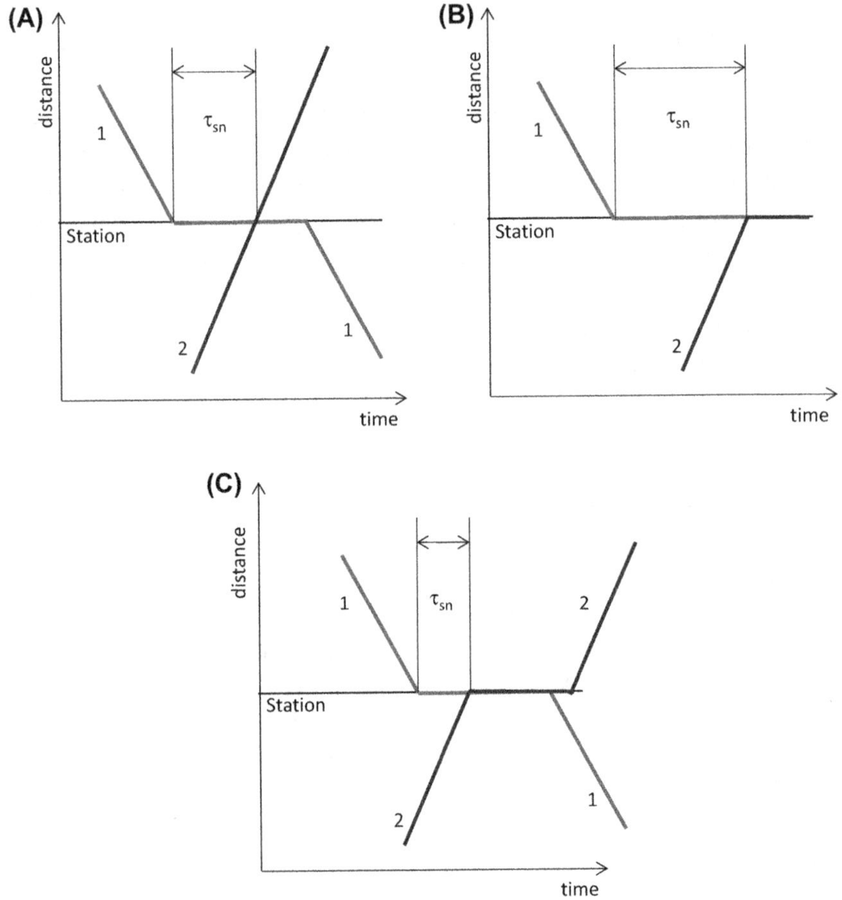

Figure B.3 Nonsimultaneous arrival of a train in the station to the passing or arrival in this station of a train from the opposite direction on a single track line. (A) Train 2 passes through without stopping; (B) both trains terminate at the station; (C) both trains stop at the station then continue.

where t_p^2 is the time required to give the exit command and start the train and t_{de} is the time required by the train to travel out of the station, over distance D_e. Figure B.5 illustrates the components required to determine D_e and D_i.

Using Figure B.5, the entrance distance, D_i (m) is given by

$$D_i = l_p + l_s + l_{di} + \frac{l_u + l_{tr}}{2} \tag{B.18}$$

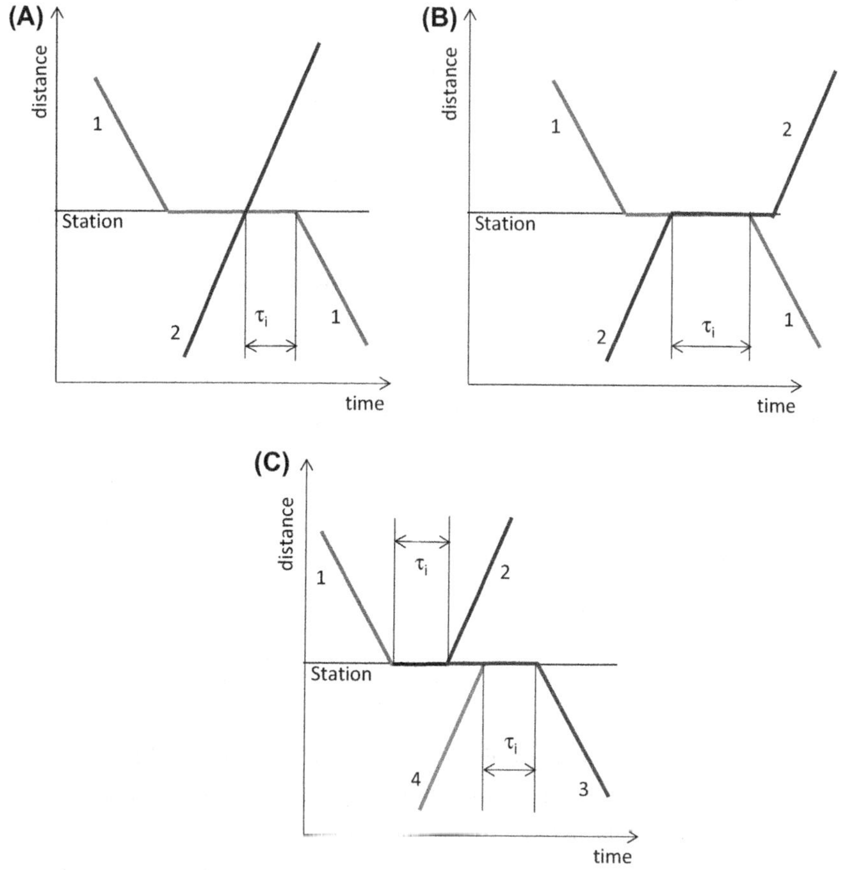

Figure B.4 Crossing interval at a station, where two trains in opposite directions arrive at the station. (A) Train 2 passes through without stopping; (B) both trains stop at the station then continue (C) both trains terminate at the station, and subsequently leave as new services.

and the exit distance D_e (m) is given

$$D_e = l_{de} + \frac{l_u + l_{tr}}{2} \tag{B.19}$$

where l_p = the distance from the warning signal to the entrance signal, l_s = the distance from the entrance signal to the first switch, l_{di} = the length of the diagonal, the distance from the first switch to the safety switch of the line the train is parked on, l_{de} = the length of the diagonal, the distance from

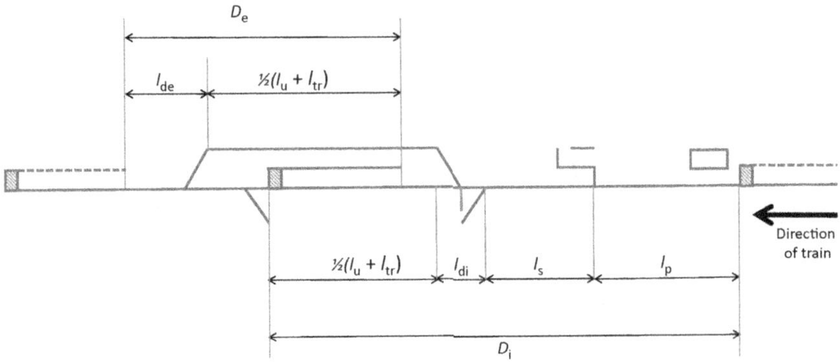

Figure B.5 Components of entry and exit station distances D_i and D_e at a station platform.

the first switch downstream to the safety switch of the line the train is parked on, l_u = the length of the parking line, l_{tr} = the length of the train.

The transit capacity of the incoming/outgoing lines is given by

$$N = \frac{1440m - \left(T_{pm}^{c} + T_{pm}^{1} + T_{pm}^{i}\right)}{t_{oc}} + N_1 \tag{B.20}$$

where N = the number of freight trains (including the local freight trains) that can daily transit the incoming/outgoing lines, m = the number of lines (except the loco lines) used for the freight trains, T_{pm}^{c} = the size of the interruption in the use of the lines, or time the freight trains are stopped over the technological norms due to the traffic of passenger trains, T_{pm}^{1} = the size of the interruption in the use of the lines due to the traffic of local freight trains, T_{pm}^{i} = the time the lines are occupied with permanent operations not related to the basic activities of the lines (stopped local cars, compose/decompose local trains), t_{oc} = the average time a line is occupied by a freight train for technological operations, N_1 = the number of local freight trains that transit in the time T_{pm}^{1}.

INDEX

'*Note*: Page numbers followed by "f" indicate figures, "t" indicate tables.'

A

T

U

V

W

Made in the USA
Monee, IL
13 September 2026

62977013R20151